BECOMING

The Emergence of Being

BECOMING
The Emergence of Being

A tale of discovery and illumination

ASHKAN TASHVIR

Best-selling author of BEING and HUMAN BEING

First published 2023 by Engenesis Publications

ISBN 978-1-922433-10-7 Paperback (Australian Print)
ISBN 978-1-922433-11-4 Hardcover (POD)
ISBN 978-1-922433-13-8 Paperback (POD)
ISBN 978-1-922433-12-1 EPUB
ISBN 978-1-922433-14-5 Audio book

publications.engenesis.com

A catalogue record for this
book is available from the
National Library of Australia

Edited by Phaedra Pym – awaywithwords.net.au

Sub-edited by Caroline New – quantumvalues.com

Book design and production by Eric and Thymen Hoek – exlibris.com.au

This book is dedicated to you, the reader,
to my daughter Diana, my son Diyan –
who is on his way to being out there in the world –
and to my wife Atefeh, without whom
none of this would have been possible.

A Word from the Author

I f you were to ask me, 'What's the biggest problem facing humanity?' my immediate response would be, 'Confusion'. Let me explain. As human beings, we are inherently vulnerable, though not all of us live life from that viewpoint. We are vulnerable to illness and disease, particularly with numerous incurable conditions in existence and undiscovered viruses still emerging. Yet, despite knowing how to take care of our health and protect ourselves against the ailments we know about, many of us don't do either. Many people don't even come close to guarding themselves against the health risks they know about, let alone the ones they don't.

We are also vulnerable to natural disasters. And although we are unable to control the environment and can't accurately predict and effectively manage volcanoes, earthquakes, floods and bushfires, etc., we choose to venture to Mars to create life there through geoengineering rather than putting all our efforts into reviving the Earth we have been irreversibly damaging. We can also be vulnerable to our own lack of awareness, naivety, our angry neighbour, our cheating partner, our unfair boss and so on. But we look the other way or resign ourselves to accept what we believe we can't change. We are indeed confused. When we combine the layers of confusion that exist in multiple dimensions of our lives and throw democracy into the mix – which at its core relies on the sanity of the crowd – you might appreciate why we are in the situation we are in today. While some are trying to take us to outer space, my intention as a philosopher and an author is to bring us back down to earth.

Although many scientists, engineers, thinkers, philosophers, leaders, artists, parents and carers, among others, work hard to articulate or address part of the confusion through their endeavours, many more keep adding to it. It seems our ability to imagine is both a blessing and a curse. Although our imagination enables us to generate new ideas and inventions that have the potential to light humanity's way out of our collective confusion, it also allows us to conjure up imaginary ideas and create constructs that deviate from our ability to strive for what I call 'authentic awareness'. This is when one's conception of reality is as congruent as possible with how things actually are. Consider that our most significant vulnerability as human beings is the nature of our perceptual system, which makes it possible for us to both see what's not there and also NOT see what's there. It is our dissociation from reality that has led to our collective confusion.

But it's not all doom and gloom. Let me complete the picture by recognising the progress we've made so far that has authentically enriched our lives. Humanity's progress resulted from our original aim to be authentically aware. That's when we were in the game of discovery to unveil what was there to be uncovered, which was the approach adopted by early philosophers like Socrates, Plato and Aristotle. In contrast, there were others, known as Sophists, who made false claims or covered things up through sophisticated rhetoric and narratives designed to manipulate and deceive, usually for their own benefit.

While acknowledging and surrendering to the nature of our perceptual system is important, that doesn't mean we should be resigned to aiming to discover more and fall into the trap of fabrication or covering up. I'm not suggesting there's anything fundamentally wrong with shared reality, which I call 'second-layer reality'. After all, without it, we wouldn't have things like currency, traffic laws or a taxation system. There is also another layer of reality, which is our personal narratives or the stories we tell ourselves. I call this 'third-layer reality', and there's nothing wrong with that either. I am simply pointing out the need to be authentically aware that there are absolutes of the world – which I call 'first-layer reality' – that we would be foolish to deny or ignore. The moment we confuse second or third-layer reality with the absolutes of the world or first-layer reality, we are in serious trouble.

In our society, I fear we may have already collapsed the three layers of reality to the point where we risk dissociating from our very nature. To minimise this risk, this book and my previous two – *BEING* and *HUMAN BEING* – together with the community and platform my team and I are building, our technology, frameworks and all the content we generate and disseminate with our platform partners, play a small but significant role in addressing the collective confusion. They do so by inviting everyone engaging with this content to go beyond inspirational, motivational or intellectual sentiment alone. Instead, the content gradually encourages people to develop authentic awareness of the three layers of reality and our intrinsic nature as human beings and then to surrender to these undeniable truths without succumbing to the existing unknowns as a form of resignation or a lack of care.

From the beginning, the primary challenge has been establishing relevance and supporting our audience to relate to the messages conveyed in this entire body of work. By making the content relatable, we're not just disseminating knowledge but encouraging people to develop their conception of it and consider adopting the metaphysics it brings forth to maximise its benefits. For me, the most significant challenge of all has been to find the most effective ways to describe the almost indescribable – the essential qualities and common traits of human beings at a metaphysical level – and make it relevant to those of us who value integrity and the fulfilment of our intentions in a dynamic, fast-paced world where most people don't pause long enough to pay attention to the things that matter most. This is getting in the way of our fulfilment, health and prosperity, individually and collectively. When I reflected on my own philosophical journey, I realised I was influenced far more by philosophical novels than by directly reading the thoughts of philosophers, particularly early on in my philosophical exploration. So, with a focus on relevance and relatability, I intentionally chose to write this book as a work of fiction.

In *BECOMING – The Emergence of Being*, the protagonist, Yoren Healy, is a man in his late thirties who appears to have it all: a lucrative career, abundant material possessions, financial stability and a loving fiancé. However, deep down, he is lost, confused, stuck and unfulfilled. Yoren is a relatable character who represents many people in society today and whose journey could apply to anyone, regardless of gender, ethnicity and cultural or religious background. You might recognise him in people you know: those who put on a mask each day to manage the impression they make as they go about their lives. You might even see glimpses of yourself in Yoren.

Through the story, you'll follow Yoren's transformational journey as he navigates the pathway to removing the roadblocks hindering him from fulfilling his dream of starting a business with the support of his coach. Along the way, you'll discover the reasons behind Yoren's state of being and lack of fulfilment, including his upbringing, family heritage, perception of societal expectations and how he relates to the world, the people in his circle of influence and himself. The coaching conversations between Yoren and his coach have been heavily influenced by thousands of hours of one-on-one coaching, team building and interactions with my students, who are mostly professional coaches, leaders, artists, entrepreneurs and investors. Many were also inspired by stories shared anonymously with me by members of our community of accredited coaches about their experience supporting their clients. So, while this book is a work of fiction, it isn't fantasy; it has its roots firmly grounded in reality.

Along with Yoren, you will learn that without authentic awareness as an approach to understanding and making sense of the world, none of us can effectively fulfil our intentions. Furthermore, you'll discover that no matter how much you want to be independent and self-made, as Yoren does, we are all dependent on others from the moment we are 'thrown' into this world. As social beings, we cannot escape this reality, no matter how hard we try or might want to. From needing our parents or carers and teachers as children to relying on a massive support network later in life, including friends, family members, neighbours, colleagues, employers, employees, the wider community, the farmers producing the food we eat, manufacturers and retailers, governments, law enforcement, financial institutions, health workers, emergency services and the list goes on, we all need others. It is inauthentic to think otherwise.

In partnering and being with others, it is critical to understand human beings, to be able to see through the facade and appreciate the authentic qualities of each person, from the life partner you intend to choose or the person you are about to hire, to the leader you plan to follow or the politician you are voting for, to name just a few. The being discourse, as described and referred to in this book, is a paradigm that supports you to do just that: understand the reality of human beings, including yourself. It is directly based on the Being Framework™, a paradigm I designed and developed with my team over the past decade, which supports us in seeing beyond identity or the surface-level attributes of skin colour and gender, to focus on the fundamental qualities we all have in common but relate to differently. Authenticity, vulnerability, commitment, courage, assertiveness, proactivity, compassion and partnership are among 31 qualities or Aspects of Being that make up the Being Framework's ontological model.

Connected to this framework – which considers each quality within the scope of performance, effectiveness, leadership and fulfilment – is the Being Profile®, an ontometric assessment tool that provides a vivid snapshot of one's state of being through an in-depth questionnaire with more than 240 strategically assembled questions. Distinctly different from any personality test, the Being Profile maps out an individual's cognitive model and identifies how they relate to each of the 31 Aspects of Being. Today, the Being Framework and Being Profile are used by individuals, teams, leaders and organisations in more than 38 countries globally, supported by an international network of certified practitioners and coaches.

Interestingly, when most people think of a support network, few consider advisors, mentors or coaches. And yet those who realise the immense benefits of having professionals like this to support them are generally the ones who go on to achieve greatness. Working with highly trained coaches from various disciplines is critical to success. In all my studies and throughout my entire career working with, learning from and coaching thousands of high achievers from all parts of the world, I have never come across a single successful leader or entrepreneur who didn't appreciate the importance of having the right coaches, mentors and advisors in their corner. In fact, most had an entire support crew. Consider that you are limited if you choose to be just you, with no friends, allies, teammates, family members, mentors, teachers, trainers, advisors, consultants and, most notably in the context of this book, practitioners or coaches to support you. After all, why would you limit yourself to your own knowledge, resources and accountability when you can have others supporting you to reach your goals and fulfil the intentions you care deeply about? It saves you time, minimises the mistakes you make along the way and enables you to optimise every opportunity, including the contribution of others.

However, I acknowledge the scepticism around coaching and understand that some of you might have reservations about it, particularly as it's an unregulated industry in many parts of the world. That's why when it comes to selecting a coach, it's important to understand that not all coaches deliver the same value. Professionals who are officially trained to leverage the Being Framework and its associated tools in a coaching capacity – known as Thrive Coaches – go far deeper than coaches who adopt other approaches that focus solely on changing thoughts and feelings or 'correcting behaviour'. While such methods might work for a while, many behaviours revert over time.

In contrast, the Being Framework focuses on who, what and how one is *being* rather than what a person is *doing*. It does so by shining a light on the deep underlying qualities that drive our decisions, behaviours and actions. Importantly, it also works on the premise that human beings are NOT simply the sum of a series of fixed traits; they're ever-evolving beings capable of transformation. When an individual or a team chooses to work with one of these coaches, the insights they gain from completing the Being Profile translate into actionable and specific areas to polish and transform to become integrous and effective.

This book is for you if you:

- want to gain an in-depth understanding of human beings, including yourself
- feel stuck or suppressed in your expression of self
- want to transform the trajectory of your life by identifying your growth potential and addressing the gaps holding you back
- are tired of thinking you'll never succeed in life or that you're destined to be the way you are and have no choice but to accept that
- believe there is a way to radically increase the probability of fulfilling your intentions but don't know how to cause the paradigm shift to become the person you know you can be
- know something needs to change but don't know where to start
- feel it's insufficient to keep acquiring more knowledge, skills, tools and resources and want to explore a whole-person approach to transformation and fulfilment
- would like to have a framework that not only allows you to see yourself with sharp clarity but also offers you a way to see through the surface of other people so you can understand them better, especially when making key decisions that impact or involve others.

This book is also for you if you are a coach. Perhaps you are looking for powerful tools and methodologies to support your coaching clients. Or you might be keen to explore a different approach to your coaching and embrace an alternative paradigm for both you and your clients. Maybe you want to implement and leverage transformative frameworks and add indispensable new tools to your arsenal. And if you're considering or exploring the possibility of becoming a coach, this book will provide an invaluable glimpse into coaching in action and what it could be like for you to be a coach with the skills, knowledge, tools and framework to support your clients in transforming beyond what they considered possible.

However, it's important to be aware that the coaching sessions depicted in this work of fiction are not intended to fully reflect real-life coaching sessions, which are typically more interactive, conversational and less prescriptive. Furthermore, every individual and coach is unique and their interactions differ. Results will vary based on many factors. I must also point out that the suggestions and recommendations made in this book are aimed at a fictitious character and should not be taken as advice or recommendations for you. Everyone's situation is different and context is critical in any coaching scenario.

Ultimately, I encourage you to approach this narrative with an open mind and heart as an introduction to the deeper philosophical body of work I am committed to bringing into the world. I hope it inspires you in your own contribution towards making the world a better place.

Contents

CHAPTER 1

A 'Brilliant' Life

I'll never forget that evening, a night that set me on the path for a journey I didn't know I needed. A life-changing journey of twists and turns, transformation, highs and desperate lows that culminated in the relatively polished man I know myself to be today – someone who is authentic, vulnerable, forgiving, compassionate and many other qualities I used to dismiss as 'weaknesses'. Thank goodness we human beings are able to transform! Hard to believe that was eight years ago. And yet, it's as vivid to me now as it was the morning after. How could one event ignite the urge to begin a process that would end up being so impactful? A process that would draw my attention to the parts of myself I had always been unwilling, hesitant and even afraid to explore. The man I see in the mirror today would have been a stranger to me back then. I cast my mind back to the information session that first awakened me to the misery and dysfunction in my seemingly brilliant life and set me on a new trajectory.

— ∎ —

Yoren checked his phone for what felt like the 100th time. 3:05 am.

Maybe I should just get up. Why am I so rattled? It was only an info session!

Although not normally one to suffer from insomnia, Yoren found sleep evasive tonight. Beside him, Mel's gentle breathing suggested her peaceful, relaxed state. But all Yoren could think of was how foolish he must have looked to the others in the session.

I must have come across as such a conceited know-it-all tonight. I thought I was better than all of them, including the facilitator! What was his name, again? Erik. Yes, that was it.

He had never felt so exposed and vulnerable, feelings for which he was totally unprepared.

Amazing how Erik seemed to be able to see straight through me, like he had x-ray vision into my psyche.

It was as though a light had been switched on, exposing a dark side within that, until that evening, had been concealed and hidden from all – his parents, friends, colleagues, staff, Mel and even himself. As he lay there, he was suddenly present to the suffering and pain that clouded his life, but which he largely denied. The newly revealed shadow seemed to grow and fester, enshrouding him until he could barely breathe. It blotted out all the blessings in his life and magnified all that was wrong with it … with him. He felt disarmed, indecisive and powerless. The 37-year-old man lying there in the darkness suddenly seemed totally alien to him.

From a very young age, Yoren Healy was told he was destined to pursue 'greatness', although, at the time, he didn't know what his well-meaning family members meant by that. By the time he reached high school, he was regarded as someone who would be very successful. And he believed it too. He was the smart, cool kid: the guy with the looks who always got the grades, the sporting wins, the best parts in school productions and, of course, the girls. At 18, his self-confidence was off the charts, and he began ticking off all the boxes he had set for himself. By the age of 30, he had the GT sports car, the Omega Aqua Terra watch, the high-flying corporate career at one of the world's top four consulting firms, the fancy beachfront apartment and the dream girl – the same girl who now lay beside him as his future wife. And yet, despite all of that, he suddenly felt like his entire life – all 37 years – had been a sham.

As minutes turned to hours and distant bird calls heralded the beginning of a new day, Yoren became present to the massive contradiction that was his life. Before last night, he believed he knew exactly who he was and what he wanted. He was perfectly content and happy, or so he thought.

Perhaps I've just been pretending to have my life all sorted, projecting a fake persona that's designed to be far more impressive than I know myself to be deep down, hoping no one will cotton on. It feels like a heavy burden. Why the hell did I agree to attend that info session anyway?

He thought back to that fateful phone conversation with Jenah, or Jen as her family and friends called her, his aunt on his father's side. It was hard to believe that was only two days ago.

— ∎ —

'Hi Yoren, how are you?' asked Jen in a cheerful tone.

'Jen! I'm great. Funny you should call now. I was just telling Emily, my PA, about you and suggesting she look you up on LinkedIn. What can I do for you?'

'Well, actually, I'm calling to extend you an invitation. It's something I think you'd get a lot out of.'

'Oh, now you have me intrigued. What is it? Some fancy soiree? You need someone with my standing to make you look good?' he joked, knowing full well that Jenah Healy was one of the most respected women in her field.

'Ha-ha, very funny. You know how I'm actively engaged with a global community that runs various seminars and events to raise awareness about human beings and supports the transformation of individuals and teams? Well, a colleague within that community is facilitating an information session that I'd love you to attend. You're going to hate me, but I've already put your name forward, so you can expect to receive an email about it.'

'What? Jen, you know I'm not into all that community stuff and always do my best to stay clear of the madness of the crowd. What's this session on anyway? Not some airy-fairy bullshit, pardon the French!'

Not waiting for Jen's response, Yoren continued, an air of self-righteousness apparent in his tone, 'With all due respect to you and your community, Jen, but all these 'personal development' programs do is try to unleash some pristine Übermensch from the shackles of their insecurities. Have you ever stopped to consider that these types of programs might be part of a larger automation of a neoliberal logic designed to continuously make individuals think they are not enough? I see so many people lured into buying programs, books or going to retreats to improve some aspect of themselves. I've never bought into any of that. Pardon me for saying so, but I am 'enough' already. I don't need to buy into training that's designed to make the rich richer. Perhaps you've forgotten that I've watched several of your community's video promotions and know what you're all promoting. So if you're insinuating that I need to become more aware, authentic and effective, well guess what – I already am!'

You might be my favourite aunt, and I admire all you've achieved in your life, but you do you, Jen, and let me be me.

'I had a sneaky suspicion you might react that way. Just hear me out and have an open mind for once in your life,' laughed Jen.

Suddenly it dawned on Yoren that he'd overreacted. After all, it wasn't as if his aunt was trying to sell him anything. He knew her better than that.

'Alright, alright! But only because you're my favourite aunt. Go ahead, hit me with it,' he said in a gentler tone. However, Jen couldn't help but notice that his voice was still tinged with a hint of sarcasm that she chose to ignore.

'It's an open night session to introduce participants to a paradigm centred on how we humans are *being*, and it's …'

'Okay, stop right there, Jen', Yoren interrupted. 'You know I'm not interested in all that psychobabble. What would I need that for anyway? I already manage a team of 16, and they all look up to me, even the older ones with a chip on their shoulders. And I'm pretty sure I know myself better than most.'

'Yes, yes, I know you think you've got it all together.'

'I'm pretty certain I *know* I have it all together, Jen. How many 30-something-year-olds have achieved as much as I have?'

'You've never lacked self-confidence, have you, Yoren? But do you remember all those times when you were growing up when you used to tell me about your hopes and dreams for the future? I often wonder why you seem to have given up on all of that. I know you're successful, and I acknowledge all you've achieved. But based on what you told me as a teenager and even as a young adult, I know that deep down you want more, and I'm afraid that what got you to this point might not be enough to take you where you want to go. I truly believe you'd benefit from looking into certain aspects of yourself that are so far beneath the surface you might not be giving them the attention they deserve. This info session might open the door to supporting you in becoming aware of those inner qualities and uncovering some of your blind spots. I'll actually be participating in the session, too, because my good friend and colleague Erik is facilitating it. I know you'd like him. He reminds me a lot of you – the real you beneath that facade you portray all the time.'

'What's that supposed to mean?'

'I think deep down you know exactly what I mean. Anyway, just sign up for the session. It's only two hours out of your day. What have you got to lose?'

'Two hours of my sanity, that's what! But yes, alright. Just for you. I'm certainly not expecting to get anything out of it though.'

'Wonderful! I know you won't regret it. Just do yourself a favour and at least try to come with an open mind.'

'You know me, Jen, 'open' is my middle name. By the way, how come you always have this way of talking me into doing things I don't want to do?'

'Ah, well I may not always tell you what you *want* to hear, but I don't hold back on suggesting what I think you might *need*. Oh, by the way, the session is tomorrow evening. See you online.'

Jen ended the call before Yoren had a chance to back out.

I love Jen, but she can be a bit off with the fairies sometimes, despite her impressive career history and professional reputation. I'll make an appearance and feign interest just to make her happy. Then I'll make up some excuse for why I can't commit to any follow-up sessions. I'm not stupid; I know that these types of 'info sessions' are always a prelude to something bigger, just to hook you in. Like I told Jen, I'm not the kind of guy who can be lured into buying training or a program designed to develop my personality or whatever it is they're trying to sell me.

— ■ —

Yoren had a reputation as someone who always got what he wanted when he wanted it. The eldest of two children, he and his sister Sophia were raised in a tight-knit family. His father, Stewart, was a professor at one of the top three universities in Australia and revered as one of the world's most reputable, progressive and respected social scientists. His mother, Sahar, was the primary carer who worked part-time as a social worker and counsellor.

Yoren had always held a soft spot for his father's younger sister, Jen. She was the black sheep of the family in that she chose travel and adventure over going straight to university after school as her brothers had done. Jen would tell Yoren all kinds of stories when he was a child and, wide-eyed and innocent, he lapped it all up, determined to one day follow in her footsteps.

After a couple of years of travel and adventure, Jen came home and was ready to knuckle down and study. The time away had made her more mature, polished and worldly than many other young women her age. She completed a double degree in economics and finance, graduating with Honours and landing a well-paid corporate job with a major financial institution. She worked her way up the corporate ladder to being the CFO of one of the largest private banks in the country and sat on the board of a number of organisations.

Despite her success and status, Jen began to sense that something was missing. After much soul searching, she chose to switch gears and, after engaging in a program of study, found new meaning in being of service to others through coaching. In recent years, she became increasingly involved in facilitating programs in personal and organisational development and coaching seasoned and emerging leaders. She found this work so fulfilling that she decided to take a risk, resign from her position at the bank and play a more significant role in the community as a master coach, facilitator, trainer and mentor. These days, she is one of their most respected leadership master coaches. At no time is she more fulfilled than when being a contribution to others. However, her years of experience in finance continue to be put to good use in the role she plays overseeing the impressive investment portfolio her father, Samuel, put together. She was initially hesitant to take on this role after spending years rebelling against what she saw as his obsessive focus on wealth accumulation, but softened after seeing it from a different perspective.

Much to his father's concern, Yoren took off after school to travel and work overseas, just as Jen had done years ago and despite topping his year in all his subjects. He was offered a place at a number of top universities, but delayed his enrolment for a year of adventure. With his chiselled good looks and outward confidence, he was a hit with the European girls. It didn't take him long to get a reputation for his partying and womanising ways. But, like Jen many years before him, Yoren quickly tired of that frivolous lifestyle and returned to Australia, hungry to build his career and live the kind of lifestyle led by the many high-achievers who inspired him.

After graduating with a Bachelor of Economics, Yoren was offered an internship with one of the world's leading consulting firms. He later completed an MBA part-time while working his way up the corporate ladder. Today he is an associate solutions specialist with the firm, a senior role typically held by people with more extensive experience. When the position became vacant, Yoren knew he had it in the bag, despite dozens of high-calibre applicants. He even bragged about it to his colleagues, even though he knew some of them were also vying for the role. He would frequently and unashamedly boast about being better than others, so his bravado in securing the position surprised no one. Later, when he was a candidate to become a partner in the firm, he was shocked to be overlooked for a female colleague.

Yoren's lifestyle matched his prestigious career. He and Mel, an HR manager for an international professional services firm, had purchased their dream home overlooking the beach in Sydney's eastern suburbs, and the couple regularly rubbed shoulders with Sydney's A-listers. Life was good. But deep down, it wasn't as perfect as it seemed. There was intense pressure to keep up appearances, maintain the lavish lifestyle he and Mel had created and pay off the debts they had amassed to purchase their expensive possessions. Alone with his thoughts at night, he would occasionally become present to a lack of fulfilment. He just couldn't put his finger on why. However, come the morning and whenever he was with others, the mask would always go back on so he could perpetuate the image of the successful man and power couple he had worked so hard to contrive.

— ■ —

Yoren was dictating a letter to his PA when he received a text message from Jen.

Hey Yoren, look forward to seeing you online at 6.

Oh damn, looks like she's not going to let me off the hook on this one!

I can't wait!

He was sure Jen could read the sarcasm in his response.

Oh well, she was the one that roped me into this.

Back home and lounging on the sofa at 5 to 6, Yoren halfheartedly scrolled through his LinkedIn feed.

No sense entering the session until the dot of 6. Hmm, I really should post more. Would be more interesting than most of the rubbish and fake news on here. Actually, I take that back. Why waste precious time dealing with online trolls? All they do is sit there and judge people like me.

By the time he looked at his watch again, it was 6 minutes past 6, so he clicked on the link to join the session.

CHAPTER 2

Moments of Reception

Yoren did a quick scan of the 40 or so participants, pausing to smile when he spotted Jen, looking impeccable and polished as ever. Then he identified Erik, the facilitator, who had everyone's undivided attention in his opening address. His manner was friendly but professional, charismatic and confident without being overbearing, 'salesy' or arrogant.

As Erik was dominating the screen, it was easy to make out what he was wearing. Yoren could see that his clothes were classy and expensive. He wore a crisp white shirt underneath a royal blue jacket that matched the vibrant hue of his eyes. He could just make out his watch peeking out from beneath his cuff-linked shirt – a silver Rolex Sky-Dweller with a classic blue dial. Casting his eyes around the other participants again, Yoren noticed many were in business attire, making him feel conspicuous in his jeans and T-shirt.

At least I'm wearing the classic Louis Vuitton T-shirt Mel gifted me on Valentine's Day. Damn it, Jen, why didn't you tell me there was a dress code! Maybe I can turn off the video, sneak away and change back into my suit …

Since he was busy sizing up the facilitator and comparing himself to everyone else on the call, Yoren was totally oblivious to the fact that Erik had completed his welcome address. Everyone's attention was now on an attractive young woman by the name of Marisa, who was animatedly expressing why she was so happy to be there.

'Thank you, everyone. I'm very excited to learn more this evening. I'd now like to pass the mike to … Yoren.'

Wait, what are we talking about?

As if reading Yoren's mind, Erik interjected. His tone was completely calm and free from resentment, despite having to repeat himself for Yoren's benefit.

'Thanks, Marisa. Yoren, please introduce yourself to the group and then let us know what you feel like expressing this evening, particularly in relation to why you're here and what you hope to get out of the session. When you're finished, please nominate someone else to share.'

I thought I was just here to listen. I didn't even know about this until last night.

Suddenly, around 40 sets of eyes were on Yoren. His palms were sweaty, his mouth dry.

Why didn't I get a glass of water? No doubt they're all judging me on how I am dressed and how unprepared I am. Maybe I can say I'm feeling sick and leave. No, I can't do that to Jen. Oh, come on, pull yourself together, man! Just tell them about yourself and impress them like you do everyone else you meet.

He took a deep breath, planted a fake but convincing smile on his face and said, 'Good evening, everyone. I'm Yoren Healy. Currently, I am an associate solutions specialist for one of the world's Big 4 consulting firms, but I am about to become a partner. At 37, I am the firm's youngest employee to achieve such a high status so quickly. I live in Sydney's eastern suburbs in a beachfront apartment with uninterrupted views I purchased a few years ago. Over to you … Julia Taylor.'

I'm glad that's over! Was that oversharing? Did I say enough?

He put himself on mute, satisfied that he had selected the most attractive female attendee to follow him and confident that he had suitably impressed her (and the others).

Erik interrupted his thoughts, 'Before we move on to you, Julia, I'd like to reiterate what I am asking each of you to do in case some of you misunderstood.'

Am I imagining it, or did he just look my way?

'Please share something you would like to express with the group in relation to why you are here and what you hope to get out of this information session this evening. Yoren, could we return to you?'

Oh, great!

'Sure. I was asked to come along to this session by Jenah Healy, who I believe many of you know. She said she thinks I'll get a lot out of it. I should warn you, though, I'm very well-read and follow the world's most renowned thinkers. And my father, Professor Stewart Healy – you may know of him – is one of the world's most highly regarded experts on social science. So you'll have to excuse me for being a bit sceptical about a program I have never heard of on human beings. And, with all due respect, you'll have your work cut out for you if you want to talk me into any follow-up program or anything else you might want to sell me. But I'm open to being proved wrong, although I have to say, that rarely happens.'

There, now they know a bit more about me and that I'm not someone who's easily led or sold to.

While the remaining participants each shared with the group, Yoren turned off his video and scrolled through his emails. He only looked at the screen whenever a new participant introduced themselves, mainly to size them up. Once they had all expressed themselves, Erik commenced his address.

Better turn my video back on, or Jen will have a go at me later.

'As human beings, we all have certain things we want, such as goals and objectives,' said Erik. 'Let's call them 'intentions'. When I say intentions, I am referring specifically to the objectives, goals and desires we want to fulfil. Obviously, not everyone's intentions are the same. We are all individuals. But generally speaking, we all want our intentions to be fulfilled, no matter how big or small. This is a phenomenological reality. Our proclivity to fulfil our intentions is fuelled by how much we care about those objectives and is a common human experience, regardless of gender, ethnicity, culture or religion. The fact that you have all given up two precious hours of your evening to be here shows that you might at least care enough to be curious about the being discourse, which is tonight's topic.'

Well, I am basically just here to appease Jen.

'Perhaps you are more than just curious,' Erik continued. 'Maybe you have a genuine and sincere willingness to learn more about yourself and others, including how these insights might support you in fulfilling your intentions and contributing more effectively to yourself, your organisation, your community, society and humanity. Perhaps you are inclined to live your life from the viewpoint of higher purpose, a state of being that conveys a willingness to sacrifice instant gratification in favour of a longer-term goal or for the benefit of a greater cause.

'No matter what your intentions – what you care about – and no matter how big or small, trivial or insignificant they might look to you or others, be it a cause or anything you're working towards, it's only natural to want to be fulfilled in that pursuit. In short, that's what we all want. We all want to be fulfilled in our endeavours.'

*I am already fulfilled and know what I want for my future. I don't
need to learn more about myself to gain clarity around that!*

'So to succeed in fulfilling our intentions, we must be effective in our
decisions and behaviours,' said Erik. 'Effectiveness is the extent to
which an intention is actualised. And the proclivity to be in a state of
fulfilment is a common human expectation; it's a state we all desire.'

An attendee from Perth by the name of Xander raised his hand to ask
a question, 'Erik, what you're saying seems to suggest that once you
reach a state of fulfilment, you have made it, that you are fulfilled in
life, that it's the ultimate goal. That doesn't seem right to me. Is that
what you mean?'

'Great question, Xander, and I can see why one could assume that.
Effectiveness is the degree to which we are successful in producing a
desired result or fulfilling an intention that we consider important.
However, fulfilling one intention doesn't mean we have reached a
state of fulfilment because most of us have many intentions we want
to realise. Furthermore, it's not a linear or one-off process. You
don't arrive at a state of fulfilment and stay there. Our intentions
continuously change as we progress through life. For example, if
you are about to become a parent, your intentions would likely be
very different from the intentions you had before starting a family.
Similarly, if you are embarking on an entrepreneurial journey, you
would set new intentions to reflect your objectives for your business
venture. Your priorities change in line with your intentions or what
you care about. Does that answer your question?'

Xander's thoughtful nod indicated he received the clarity he had been
seeking. Meanwhile, Yoren was only halfheartedly listening to the
conversation, every now and then zoning out completely to check his
missed calls and messages. He was so engrossed in one particular
message that he failed to notice that Erik had recommenced his
presentation.

'So, for us as human beings, the prerequisite to being able to fulfil
our intentions is to be effective in our decisions and endeavours,'

continued Erik. 'And for us to be effective, we need to be integrous – to be whole and complete or 'of integrity'. We're no different than any other system or organism in that regard. These are ontological laws of existence that apply to everyone and everything.

'Imagine if one of your organs malfunctioned – let's say one of your kidneys failed or you had a heart issue. The performance of the overall system would be impacted. The same principle applies to animals, plants, hardware, software, organisations, societies, in fact, any system. For example, if a cog breaks in a mechanical watch, it will malfunction. The same goes for a bug or error in a software program. Obviously, I'm not comparing us to machines. But when you consider that the human body is also a system in that it is made up of multiple constituent parts, you can see that any breakdown within the system will cause suffering and dysfunction.

'So, we can conclude that a state of integrity is necessary for any being, system or organism, including us humans, to be effective and perform at an optimum level. When you perform at an optimum level, the probability of you being effective is increased, which then enhances the chances of you fulfilling your intentions.

'There are certain underlying qualities inherent in all human beings that either contribute to or compromise our integrity or wholeness and which drive our decisions, actions and behaviour. When we lack wholeness or integrity, we can't be effective. And without effectiveness, we can't possibly fulfil our intentions. Any questions so far?'

Peter, a middle-aged businessman from Singapore, raised his hand and asked, 'Could you please explain in more detail what you mean by integrity in this context, Erik? It seems to be different from the definition of integrity that I am familiar with, which is to be honest and to have strong moral principles.'

'Good question, Peter. I agree. Integrity is one of those words that is commonly used in multiple different ways, so let me clarify. To put it simply, by integrity, I am referring to the state of being whole and undivided. It's when all the parts that combine to form a whole and complete human being are working at an optimum level. Think of it like a piece of machinery that relies on all the parts to work properly for it to run efficiently. If some parts are deficient, the machine might still run, but not as effectively. In the context of human performance, which we are discussing here, integrity is how an individual relates to the various constituent parts or qualities that bring workability and effectiveness to their lives – qualities like authenticity, commitment, assertiveness, anxiety and so on. In this way, integrity supports us to fulfil our intentions.'

Scanning the participants to gauge how his explanation had landed, Erik could see there was some confusion. Before he had time to clarify, Lakshmi, a young woman from India, raised her hand and said, 'Erik, I'm confused by what you just said. It seems to me that you are suggesting that a human being must be whole and complete to be integrous – that all the parts need to be working at an optimum level. Is that state even real? Isn't it a bit utopian and dreamy? Are you saying one can achieve the state of full integrity and completeness and the journey stops there, when one is perfect?'

'Thank you for your question, Lakshmi,' replied Erik. 'I can see where the confusion lies, and I can also see that you might not be alone in your confusion. Let me explain. When I talk about integrity, I am referring to the integrity of one's being. It relates to the qualities that lie within, the drivers of our decisions, behaviours and actions. More specifically, the healthier your relationship with those qualities, the more integrous you become. It is also worth noting that integrity is not a static state to reach and remain in. In other words, it's not a quality to just be in constantly. It's something we must continually work towards or strive for.

'Let me clarify further. Our integrity is constantly being challenged by situations and circumstances life brings our way or that we cause ourselves by our decisions. Indeed, the integrity of any system or entity is constantly being challenged, and it takes something to maintain it. For example, we get our car serviced regularly by the mechanic, and we clean our homes and tend to our gardens to maintain their integrity. The same goes for our physical and mental health. The idea is not to be in a state of total integrity all the time but to live life from the viewpoint of valuing and caring so much about integrity that you choose to work towards it. This also requires you to have a sense of integrity so that you can discern when your integrity is challenged and take steps to restore it.

'We are constantly exposed to matters and experiences in life that can move us out of integrity. For example, divorce, a serious illness, going broke while attempting to build a startup, and not having enough money to pay the bills and put food on the table are all examples of circumstances that would challenge anyone. A person with a relatively healthy relationship with integrity is committed to restoring their being to a state of integrity any time it is challenged. They would respond rather than react to a challenge, regardless of whether they are the source. It's up to us to become aware of those times when we move out of integrity and care enough to restore it. Does that make sense, Lakshmi?'

'Yes, it does. Thanks, Erik,' she smiled. Erik could see that he'd clarified it for other participants too.

> *Hmm, to be of integrity is to be whole and complete, which requires the constituent parts to work at an optimum level ... interesting. And it's also something to constantly have a sense of and keep working towards when it's challenged. I've always considered myself a man of integrity. But this puts a totally different spin on it. It's kind of weird, though.*

'Let's return to our intentions – which, as I mentioned, represent the things we most care about and therefore determine our priorities,' continued Erik. 'Becoming aware of your intentions and what it takes to fulfil them is the first step. Let's say your intention is to be an Olympic swimmer. Then you'd need to care enough about that intention to be fully committed to daily swim sessions and work with a professional swim coach. You'd need to be responsible by actively *responding* to the circumstances rather than *reacting* like a victim.

You'd need to have the courage to step forward despite your fears, anxiety and discomfort. You'd need to be vulnerable enough to be coached and to shape a congruent conception of what it takes to become an Olympic athlete and authentically aware of all there is to learn and overcome. You'd also need to be proactive and resilient in the face of all the difficulties along the way, such as overcoming injuries and intense competition from other swimmers, and the list goes on.

'Let me make this conversation more tangible by referring to something we can all relate to: focus. There are times when many of us have unrealistic expectations. We talk about having a side project and say, "If it works, then I might take it seriously." The more effective logic is to flip that on its head and tell yourself, "I am taking this project seriously so that it might work!" Now, if you have too many priorities – or matters that you care about – you may as well care about nothing at all. That's because your energy and attention would be so scattered that you end up with less energy and focus for each endeavour, leading to reduced effectiveness. There could be various reasons behind your lack of focus, including how you relate to care and commitment. Indeed, a lack of focus occurs when one's integrity is challenged because of one's relationship with care and commitment. It takes sacrifice to commit to a select number of matters. In other words, you'll need to sacrifice certain things that you enjoy, at least for the time being, so you can commit to devoting the time and energy required to focus on what really matters, the things you most care about. This simple ontological fact will significantly increase the probability of fulfilling your intentions.'

Yoren suddenly sat up and took notice.

> *I've never thought about it this way. I always saw myself as a very caring person who gives so much attention to everything and everyone in all aspects of my life. Surely that's why I have it all together. But have I really given the most important things as much focus and attention as I should? Have I been as effective as I could be? Maybe I have too many priorities. Maybe I'm just*

trying to do too many things at the same time. Perhaps that's why I never seem to have time to work on my personal projects. But hang on a minute. For any of my most significant achievements, I was intensely focused, at least for a certain period of time. I cared enough to be committed till the very end, till I achieved the outcome I was striving for. So why don't I apply this logic to other things I want? I know I could bring greater care and commitment to those things, so why have I been choosing to neglect and ignore them? I must admit, this is more confronting than I thought it would be. What if I'm the one getting in the way of what I really want, the business I always wanted to build, a business of my own?

Erik's words had touched on a nerve and made Yoren glimpse the inauthenticity in his belief system and value structure.

One cannot care about everything at the same time. Such a simple idea. But hang on a minute; that's not fair! I want to care about several things at once. I've never let that limit me in the past, and I don't intend to start now. Why would anyone sacrifice many things for the sake of just a few things they care about?

Yoren tried to get his head around this new information and apply his typical logic to disprove it. Erik looked around at the participants' faces and could tell that many had shifted into deep thought. While he knew the information was confronting for many of them, he chose to proceed.

'Let's go back to integrity and explore that a little more in relation to fulfilling your intentions. As I mentioned when responding to Peter's question earlier, when I refer to integrity, I'm not talking about one of its conventional meanings, which is being of high moral standards. I'm talking about another definition of integrity, which is being whole, complete, unbroken or undivided. Let me elaborate. There is a fundamental law of existence whereby parts combine to shape a whole. This 'whole' can then combine with other 'wholes' to shape a new, more complex being – a higher-level 'whole'. We call this continuous and iterative pattern 'transcendence and inclusion'.

'Let me bring it home with a simple biological example. Atoms gather together and transcend to a higher being called a molecule. Once that happens, the molecule as a 'whole' includes the atoms. Then the molecules gather together – as parts this time – and they form a higher being called a cell. Then the cells come together to form different parts of an organism, and so on until a complex being, such as a human being, is formed.'

Why are we being given a biology lesson? What do atoms and molecules have to do with integrity and fulfilling our intentions?

As Yoren considered his judgements of the presentation, he was oblivious to the fact that Erik had moved on. Consequently, he missed the next part of his talk.

'The same process applies when it comes to consciousness. As individuals, we continuously expose ourselves to various perceptions of matters in life. And if we are capable, we develop our understanding or conception of those matters, so these conceptions are the 'wholes' being created. Just as our physical bodies are constructed from numerous constituent parts, it is a similar process when it comes to intentionally developing our consciousness,' said Erik.

'It all begins when you receive new pieces of information – well, not necessarily new, but new to you, to your individual consciousness. That information could have been out there in the world, but you were either ignorant to it – in other words, you were *ignoring* it – or you were oblivious to it. Or perhaps you didn't care enough to be present to it, so you neglected it. Receiving information – which we call reception – is like an ah-ha or lightbulb moment. It's when you are suddenly *informed* about something, which is why it's called information. Imagine that you suddenly become present to the fact that the way you've been relating to money is the reason you've been struggling with your finances. In other words, the perception you hold or the conception you have of money isn't congruent with reality, and you've paid a price for your ignorance. Now that you've experienced this lightbulb moment of reception, you suddenly start paying more attention. This new information suggests that it might be best to transform your current conception of money. And if your goal is to be wealthy, you'll need to learn what it is and how it works.

'The next step after receiving the information – or, to be exact, after being informed about something – is perceiving it as knowledge. That's when you *choose* a perception of it directly through your senses. In the example of money, you are now perceptive to articles and YouTube videos, etcetera, on how money works, and you choose who to follow and what to read, watch and listen to on the subject in order to gain objective knowledge.

'As time passes, we are all constantly learning and adding more to our web of perceptions. This is a metaphor that describes the perceptions we adopt over time. It can be compared to a web because it's easy to get stuck inside our own web of perceptions rather than be open to exploring other perceptions. For example, you might have a particular perception of marriage, money, life, God, commitment, love, assertiveness and so on. As you learn more about them and put all the pieces of the puzzle – or parts – together, you shape the whole. This 'whole' ultimately becomes your intentional consciousness, which we call awareness.

'In this constant process of transcendence and inclusion in the realm of consciousness, there are times when certain parts get missed or are not carried over. The parts that are left behind create a void or gaps within the development of the 'whole'. For example, it could be the way you interpreted a particular event in your life, such as an interaction with your parents when you were a child, feeling unloved by a partner, or seeing unfairness in the world. We're often not aware of these gaps as they may sit in our unconscious, but they get in the way of our integrity. The high-level solution is to bring those parts to our awareness so we can identify, address and integrate them, either by resolving them or gracefully carrying them over as part of the whole.

'Over time, you choose your opinions and beliefs based on a collection of experiences, and you gradually form a narrative lens of all your life's stories and interpretations of the events and viewpoints you have been exposed to. These come together to shape your worldview and establish the way you relate to existence and everything in it. As time passes, you continually put these pieces together, which leads you to keep moving to a higher degree of awareness. Over time, you may become more acutely aware of yourself, your talents, emotions, preferences and characteristics. You might even become aware of your troubled sides, which we call the shadows. This might lead you to become more attuned not only to the shadow parts of you as an individual but also to the shadow side of human beings on a collective scale and how this impacts humanity.'

Triggered by the shadow conversation, Yoren was suddenly paying attention again.

> *Now, this is really starting to go off on a tangent. Shadow … really? I can't believe Jen, of all people, is so into this!*

'Some of us simply choose our perceptions based on our environment or what we were told at school, or by our parents, friends, colleagues, religious leaders, or what we hear or read in the media or from opinion-makers, influencers, TV and so on,' continued Erik. 'Simply put, many of us choose to outsource the heavy lifting involved in perceiving new knowledge and, to a certain degree, our sanity to others.

'But there are some people who choose to do it differently. Instead of simply relying on what they pick up at an event, online or in a conversation in a shallow, unsophisticated way, they choose to shape a *conception* of a matter. This is a lengthier, far more thorough mental process than simply choosing a perception in an instant. We shape a conception of a matter over time through logic, reasoning, conversation, analysis, reflection, contemplation and so on. As critical thinkers, truth seekers and those who choose authentic awareness as an approach to comprehending the world as it is, we relate that knowledge to the context of our lives or what we care most about, our priorities. Returning to our money example, such a person would take the time to learn all they can from various sources about what money is and how it works to ensure they can be effective in their desire to grow their wealth. They would not simply choose a perception or rely on what they may perceive through their direct senses; they would shape their own conception of it.

'Consider that the most effective people tap into and leverage as many ways of examining matters as they can in order to shape authentic and congruent conceptions of different fragments of reality. They are authentic in their awareness and are not lenient or fickle with their opinions and beliefs. Some of us gradually develop the ability to conceive instead of being satisfied with just perceiving a meaning. That's when, instead of just picking an available perception of a meaning, we go through an objective knowledge-filtering process. We reflect on our perceptions and then ensure that we relate our well-investigated knowledge to our lives. This approach often paves the way towards developing wisdom and practical knowledge that can significantly drive our decisions, actions, behaviours and, ultimately, our outcomes and accomplishments.'

Reading the attendee's faces, Erik suddenly realised that a few of them were confused.

'I acknowledge that some of this content is challenging to grasp. As I mentioned at the beginning of the session, there's only so much we can cover in two hours. However, there are various ways to continue the conversation and learn more if you want to because you find it relevant and useful. For now, though, please bear with me as I explain further, and feel free to raise your hand if you have a question.

'As time passes and we keep developing higher levels of awareness, we may leave behind certain unresolved and unintegrated matters, which can lead to misunderstandings, misconceptions, unhealed traumas, incomplete experiences, unforgiven mistakes, resentment and more. These troubled, unintegrated and incomplete parts represent our shadow side, which can compromise our overall integrity. And, as I said earlier, if the integrity of any system is compromised, it leads to pain, suffering, dysfunction, mistrust and a lack of workability. This is precisely why it is so important for us to cast light on our being to identify these troubled parts and expose the shadow. Although it might be painful – after all, facing our troubled parts is never easy – if you choose a life of growth and prosperity, if you want to thrive, fulfil your intentions and actualise your potential, then facing your shadow is not negotiable. Any questions so far?'

As much as I wish to beg to differ, it all seems to make total sense. I've always chosen the path of growth and prosperity. But I've always believed that I need to maintain a positive mindset and push aside any inner troubled parts or disguise them to achieve that outcome. Hmm, facing your shadow is not negotiable. Is the fact that I'm struggling to sleep at night an indication that I know there's more to me than the life I'm leading?

Erik's words on the shadow had hit a nerve. But Yoren was not about to expose himself by asking a question, let alone be open about his revelation.

When nobody raised their hand, Jen unmuted herself and made a suggestion, 'Erik, earlier you mentioned that human beings are made up of a number of constituent parts. Could you explain to the group which parts we need to become aware of that impact how we perform?'

'Sure, Jenah, thanks for the reminder,' replied Erik. 'Our studies have identified 31 qualities or Aspects of Being that are the most critical and influential when it comes to integrity and effectiveness. In our model, these qualities are broken down into Moods and Ways of Being. The Moods are vulnerability, care, fear and anxiety, while the Ways of Being include responsibility, authenticity, peace of mind, higher purpose, compassion, love, presence, confidence, assertiveness and reliability, just to name a few. They are all qualities we should have a healthy relationship with if we care about the integrity of our being so we can be effective and fulfil our intentions, those matters or endeavours we care most about. By now it should come as no surprise to learn that, unless we become aware of those constituent parts to see how we are being and identify the shadow parts, it's impossible to address them, integrate or heal them. In other words, we cannot intentionally become effective at something we're unaware of. So the first step is always awareness.

'Let's now take a step back and talk about why any of what we've discussed matters. Unlike what some schools of thought might have us believe, as human beings, we are not destined to be how we are forever. We are not defined by our personality type or whether we are introverts or extroverts. We can and do transform. When I say transform, it's not about changing *what* we are as human beings; it's about changing *how* we are being. We can become more committed, courageous, assertive, proactive and compassionate, among other qualities we have the power to transform. Employees can transform to become successful entrepreneurs. Mediocre sportspeople can transform to become Olympic athletes. Someone living below the poverty line can transform to become a high-net-worth individual. Small family businesses can transform to become scalable global enterprises. These are just a few examples of transformation, and none of them is unprecedented.

'For transformation to occur, we go from a degree of awareness to a degree of effectiveness. As I mentioned earlier, awareness is always the starting point because you can't become effective in something you are not aware of or have misconceptions about. Furthermore, we cannot move to a degree of effectiveness unless we are aware of any constituent parts that cause us to be out of integrity or wholeness. For each of us, life is a constant dance between a degree of awareness and a degree of effectiveness as we move in and out of integrity.

'To recap, awareness begins with reception. This is the lightbulb moment when you are informed: when something has been brought to your attention. You may then choose a perception of the matter, based on what you hear, read or see about it. Some people are satisfied at this level and choose to look no deeper. However, others – the critical thinkers and truth seekers among us – will take the time to shape a conception of the matter, studying it and learning as much as they can about it until they are satisfied that they have investigated it thoroughly. When you develop a conception of something, you also contextualise it by relating it back to your own life and priorities. Any questions?'

'Can you give us an example of someone moving through those three degrees of awareness?' asked Ahmed, a young man from Melbourne.

'Sure. Imagine your attention is suddenly drawn to climate change by an external trigger such as a billboard or posts on social media. This is the reception stage of awareness. Your interest is piqued and you spend time investigating it online. The more you discover, the more you want to learn. Your focus turns to trying to validate the studies you read on climate change. This is the perception phase. In other words, you're developing an authentic perception of climate change. Once you're satisfied with the perception you've chosen, you store that in your memory bank until you find an opportunity to draw on it and apply it in a practical way.

'A few months later, you're thinking about buying a block of land on which to build your dream home. You draw on your perception of climate change in determining where to buy and where not to buy. You then decide to take the time to investigate the matter thoroughly in order to shape a well-informed conception of climate change and how it relates to you in the context of purchasing the right block of land. Once you're satisfied with the knowledge you've acquired, you decide that buying in a one-in-a-hundred-year flood plain is too risky. At this point, you're applying your knowledge of climate change to your life. Not only do you know about climate change, but you're applying your now well-investigated knowledge or conception of it to your decision about buying property. Does that make it more tangible for you, Ahmed?'

'Absolutely,' responded Ahmed, while other participants nodded in agreement.

Hmm, I follow a lot of well-known thinkers, but I've never thought to look into the validity of what they're sharing. Perhaps I've been missing the conception stage and just adopting a perception I was being presented with and jumping straight to applying what they told me to my life.

'Effectiveness demands awareness too,' said Erik. 'You could not be effective at building a bridge or an aeroplane, for example, if you were unaware of the laws of physics. Similarly, you cannot be an effective surgeon without extensive knowledge of human anatomy. I'm sure you get my drift. However, just as there are degrees of awareness, the same is true for effectiveness.'

Erik checked his watch, conscious of time, and decided to start wrapping up.

'We're approaching the end of this session, so I'd like to recap the key points and also leave you with some food for thought. We all have matters or intentions we care about and want to fulfil. And when we care about something (or someone), we want to make that thing or person a priority. To be fulfilled in our intentions, we need to be effective in our decisions, actions and endeavours. And to be effective, we need to be integrous, and that means we need to first be aware of the health or otherwise of our constituent parts: the qualities we have a healthy relationship with and the ones we don't – the shadows. Finally, we need to work on the shadow parts to transform them and restore integrity. And remember, this is not a one-off process. We are constantly moving in and out of integrity and should work towards restoring it when it is lacking.

'There is a law that applies to all beings; we're either growing or dying. Things in the world are constantly transforming, whether we are intentionally conscious of it or not. So we're always moving towards growth or regression. Being a leader who is responsible and relatively autonomous means being aware of our role in this transformation process and being an active agent in our life rather than a passive victim.

'You may question why you should bother transforming your being. And the simple answer is because you *care*. We all do. We care about fulfilling our intentions, both individually and collectively. When you set an intention or objective, you care about it deeply. It becomes your priority. So, on the one hand, you have the intentions you care about, and on the other, you have your current being. Put simply, this is how you're being right now: how committed, responsible, assertive and courageous you are, along with all the other qualities. The healthier your relationship with all the qualities that count when it comes to human performance and effectiveness, the more integrous you are and the more likely you will succeed in aligning your being with the intentions you wish to fulfil. In other words, your being must be aligned with what you want to achieve.

'Every single one of us has three choices when it comes to fulfilling our intentions:

1. You can let go of your intentions and choose the pathway of contentment, staying as you are, which means your current state of being remains untransformed.

2. You can hold onto your intentions, make them priorities in your life and be willing to transform your being to become the person you need to be who has a higher probability of achieving them.

3. Or you can cling to your desires but not be willing to transform how you're being to increase the likelihood of achieving them.

'Most people choose the third option. They want to stay the way they are and maintain their existing lifestyle. And yet they expect life to miraculously bring them different results. The fact is, you can't have it both ways. If you're drawn to an intention or calling, but your current state of being is luring you to stay as you are, you're being pulled from two directions. And this commonly leads to a life of dissatisfaction, misery and stress.

'The majority of leaders and high achievers, on the other hand, intentionally choose the second option. They understand that everything is constantly changing and transforming, including themselves. And they respond by aligning their being with those changes, taking charge of their own transformation in order to influence their personal reality and potentially also the shared reality around them.

'Human beings are social creatures, so it's inauthentic to live life as if we can function completely independently from others. Our true power resides in our ability to organise ourselves in groups and communities. From an anthropological perspective, this has given us an enormous advantage over other creatures. How effectively you get to know yourself and other human beings is vital, no matter whether you're building a career, a family, an organisation, a community or whatever you're up to. It's surprising how little we know about human beings and how we are being. This lack of authentic awareness is one of the major reasons we jump into toxic or unworkable relationships, marry the wrong person, hire the wrong person and so on, leading to suffering on a massive scale. Many great thinkers emphasise the importance of having the right spouse, partners and team members, and most successful business leaders say that having 'great' or 'talented' people is critical for growth. But what does this mean? What defines a great or talented team member? Those terms are vague and ambiguous. The being conversation addresses some of this ambiguity and helps us to see through ourselves and others.

'We've covered a lot of ground today, and I acknowledge that you might be feeling overwhelmed. I know I did when I was first introduced to this content. But fear not; this is just the beginning! There's only so much we can cover in two hours. So if you walk away with nothing more than a high-level understanding and the curiosity to learn more about who and how you and others are being and what it takes to fulfil your intentions, then I've achieved my objective for this session.

'I'll finish by reiterating that life is a constant dance between a degree of awareness to a degree of effectiveness. In the middle of that dance is your integrity. And the things causing you to falter and lose step are your troubled parts or shadow. By casting light on the shadow, facing and transforming it, you can dance through life with greater ease and flow.'

As Yoren shut his laptop, his mind was a whirl of emotions. Confused and feeling slightly anxious, an unaccustomed sensation, he had more questions than answers.

Has all my success to date been authentic? Am I being effective and integrous? I'm up to my eyeballs in debt and have a massive mortgage hanging over my head. But nobody knows about any of that because I've done such a great job of only revealing what I want people to see. Isn't that what all high achievers do? So why do I suddenly feel like an imposter? Like all my so-called successes are on the surface, and the person within, the real me, doesn't know what he wants, doesn't even know who the hell he is anymore, let alone where he's heading!

The biggest shadow of all suddenly dawned on Yoren … *Am I the best I could ever be?*

CHAPTER 3

The Seed is Sown

Yoren did his best to push aside the disturbing and unfamiliar thoughts and feelings that had threatened to derail him for the entire week since the information session. He'd been reasonably successful at ignoring them while at the office, but the nights were a different story. That's when he would sit up late, pretending to work or lie in bed, wide awake, mulling over the presentation and trying desperately to find fault in what Erik had shared. The lightbulb moments of reception he had experienced kept playing over and over in his mind like a showreel on repeat that he couldn't switch off.

Erik had ended the information session by walking attendees through a few pathway options for those who found the information relevant and useful, and who might like to delve deeper into the being discourse. This was the first step to contextualise the learnings from the session in a practical and personalised way. He said undertaking a self-discovery process would support them to 'look into a mirror' and see how they relate to all the fundamental qualities that play a significant role in their overall integrity, performance and effectiveness as human beings. He also said this process would cast a light on their being and support them to become aware of and present to their shadows – the troubled parts getting in the way of their integrity. This was the part that particularly intrigued Yoren. While he portrayed a persona of bravado and superiority around others, deep down he often felt he was not good enough.

I'm so tempted to call Jen and pick her brain about it, but I don't want her to think I'm interested in delving deeper into how I'm being. But I can't help being a bit curious about the self-discovery process the facilitator (what was his name again?) mentioned towards the end of his presentation.

Yoren was sceptical at the best of times and now was no exception. However, deep down, he couldn't deny that the information session had made him receptive to the possibility that something within himself was out of place and was preventing him from fulfilling his intentions. Despite his misgivings, he told himself he was merely curious rather than hopeful. The last thing he wanted was for anyone, including Jen, to think he had any weaknesses. So he procrastinated in calling her.

It wasn't unusual for Yoren to defer or avoid taking action or making decisions, especially if he felt it might impact his reputation. He would often project a fake persona if he thought that would appear more acceptable and impressive to others, maintaining an air of bravado if he thought he might look foolish. He was also generally more concerned with being seen to do the right things than actually doing what he knew to be right. In most situations, Yoren took criticism personally and sometimes attempted to create unrealistic boundaries to maintain a 'safe' distance and avoid the unknown. This would occasionally cause issues at home between him and Mel and create problems at work.

What will Jen think if I ask her to connect me with a coach? She might think I'm weak and that I can't take care of my issues on my own, just like Dad when it comes to the household finances.

— ∎ —

Yoren had always had a somewhat strained relationship with his father, Stewart. From the time he was a teenager, his father had done his best to influence his firstborn to follow in his footsteps. He had high hopes for Yoren to attend the best university, achieve top grades and move into academia to contribute to the world through research and knowledge. The last thing Stewart wanted was for his son to emulate his grandfather and become a 'greedy, money-making businessman', which is how Stewart had always perceived his own father. His attitude later influenced Yoren's perception of his grandfather too, but not in the way Stewart wanted. Ironically, Stewart's own relationship with money was less than healthy and he struggled to manage his finances, despite beginning his career in economics. Later, Yoren vowed that he would never be like his 'socialist' father. He would prove his father wrong and become someone important. It was like history repeating itself because Stewart had shown similar disdain towards his own father when growing up. So Yoren read every book he could lay his hands on about the best ways to make money and grow rich.

Stewart Healy was born in Israel to immigrant Jews who moved to Israel after the Second World War. The eldest of three children, he had a sister, Jenah, who was four years younger and their brother, Igor, arrived two years later. Their father, Samuel, was originally from Dublin, Ireland. Born in 1942, Samuel was eight years old when he, his younger siblings and their parents migrated to Israel. Street-wise, masculine and physically strong, Samuel was not a man to mess with. He had been through the school of hard knocks in Israel before creating his own wealth through a series of astute investments and business ventures. Well-connected and shrewd, Samuel believed in having good lawyers and accountants behind him. Nothing was more important to him than protecting his family and ensuring they had the best of everything. He worked hard to give them a better life than he had experienced growing up. They lived in a multimillion-dollar mansion with its own helipad on the roof in Sydney, where he ran a diamond wholesale company and wedding catering business. The family also owned a motorhome and a luxury yacht, both of which were seldom used since Samuel was always working.

Ironically, Samuel's efforts to create a cohesive family and multi-generational investment portfolio and businesses seemed to have failed since all three of his children ended up going their own way. Only Igor made a half-hearted attempt to replicate his father's success. However, his desire for shortcuts eventually led him into politics, a move his father derided as 'the pathway of corruption and hypocrisy'. Samuel was bitterly disappointed that none of his children had followed him into the family business.

Samuel met his wife Uriel through a matchmaker in Israel when he was 19 and she was 18. Uriel had been raised in the Jewish Orthodox tradition and she and her family had fled Ukraine for Israel in the same year that Samuel's family had arrived. Samuel was drawn to her wholesome values as much as her natural beauty. They married a year later and started a family almost immediately. Uriel was a proud stay-at-home mother who loved nothing better than to cook for her family, provide them with a lovingly-maintained home and instil the kind of core values in her children that she believed no one else could. Even years later, when the family could afford all the domestic help they wanted, Uriel disliked having strangers in her home and preferred to look after the household and her children herself. She ran a tight ship and always kept her children close to protect them from what she saw as the unhealthy influence of others. Uriel's humble, wholesome persona, overprotective nature and simple way of life belied her innate wisdom and integrity. Her calmness, patience and contentment drew people towards her like a magnet, including her children, who would often find comfort in her arms or through conversation at the kitchen table when they were growing up.

As the eldest, Stewart was highly studious and excelled at school and university. From a young age, he was heavily influenced by Karl Marx and later by various neo-Marxist thinkers and theorists from the Frankfurt School of Thought, like Herbert Marcuse, Erich Fromme and Theodore Adorno. He later learned about postmodern philosophers such as Michel Foucault and Jacques Derrida and also began to follow people like John Money and Alfred Kinsey, developing a keen interest in topics like power dynamics, identity politics, gender studies, emotional safety and political correctness. He proudly identified as a left-wing socialist with progressive anti-neo-liberal views coupled, ironically, with conservative family values stemming from his Jewish upbringing.

His sister Jen looked up to her older, 'wiser' brother and, in their teens, would spend hours listening intently as he lectured her about the latest philosophical book he was reading. Full of dreams and ambitions, and with a quirky sense of humour and cheerful disposition, Jen would often tease Stewart for his serious ways. However, by the time she was 18, she had grown weary of her father's constant attempts to convert what he called her 'fanciful ambitions' into serious money-making ventures and his constant comparison between her and her 'focused and academic brother'. A rebellious, free-spirited young woman, Jen didn't want her dreams to be stained with money. So, against her parents' wishes, she left the nest to explore the world on her own terms. She travelled to Europe and then to India, China and other parts of Asia, lapping up the different cultures and cuisines. When, after three years, she was finally ready to settle down, she returned to Australia and landed her dream role with a multinational finance corporation. This role saw her travel extensively for business, particularly to the Middle East.

Jen was seen as the black sheep of the family because she didn't choose to become a business owner and investor like her father or a socialist intellectual like Stewart. Regarding herself as a feminist, an identity that was amplified by the corporate environments in which she worked, she frowned upon her mother's decision to be a homemaker in what she considered to be a male-dominated patriarchal household. Eventually, in her early forties and after her extensive travels, she developed a greater appreciation for the many opportunities her mother's surrendered way of being had afforded her.

Some years later, after looking inwardly, polishing herself and going through several rounds of transformations, Jen realised how she had misunderstood her parents and developed a deep sense of gratitude for who they had been in her life. She no longer saw her mother as 'just a housewife' but as a powerful person who consciously chose her pathway and lifestyle with awareness, contentment, integrity and surrender. Despite all her studies, worldly experience and self-assurance, Jen didn't realise the maturity and wisdom her mother had had at half her age until she was a middle-aged woman herself. She eventually also came to understand that her father had been right. He'd never wanted her to focus solely on money, but for her to appreciate the importance of economics in pursuing her goals and dreams. As a realist, he knew only too well that capital was one of the key ingredients his ambitious daughter needed to fulfil her intentions and amplify the impact she could make in solving some of the world's problems through business and, particularly, entrepreneurship. Knowing she couldn't rewrite history, only pave a better way forward, Jen chose to forgive herself rather than be crushed by regret.

— ■ —

Faced with Yoren's overly confident exterior, few people realised that he struggled in uncertain situations. Although his tendency to procrastinate or delay making decisions sometimes made others consider him passive or lacking discernment, he also knew deep down that he could be overly sceptical and focus too much on what could go wrong. And there were also times when he was simply nonchalant and failed to consider the consequences of his actions or inactions.

Despite his tendency to be uncertain and, at times, oblivious to the consequences of his actions, Yoren's relatively healthy relationship with care wouldn't allow him to ignore the insights he gained from last week's information session. And despite the resistance he'd felt to Jen's invitation, his relationship with care prompted him to show up. And now, he couldn't stop thinking about the moments of reception he experienced in the session and didn't want to let them go. Indeed, his relationship with care was one of the major factors that had led to his current level of success and it was now compelling him to call his aunt.

So, exactly a week after the information session, Yoren decided to bite the bullet and call Jen. It was almost midnight, and Mel had been sound asleep for the last hour and a half. He knew it was late, but an urge had been ignited. Ignoring it would be like paying no attention to an itch that needs scratching. So, without considering that Jen might be asleep, he grabbed his phone and made the call. Unaccustomed as he was to asking for help, he felt nervous and awkward as he waited for her to answer, almost cancelling the call twice before she picked up.

— ▪ —

'Hi, Yoren, what's up?'

Yoren paused, awkward and unsure of what to say.

'Hello? Are you there, Yoren?' asked Jen, checking her phone to ensure it wasn't on mute when there was no immediate response.

'Yes, I'm here, Jen. How are you?'

'Ah, there you are. I'm fine. The question is, how are *you*? It's not like you to call so late. You do know it's almost midnight on a weeknight, don't you? Isn't it well past your bedtime, young man?' she teased lightheartedly.

'Sleep is overrated,' said Yoren. 'Plenty of time for that when I'm dead. Anyway, I had a feeling you'd still be up, and I was just thinking it mightn't be such a bad idea for me to experience that discovery session, or whatever it was called, that the facilitator mentioned the other night ...'

'Sure. Do you want to know a bit more about it? I'm sure you have a few questions,' said Jen.

'I don't, actually,' Yoren responded. 'I was just thinking of giving it a go ... no harm in seeing what it's like.'

Although they weren't speaking face-to-face, Jen could tell that Yoren was hiding his genuine interest and curiosity. She knew her nephew well enough to know that his nonchalance was a front for his under-lying care and hope that the discovery session might actually benefit him.

Not wanting to let on that she could see straight through him, Jen said, 'I see. Look, this is not a conversation we should be having at midnight, especially as I have a very important session at seven that I am still preparing for. Do you think you could step out of the office for a couple of hours on Friday and come over for morning tea, say at 10?'

'Sounds great!' Yoren said enthusiastically before hastily clearing his throat and toning down his expression to ensure Jen didn't think he was too keen. 'I have a meeting that morning, but I'll have my PA reschedule it. See you then.'

CHAPTER 4

The Garden Walk

Jen lived with Nader, her husband of 10 years, in a charmingly rustic 1940s homestead they had lovingly restored together on a four-hectare property on the outskirts of Sydney. Born and raised in Iran, Nader had come to Australia on a student visa after finishing high school. While backpacking around the country, he met Juliette, an Australian girl around the same age, and they fell madly in love. The couple married in their early twenties and settled in a small hinterland community near Byron Bay on the New South Wales north coast, where Nader taught yoga and played music for a living, writing poetry, surfing and painting landscapes in his spare time. They were blissfully happy together and even happier as their family grew. Their firstborn, a son, was like his father in many ways but had his mother's curls and steely-blue eyes. Three years later, twin daughters made their family complete. When the twins were just three years old, Juliette was diagnosed with terminal cancer, succumbing to the disease after only six months and leaving Nader to raise his young family alone.

Jen and Nader met online 18 years after Juliette's tragic passing. They instantly hit it off when they met in person and married a year later. Jen, who'd been involved in several short-lived relationships and had never married, had always lamented the fact that she'd never had children. As a woman in her mid-forties, she knew that ship had well and truly sailed. So, she was delighted to be welcomed as a stepmother by Nader's adult children and loved them like they were her own.

Yoren arrived at Jen and Nader's place a quarter of an hour after the scheduled time. It was a glorious morning, and Jen was seated at an elegant outdoor table. Daisy, her much-loved rescued Saluki, and Bella, a beautiful white Persian cat, were lazily sprawled out in the sun by her side. Despite his tardiness, Yoren observed how relaxed Jen looked. Her radiant smile as she got up to greet him was warm and welcoming, and she made no comment about his late arrival. She motioned him to take a seat as she went inside to get the tea and cake she had prepared. As Yoren waited for Jen to return, he cast his eyes over the gardens, noting how immaculate everything looked.

Jen returned with a tray bearing a delicate bone china tea set and three slices of homemade chocolate cake. She placed them on the table, poured them both a cup of tea and offered Yoren a generous slice of cake. Without taking the time to acknowledge Jen for preparing such a beautiful spread, Yoren got down to business.

'So tell me about this discovery session. What's it about, how long does it take, and exactly what would I be getting myself into if I decide to go ahead?' he asked, tucking into the cake.

'Before I answer your questions, Yoren, I want to bring something to your attention,' said Jen.

Oh, here we go. Why can't Jen ever just answer a direct question?

Jen paused as she smiled lovingly at Nader, who tipped his hat and blew her a kiss from the nearby rose garden he was tending. Yoren acknowledged Nader with a brief wave, mentally noting how affectionate they still were with one another and how different that was from the relationship dynamic between his parents. From the corner of his eye, he spotted two gardeners who were trimming hedges nearby and another who was preparing a new garden bed.

Jen and Nader must be doing well. The place looks amazing! And they can afford to have help to look after it too. Not bad!

'Last night, you were thinking about the info session and what Erik was taking us through, right?' asked Jen, drawing Yoren's attention back into the conversation.

'Um, no, not really. Well, it might have briefly crossed my mind …'

'So, is that a yes or no?' asked Jen in an assertive tone, the warm smile never leaving her face.

'Yes,' responded Yoren. He sat back in his chair, his arms folded, a guarded expression on his face.

'Relax, Yoren,' laughed Jen. 'No one's judging you here. I know it's been on your mind. You didn't call me close to midnight to make small talk! But for some reason, you were holding yourself back from telling me what was going on.'

Realising there was no hiding his true feelings from Jen, Yoren momentarily offered a glimpse into the vulnerable, authentic side of himself.

'You're right, Jen. I admit there are certain aspects of my life that are not how I'd like, despite all my external successes. I'm hoping this next step might help.'

However, as quickly as the walls came down, they shot back up again.

'Just as long as you don't expect me to do a personality test or listen to some fanciful inspirational talk,' he quipped.

'Hold on a minute, Yoren. Bring yourself back to where you are and who you're with right now. You're here with me, enjoying tea and your favourite chocolate cake, which I baked this morning – especially for you, I might add. All I'd like to do is bring your attention to what we refer to as being vulnerable. Consider how you were being just now when I gently confronted you. There was a moment when you chose to be vulnerable, when you openly and authentically shared your pain, suffering or perceived problem. Then you suddenly flipped and became closed, guarded and opinionated about something you have never experienced or studied.'

Before Yoren could interrupt to make excuses, Jen continued, 'It's all good, Yoren. All I ask is that you reflect on this later and compare the two ways of being – how you were being when in acknowledgement of being vulnerable, which is a mood, and how you were being when you were not. Now, please have this last piece of cake to save me from eating it later!' she laughed.

They finished their morning tea in amiable silence before Jen suggested they go for a walk so she could show Yoren a new section of the garden Nader had just finished creating and they could continue their conversation. Without waiting for Yoren to get up, Jen leapt out of her seat with the agility and grace of a woman far younger than her 56 years, her flowing floral dress spinning to reveal bare feet as she walked briskly towards the gardens. Yoren smiled as he got up and followed his aunt.

It's like she doesn't age! How on earth can someone so childlike and playful be considered such a significant and serious player in their field? She's not even wearing shoes, for goodness sake!

They chatted about the gardens as they walked, Jen pausing from time to time to smell a rose or some other fragrant flower in bloom.

'Jen, you mentioned earlier that vulnerability is a mood. By mood, are you referring to how I feel?' Yoren asked.

'Your mood is beyond what you feel, Yoren. It's your state of mind. It's how you are, or, to be more exact, it's how you disclose or express yourself. Another example of a mood is care. You obviously cared enough to come all this way to discuss all of this.'

'Yes, I suppose you're right. So could you please clarify why care is considered a mood?'

'Sure. There is significant literature on care as a mood. It's often referred to as love, but not in a romantic sense. It's been talked about a lot. For example, the German philosopher Martin Heidegger referred to care as one of several ways through which human beings disclose themselves. His view was later interpreted and discussed by other thinkers. As I said before, care and other moods like vulnerability can be seen as one's mode or state of mind. Let me read you the distinction we have for care to avoid confusion and ensure you know what I'm referring to when I use the word care.

She reached for her phone, tapped on the screen and began to read.

> *Care* impacts how you relate to what matters to you and influences you in such a way that you ensure the matters and people you *care* about are supported, protected or dealt with in the best manner possible. *Care* leads you to address whatever is necessary to nurture the person or matter and dedicate the appropriate level of time, resources and attention to them. *Care* is considered the epicentre or focal point of being as, without care, nothing of importance can be achieved. When you *care* about something, you pay attention to it; you value it and it becomes a priority. *Care* influences how likely you are to make decisions or take action based on the level of value you ascribe to that person, relationship or matter.

Frustrated, Yoren interrupted his aunt. 'I knew I'd regret that question. I was hoping for a concise answer, not a lecture.'

'A lecture?' Jen laughed. 'I may not be answering your questions as quickly as you'd like me to, but please bear with me, Yoren. This is important, and I'll explain why shortly. Are you okay with that?'

'Sure, go ahead,' he sighed, raising his eyes in exasperation.

'You'll recall that Erik talked about having a healthy or unhealthy relationship with each of our Aspects of Being. Care is one of those qualities that we relate to in a healthy or unhealthy way. Let me read you what it looks like when someone has a healthy relationship with care,' said Jen as she turned to her phone again.

<blockquote>A healthy relationship with *care* indicates that you have clarity around your value structure – what you value most – enabling you to prioritise matters effectively. You give those matters the requisite consideration and attention to achieve the intended outcome while avoiding damage or minimising risk. This may extend to those areas to which you choose to attach importance, influencing you to make decisions and take relevant action regardless of whether it affects you directly.</blockquote>

'Now, you will also recall that Erik touched on the shadow, the troubled parts of us, which we all have to varying degrees. That's when you relate to an Aspect of Being in an unhealthy manner,' continued Jen as she took a seat on a sandstone bench in the garden and motioned to Yoren to join her.

'Hang on a minute, Jen. Healthy or unhealthy based on whose metric?' Yoren's body language signalled his scepticism.

'Based on a comprehensive, qualitative study of the world's highest achievers and effective leaders and the qualities they share. It turns out that many of these qualities are admired and considered 'virtuous' across cultures and religions worldwide. I can go into the details of that study with you at another time. For now, I'd just like you to have an open mind and hear me out to see if you can relate to the healthy and unhealthy sides of care. Let me read to you what the shadow side of care looks like, which is when someone has an unhealthy relationship with it.'

<blockquote>An unhealthy relationship with *care* indicates that you may often defer making decisions or avoid taking action in certain areas, particularly outside your sphere of perceived interest. You may be inclined to neglect, pass or abdicate *responsibility* and be apprehensive about the future. Others may consider you biased or that your judgement is clouded in areas of particular interest to you. Alternatively, you may be distracted, as everything becomes your priority. You may refuse to let go of whatever matters come your way as you are constantly fearful of missing out. Consequently, you may flit from one matter to another, leaving most of them incomplete while forsaking fulfilment.</blockquote>

'All these qualities you refer to – what did you guys call them … Aspects of Being? Aren't they just common sense? What's new about them?' asked Yoren.

'It's interesting that you seem to be after *new* things, Yoren.' responded Jen with a wink.

'Of course. I'm always interested in learning new things.'

'You're correct in assuming that these Aspects of Being are common to all human beings,' said Jen. 'We all relate to things like fear, anxiety, vulnerability, care, authenticity, responsibility, commitment, assertiveness, confidence and so on, in one way or another. There is so much emphasis out there on our differences, but in our work, we mainly focus on commonalities, the aspects that unite us.

'Basically, we're looking at what's real about human beings, both in terms of nature – the primal qualities that make us human beings of the same species – and the shared and common experiences we may end up having. So you're absolutely right. They are common sense. But here's where it gets interesting. As you can probably guess, ironically, a healthy relationship with these qualities is not very common! It seems that while many of us are familiar with them, we're not necessarily *being* them.

'The empirical data and our experiences as coaches working with different people from various backgrounds reveal that not many people are actually authentic, responsible, vulnerable, forgiving, assertive, confident, proactive, courageous and so on. And that's despite the fact that these qualities are commonly valued and espoused by religions, societies, cultures, research and philosophers. So it's not about needing to invent or fabricate *new* qualities but instead harnessing our energy to polish our relationship with these existing fundamental qualities that have stood the course of time so that they contribute to our overall integrity as individuals.

At the end of the day, there's so much pain and suffering in the world. Consider that the high-level solution to most of the problems we human beings face is to improve our integrity as individuals.' Jen was visibly moved by her own explanation.

'What about bigger global issues that are far beyond individual responsibility and integrity?' asked Yoren. 'With all due respect, Jen, it's easy to make banal statements. But are they practical?'

'Well, let me do my best to answer a question that contains the word 'banal' politely!' responded Jen, the twinkle in her eye indicating a hint of amusement. 'Who do you think designs the systems and sets the policies and regulations? Who then executes these processes, policies, regulations and procedures within government bodies and corporations? And who votes for the decision-makers that create the rules that apply to all of us? It's us human beings! We, as individuals, are the ones who do all of that. Integrous people design integrous systems and processes. No matter which way you look at it, it all comes down to the integrity of individuals. Now, before we attempt to solve all of humanity's problems and challenges and analyse the structure of existence itself, let's continue walking and return to the issues that brought you here, shall we?'

They continued to wander through Jen and Nader's beautifully manicured gardens.

'Walking through the gardens as we talk about human beings makes me feel a bit Aristotelian,' laughed Jen.

'Why? What does any of this have to do with an ancient philosopher?' asked Yoren in a bemused tone.

'Well, Aristotle was known for his penchant for teaching outdoors, walking and talking with his students rather than being confined to the classroom as he and others were with his teacher, Plato. This is how the Peripatetic School came to be, which impacted much of what we know today.'

'What does peripatetic mean? I've never heard of it,' asked Yoren.

'Fair question, given it's not a commonly used word. I think the dictionary defines the noun 'peripatetic' as a person who travels from place to place, especially a teacher who works in more than one school or college or an Aristotelian philosopher. In fact, the root of the word dates back to late Middle English and comes from the Old French *peripatetic*, via Latin from Greek *peripatētikos*, which means walking up and down.'

'The root of the word … haha, you kill me with your passion for etymology, the way you love digging into the origin of words,' mocked Yoren. 'But don't you think we are straying way off track?'

'I realise there are times when you may not see the relevance in what we're discussing, at least not yet. So let's return to why you are here, which I know is not just to visit your favourite aunt and enjoy my chocolate cake! Tell me, are you at all anxious about the real reason you are here?'

'Anxious? Have I ever come across to you as a person who suffers from anxiety, Jen?' asked Yoren, visibly irritated by her question.

Smiling, Jen clarified, 'Oh no, there seems to be a misunderstanding. I am not referring to anxiety disorder but simply to *being* anxious, which is a natural way any human being would feel in the face of potential danger or uncertainty. We all feel anxious in the face of matters that may make us vulnerable to the what-ifs or the consequences we might face as a result of how we are being or what we are doing now or might be doing in the future. Let's take the other night, for example. Surely you must have mulled over various what-if scenarios before calling me just before midnight. The fact that you're here to discuss the possibility of learning more about your being suggests the presence of anxiety, which, by the way, is a mood like care, which we talked about earlier.'

'Yes, I'm sure I thought about several what-if scenarios before calling you and coming over. So what? I'm an analytical person. It still doesn't mean I'm feeling anxious,' he retorted.

'You're not alone in your uncertainty about the future, Yoren. We are all uncertain to varying degrees. Anxiety is yet another mood through which we disclose or reveal ourselves at times. And we are all vulnerable to many things because we don't have full control over all matters in life. We're not even the source of many of them, and yet they often impact us. And we're also vulnerable to being misunderstood when trying to freely express ourselves or to not knowing or misunderstanding, which can lead us to make ineffective decisions that we later regret. Can you see how vulnerability around an unknown future can lead us to be anxious?'

'Yes, when you put it that way, Jen, it does make sense,' admitted Yoren.

'Great! Good to hear you being a bit more vulnerable in acknowledging that,' said Jen with a smile. 'Most people don't, at least not the majority of the time!' she added with a wink.

'Well, I'm *always* open and vulnerable,' said Yoren.

'Are you sure about that, Yoren? Over morning tea, I suggested you contemplate the difference between when you have been vulnerable and when you have not. Would you mind trying it now as a quick exercise?'

'Okay, I'll give it a shot. What exactly do you want me to do?' asked Yoren.

'See if you can identify some of the instances in your life when you know you were being vulnerable and open and compare those to instances when you were closed and guarded. Consider the difference in how you felt at those times and also the outcomes or consequences.'

'Sure, I can do that,' he said.

He cast his mind back to the first time he met Mel. They were at an event hosted by a mutual friend, and there was instant chemistry when their eyes met across the room. He swiftly made his way through the couples on the dance floor to introduce himself and buy her a drink. They found a seat in a quiet corner and struck up a conversation. Keen to make a good impression, Yoren boasted about his accomplishments, where he lived and the people he hung out with. Based on his lack of vulnerability, Mel assumed he was arrogant and not at all her type. So she politely declined his request for her phone number and left to join her friends. Six months went by before their paths crossed again. This time, Yoren was determined not to let her get away, so he made a conscious effort to be open and vulnerable with her. He was polite, asked questions, listened attentively and even opened up a little about his hopes and dreams for the future. By the end of the evening, she not only shared her number with him, but suggested they go out for coffee the next day.

Jen could see that Yoren was doing as she had asked. After a few moments, she said, 'Now, consider the relationship between vulnerability and anxiety in your scenarios,' adding another layer to the exercise.

'What do you mean by the relationship between them?' asked Yoren, puzzled.

'How they are connected,' she responded.

As they continued walking and talking, a garden bed of lavender in full bloom suddenly caught Jen's attention. She bounded gleefully towards it to pick a small bunch for her kitchen table.

'Oh, I just adore lavender! Such a beautiful perennial with a soothing, calming scent.'

'What's a perennial, Jen?'

'There are two types of plants: perennials and annuals. The main difference between them is that perennials regrow every spring, while annual plants live for just one growing season and then die. I know you're not a gardener, Yoren. But you do appreciate beautiful things, and I notice you have an eye for things that will stand the test of time. As a perennial, lavender starts blooming in late spring. But when grown in favourable conditions, as they are here, they often bloom more than once and live a very long time. These ones have been here for more than a decade. The point is, don't you think life and existence are wondrous? For instance, that each lavender blossom lives for a season or two and then dies to be replaced by another flower, and so the cycle continues?'

Oh, Jen, what are you on about now? How are perennial flowers relevant to what we're here to discuss? The same goes for Aristotle and peripatetic! And what do they all have to do with care, anxiety and vulnerability?

Rather than raising the questions and doubts in his mind with Jen, he remained silent and waited for her to continue, inwardly hoping she would come back down to earth.

Stepping out of the lavender garden and back onto the paved pathway that meandered through the extensive grounds, Jen said, 'Now that we have discussed care and anxiety and touched on vulnerability, let's zoom out for a moment. Picture life as a symphony orchestra in which every living being is playing their instrument. We all have our role to play in this orchestra of existence. Whether you play that role consciously or unconsciously, you have made a decision to live, finding the possibility of existence – of being out there in the world – something worthwhile, something you hold so dear that you have decided to work to improve it, at least on an individual level. And I'm doing the same in my own unique way. Consider that you're having this conversation with me today because you care and are curious. Something is calling you from within. Why else would you have bothered to call me the other night and postpone a business meeting to come here today? Now, aren't you curious to know about the fourth mood?'

'Sure, go ahead and tell me,' said Yoren, his curiosity heightened.

Jen playfully spun around, touching him on the nose with a sprig of lavender. 'Before I tell you, why do you want to know?'

'Because I'm curious,' he said, wondering what she was up to.

'Just curious?'

'Isn't that enough, Jen? What do you want me to say?' By now, Yoren's frustration was getting the better of him.

'Well, curiosity is necessary, but not enough if you *really* want to conceive what you perceive!'

'What? This is getting ridiculous! If curiosity isn't enough, what would you suggest, Jen?'

'To answer that question, let me first draw your attention back to what Erik touched on when he talked about the different levels of awareness. Remember when he introduced reception, perception and conception? When you receive new information, you're being informed about something. It's your ah-ha or lightbulb moment. It means your care and attention are being directed at something, which leads you to become newly informed about something you didn't know or didn't give much attention to before. I imagine you experienced a few of those receptive moments in that session, which I'm guessing is what sparked your curiosity to want to know more and led you to call me.'

'Yes, sure. Some parts grabbed my attention more than others,' said Yoren.

'The next step in the awareness process is perception. This is when you use your senses to learn about something, for example, seeing something online or listening to a news report. This is where you're *choosing* a perception to store in your memory bank to draw on when you need it. The third step, conception, is when you come to gain an *understanding* of the information you're gathering. It's when you tap into logic, reasoning, reflection, conversations, comparisons and so on to develop an informed understanding of the knowledge you have acquired. If you choose to conceive rather than merely being satisfied with a chosen perception, you will eventually relate what you have come to know – this objective knowledge – back to your own life and circumstances or the matters you care about. You put it in context so you can work out how to apply the knowledge in a practical way to address real issues that matter to you – your top priorities. These are the intentions Erik talked about that you want to fulfil. So to answer your question, I would suggest you need *sincerity* as well as curiosity.'

'Isn't it enough to be curious for now, Jen?' asked Yoren in an exasperated tone.

'Curiosity is indeed necessary, but it's not enough, Yoren. Let me use an analogy to explain why. Imagine you enter a room and see a small wooden box on a table. If you are just curious, you would open the box to see what's inside it. Once you know what's in it, mission accomplished! You were curious and now you know. But if you're coming from a place of sincerity as well as curiosity, your approach would be different.

'Let's say you've lost a button from your favourite shirt. You've searched everywhere for it to no avail. Now when you see the box, you are not only curious to know what's in it, but you also have a sincere desire to discover if it could hold your lost button. You open the box and sure enough, there it is – the missing button! Your shirt, which was out of integrity due to a missing button and therefore not fit to be worn, can now be made whole or integrous again because you have found its missing part! Now the shirt is usable again.

'When you form conceptions of matters, you make them relevant to you by linking them with something you care deeply about. That is true wisdom because it leads you to take action – to act upon your newly conceived knowledge. Without action, the knowledge would simply be stored in your memory bank as an idea, an opinion, a belief or a perception, none of which would have any impact on your life. So while perception is the result of knowing, either directly through our senses or by taking on what others say, and is often an instant process, conception involves using our intellect to think, reason, converse, contemplate and analyse. Take hearing, for example, which is a direct sense. When you hear something, you are consciously perceiving it. However, listening is more than just hearing. Listening demands attention, intentionality and presence. It requires your intentional mental effort or awareness. So hearing sits within the realm of perception, while listening is part of conception.'

Jen could see from the expression in Yoren's eyes that a light had been turned on. 'Okay, Yoren, I can see that you sincerely want to know now. So let me tell you what the fourth mood is. It's fear.'

'Is that it? Is that what you had me waiting for with bated breath, Jen? What's fear got to do with me? There's not much I'm afraid of. In fact, most would consider me to be fearless with the kinds of calculated risks I take.'

'In reality, there is no such thing as being fearless, Yoren. When I refer to fear, I am referring to how you *relate* or *attune yourself* to it. After all, there will always be fear-generating things out there, so every human being has a relationship with fear,' said Jen with a smile. 'I could talk about this for hours, but I'm conscious of your time and mine. Let's talk about the real reason you called me – to ask my opinion about exploring what you learned further with a coach.'

> *I was wondering how long it would take to get to this topic. I hope Jen realises I'd rather talk to her than have some guy I don't know try to psychoanalyse me. But then again, I also don't want her to know everything that's going on in my life. Imagine if she finds out about some of my innermost secrets, the ones I've never shared with anyone or, worse, accidentally divulges some of those secrets to Dad!*

Yoren's inner musings about who he would prefer to have coach him were abruptly brought to a halt with Jen's next words.

'Naturally, I'm not the best person to coach you because, as your aunt, I am too close to you. The best person to walk you through the four Moods, as well as other Aspects of Being, is a trained coach who is not related to you.'

Unsettled by the idea of having to open up to a complete stranger, Yoren feigned indifference, 'Jen, I really don't need or want a life coach or mentor.'

'I didn't mention either of those, Yoren. I'm not referring to a life coach or general mentor. I'm talking about an accredited coach who has undergone professional and rigorous training in the being discourse. This is someone who has the expertise to support you in getting to know and understand how you are being and coach you over time on how to translate those insights into actionable and specific areas to focus on in pursuit of fulfilling your intentions. Anyone who wants to be a high achiever but thinks they can do it alone is missing out because they're not tapping into the power of coaching and other support measures. Imagine a person who wants to get in shape and hit their objective without a personal trainer or fitness coach. It might be achievable, but it certainly wouldn't be easy. Now imagine a person who dreams of becoming an Olympic athlete but refuses to work with a team of coaches! As you know, I'm an accredited master coach, but I also have a coach. In fact, I've been coached for years.'

Yoren was surprised to hear that Jen had a coach, despite being a master coach who trained and mentored others.

'I'm not sure I'd be willing to fork out an arm and a leg for coaching,' he scoffed.

'Another perspective on coaching is that it's an investment in yourself rather than an expense,' said Jen. 'I know many people from all walks of life who understand the value of effective coaching, which is why they choose powerfully to invest in themselves through coaching support. When they see the benefits coaching delivers, they realise how its return on investment contributes to their financial wellbeing and other dimensions of their life.'

'I can see how some people might rely on ongoing support to keep them on track,' said Yoren. 'But I'm a fast learner and quite capable of holding myself to account. Once I have the information I need, I don't need anyone to help me decipher it and relate it back to my life. I'm an independent guy and perfectly adept at working things out on my own.'

'Really, Yoren? Do you think it's authentic to live life from the viewpoint that you're an isolated individual who doesn't need others?

The fact is, we're all connected as human beings. This connection is referred to by many of the world's most renowned thinkers as 'common being' or 'unity of existence'. Martin Heidegger also used the term *mitsein*, which translates to 'being with'. As social beings, it is in our nature to align ourselves with others.

'In the pursuit of fulfilling our intentions and hitting the targets we set for ourselves, we need to partner with others in one way or another. We need other people's contributions; we need effective and efficient teamwork, and we might need to form partnerships with others whose vision is aligned with or complements ours. For any business to succeed, trust and effective communication must be established and maintained internally with the team members and externally with all stakeholders to ensure the company's value proposition is clear to potential customers. So, as you can see, this isn't an abstract theory; we are all dependent on each other.

'We depend on the farmer, the butcher, the greengrocer, the plumber, the electrician, the carpenter, the mechanic and so on. One of the greatest shadows we humans can, at times, buy into is a desire to be totally independent of others. The reality is we're not! Living life as if you can do it all alone and be left to your own devices is inauthentic because it's incongruent with reality and, therefore, ineffective. This viewpoint sets you up for failure and disappointment. If you're up to something big, like starting your own business, it's unrealistic to expect that you'll achieve your objectives on your own, don't you think, Yoren?'

Yoren was silent for a moment. Jen's words had once again struck a chord. This time, they made him receptive to his lack of effectiveness in managing projects and his team members. While he was accustomed to taking all the credit for successful projects, he had always known deep down that they were, in fact, the result of considerable contribution and collaboration. He had never acknowledged that he could not have delivered those outcomes without the efforts and cooperation of his team. This meant he also rarely acknowledged his team for their contribution. This realisation made him suddenly present to why they lacked cohesion and were sometimes not as effective as they could be.

Interrupting his thought process, Yoren suddenly remembered Jen had asked him a question. 'Well, sure, I work with others every day. But I don't see how this relates to me being coached.'

'Let me explain, Yoren. But first, bear with me for a moment. I want to share something really important with you about why any of this matters.'

Yoren feigned a yawn, and Jen playfully nudged him on the shoulder as she prompted him to start following her back to the house. She began to speak more softly but earnestly. It was clear to Yoren that what she was telling him mattered greatly to her, so he listened in respectful silence.

'Different people and disciplines of thought narrate radically different stories around how we came to be as human beings,' Jen continued. 'Some believe we were once apes and evolved to become how we are today. Others maintain we descended from a man and a woman created by God. Those are just two of several views on how we originated. No matter what you choose to believe or how we actually came to be, the fact is, we are here. We are thrown into this world, we are here for a while and then we depart.

'Where this gets really interesting is that during our limited time here on Earth, we are each constantly expressing ourselves to the world. We refer to this as the 'projection process'. It's not a journey but a process. Imagine that every time you project yourself, it's like releasing a drop of water into the ocean of existence. With every drop released, you cause a ripple effect over time. How you think, the decisions you make, the actions you take, your behaviours and what you say all have an impact, whether or not you are present to and intentionally conscious of it.

'Herein lies a paradox. We call it the 'paradox of importance'. On the one hand, you might tell yourself that your existence and the impact you make don't matter much because you are insignificant in the grand scheme of things, like a grain of sand in a desert. On the other hand, you could choose to live life from the viewpoint that you are to leave your own special mark on the world, a one-of-a-kind unique expression of your authentic self. This way of living would almost certainly support you in shaping your unique contribution to the world.

'While you are, to a great extent, the primary cause in responding to matters in life and are in the driver's seat, this is not just about you. You are not the epicentre of the universe. This paradox of importance is a reality. It's important to balance these two seemingly paradoxical views so that you don't land at either end of the spectrum. Finding that balance will lead to a relatively polished and authentic view that you are neither the epicentre of the universe nor insignificant in the grand scheme of things. It will make you realise that you are a distinct, autonomous individual and are here to actively express your unique being to the world. If you don't, the world and our shared reality will lack something. It will lack the remarkable, one-and-only *you*, and a world without you in it would be different. Imagine a world without the Internet, smartphones, Beethoven symphonies, literature, all the music ever composed, the poems and artworks ever created, all the inventions, and so on.' Jen paused to wipe a tear from her cheek.

Deeply present to Jen, who was speaking with passion and conviction on a subject close to her heart, Yoren was taken aback by his own emotions. He was simultaneously overwhelmed and moved, both feelings he was unaccustomed to. As if reading his mind, Jen paused momentarily to let him process her words and his reaction.

Then, picking up that he was ready to hear more, she continued, 'All beings out there in the world have surrendered to their role. The dog is being a dog, and the cat is being a cat. The sun, the moon and the stars are all playing their parts without question, making their unique contribution through the manifestation or projection of their unique being. They are present and surrendered to be what they are meant to be. Now, I realise that they don't have a choice. The moon doesn't grab existence by the collar and demand to know why the sun gets to be the source of light and warmth and she only gets to reflect his borrowed light at night.

'It is we human beings who, by our very nature, have a significant capability to choose our own destiny. Our relatively high level of autonomy means we can choose our path and lifestyle with conscious discernment, choosing whether or not to surrender. The key is to become present to our nature, our essence – or what we call our Aspects of Being – collectively and as individuals, and get to know ourselves more accurately. As human beings, we're uniquely capable of becoming receptive to whatever is calling us. And if we hear the call, then we can consider ourselves blessed as that might just give meaning to our lives and allow us to contribute to others.'

As if suddenly realising Yoren might consider her narrative overly spiritual, Jen swiftly returned to the matter at hand. 'The important thing to understand now is that unless you get to know *what* and *how* you are being, you may never know *who* you are deep down and what your calling is. That would potentially result in you neglecting, ignoring or overriding what is there for you to express.

'And it's not just about knowing how you are but also getting to know the commonalities we have as human beings so that you can under-stand others better too. Why is this important? Because you need to assess others before hiring them, partnering with them, trusting them, integrating them into your teams, interacting with them, designing the right ideas or products to sell and so on. Being naive to the fact that you need to assess and understand human beings better will most definitely prevent you from moving forward and being a high achiever, particularly as I know you've always wanted to have your own business, Yoren. Creating that level of alignment and engagement demands an understanding of human beings, yourself and others. This is where having access to a tool and framework that guides you on where to look is highly beneficial.

'Too many people spend their entire lives copying others or replicating other people's ideas, oblivious to the fact that the single most valuable thing we all have is our unique being. Nobody else is you, and *that* is your power. A coach can support you to discover and tap into that power, Yoren. Now, as I said earlier, I have someone in mind that I'd like to connect you with. If you agree to that, you can rest assured that you'll be in the right hands.'

Arriving back at the house, Yoren hugged Jen and thanked her for giving up her time to meet with him and for the delicious morning tea. On his drive back to the office, he was lost in thought as he dealt with various mixed emotions. He felt incomplete in the conversation and his mind was racing.

> *I wonder who this coach is that Jen wants to connect me with and what he's like. I still would've preferred to go through this whole coaching thing with Jen, though. I really can't see the issue with her and I being related. But then again, do I really want her to know everything about me? Let's see who she refers me to. I'll be sure to check him out thoroughly online before our first meeting – if I agree to go ahead, that is.*

Yoren found it challenging to focus for the rest of the day, so he decided to finish early, put on his favourite playlist and hit the weights at his local gym to take his mind off his earlier discussions with Jen. Later that night, he checked his emails, responding to the ones that couldn't wait until morning. Suddenly, he came to an email from Jen. The subject line simply read 'coach details'. He opened the email to find it short and straight to the point, with nothing more than the coach's name and phone number. Her name was Grace.

CHAPTER 5

Testing the Water

Damn it, Jen, a female coach! Really? Yoren thought to himself as he typed 'Grace de Jong' into the LinkedIn search panel. Finding her, he scrolled through her profile details. *Hmm, at least she seems well-qualified and connected. She's not bad looking either! Might be best not to tell Mel about this. No sense in her worrying and thinking I need help anyway.*

Lying in bed later that night, Yoren struggled to sleep as he thought about everything Jen had discussed with him.

Should I go ahead with this? Should I contact Grace?

He thought about several excuses to avoid contacting her. But he couldn't come up with a reasonable explanation that wouldn't make him look foolish to Jen. And in his more vulnerable moments, he couldn't ignore the fact that he was curious.

Maybe I should go ahead and do it, just out of curiosity. What's the risk, anyway? Nobody aside from Jen needs to know.

The next morning, after an almost sleepless night and two strong coffees, he mustered up the courage to call Grace. She answered the phone almost immediately.

'Hi Grace, it's Yoren Healy. I believe Jenah spoke to you about me. I was wondering if we could have a chat about coaching and what's involved.'

'Hello, Yoren. Yes, I've been expecting your call. Let me start by asking you some questions. Would that be okay?'

Yoren responded in the affirmative, but wondered why Grace wasn't just answering his question by letting him know about the coaching process. He still wasn't sure he wanted to proceed.

Grace's tone was warm and friendly, yet professional, direct and assertive. It struck Yoren as she asked him a series of questions that she might have been assessing whether he was the right fit for her as much as he was working out if he wanted to proceed. He had always assumed a coach would be grateful to accept any new client, but her questions made it clear that this was not necessarily the case. He never imagined that there was a possibility he could be turned down.

After Yoren had responded to Grace's initial questions, she asked, 'Have you ever completed a profiling assessment, Yoren?'

'Yes, I once completed a personality test, but I didn't really get anything out of it because it didn't give me any insight into how I could change or improve. It really just confirmed what I already knew and gave me a few irrelevant insights. Since then, I've been offered the opportunity to complete many other tests, but I've declined them all. I already know my personality type, learning preferences and leadership style, so why would I waste my time on another test? To be honest, I think these kinds of tests are interesting at best, but not particularly useful. In my experience, people who like psychological tests are usually the type who are also into things like astrology and numerology.'

While it was clear to Grace that Yoren had his guard up and was resisting before listening to what she had to say, she read between the lines and could tell he was sincere in his curiosity and desire to want to know more about himself, particularly when he said the personality test he completed had not given him relevant insights into how he could change. Furthermore, Jen had touched on what to expect and told her that the information session he attended had raised many questions for him. So Grace proceeded to explain the ontological assessment tool she used with her clients and how its completion was not negotiable if someone wanted to be coached by her.

'The first step, if we choose to work together, is for you to complete an online profiling assessment. I use it with all my coaching clients as a prerequisite to any coaching conversations. Rest assured, the assessment I'm referring to is *not* a personality test,' she said.

'What makes your assessment tool so special?' asked Yoren, doubt and scepticism clearly evident in his tone.

'I understand your concern, Yoren. Many of my clients feel the same way at first. But in my experience, this tool and its associated framework are the most effective for the coaching I offer. While I have found most profiling tools have some merit, I am also sceptical about their benefits when it comes to change, particularly for sustainable transformation. The assessment tool I use – and the one that Jen uses with her clients too – is an ontometric tool that maps out the qualities of human beings known to have a significant impact on performance, effectiveness and the fulfilment of an individual's intentions.

'It maps out part of your cognitive model by revealing, with a relatively high degree of accuracy, how you relate to a set of fundamental qualities and, most importantly, how you act upon your understanding of them based on the answers you provide. For example, it identifies how you relate to and act upon awareness, integrity, authenticity, anxiety, vulnerability, commitment, assertiveness and proactivity, among others. How you relate to and act upon these qualities, or Aspects of Being, influences your decisions, behaviours and actions. Consequently, these Aspects of Being, to a great extent, determine your outcomes and results in life. And this assessment is also highly effective for teams.'

Yoren recognised a lot of the terminology Grace used in her explanation because it had been discussed by Erik during the information session and also by Jen in their follow-up conversations. He was gradually shaping a more congruent and authentic conception of where the assessment could fit into the whole equation, as opposed to seeing it as an isolated, standalone 'online test'. However, he was still not completely convinced.

'I understand what you're saying about the qualities your assessment looks at and how it reveals the relationships one has with those qualities. But how does it help people solve their challenges and change, or transform, as you put it?' asked Yoren.

'Good question, Yoren. This assessment tool is highly effective at uncovering the *underlying* qualities and drivers of your decisions, actions and behaviours, the root causes of the challenges you face. These are the qualities or Aspects of Being that lie deep beneath the surface, so deep that you might not be present to them. You may find some of the questions challenging or confronting. I know I did, especially as they had me look into areas I hadn't thought about before. Completing the assessment will enable you to look at yourself through a different lens. Once you have that new perspective, you can use the results in your profile report to identify the areas you wish to transform. Alternatively, we can do that together if you decide you'd like to pursue coaching and we determine we're the right fit for one another.

'Unlike other tools that identify fixed traits, all the qualities measured by our assessment tool can be transformed. Should you choose to continue working with me as your coach after completing the assessment, we'll use it as a reference point and benchmark throughout the coaching journey as a way to evaluate the progress you are making in the areas you choose to work on. Does that answer your question?'

Yoren agreed it did, but persisted in asking several additional questions, such as how the assessment was formulated and by whom, the extent to which the tool had been validated or proven, whether it was backed by science and how many people had been through the process. Grace patiently listened and responded to his questions with finesse.

'Thanks, Grace. I agree the tool sounds interesting, and it seems like it's been extensively tested and validated. But I feel I know myself well already, including how I relate to those qualities you mentioned. So can't we just go straight into coaching?'

'We could,' responded Grace, 'But it would be a lot less effective than using the results of the assessment as the foundation for our coaching conversations. While we all have a degree of self-awareness, there are always blind spots we don't have immediate access to. So it's important not to fully rely on your current understanding of yourself or even purely rely on me as a coach. We human beings can be overly subjective, self-absorbed and biased or simply misunderstand ourselves and others. The assessment tool, and the algorithm behind it, have been intentionally designed to be as objective as possible and relatively unbiased.

'Put simply, we would be trying to find answers in the dark instead of knowing from the start the key areas we need to focus on to be most effective. So while you might think you know yourself well – and I am not suggesting you don't – it takes a lot to see the deep, underlying qualities that drive your decisions, behaviours and actions. Consequently, most people only work on addressing those surface-level qualities and completely miss the *drivers* of those decisions, behaviours and actions. That's why few people achieve the results they are seeking, or they might see results for a while and then slip back into old habits. Does that make sense, Yoren?'

'Yes, it does. But can you tell me how it works to achieve all of that?'

'Sure. The assessment is designed to break down the integrity of a human being into smaller, more digestible and communicable constituent parts. Those parts are our Aspects of Being. I believe Erik explained integrity in relation to who and how we are being during the session you attended, so I think you would get where I'm coming from when I use that word. When you know there is dysfunction in part of your life, the assessment tool supports you to track down the root causes behind that dysfunction by highlighting the exact parts that need to be addressed.

'To use a metaphor, it shines a light on your being and casts a shadow. In other words, it reveals the shadows or troubled sides of you, and those are the areas that, if polished and transformed, will contribute to your integrity. We can take a stab in the dark and guess where those shadows are, but completing the assessment makes the process of identifying where to focus in our coaching conversations easier, more reliable and much faster. It would take a very long time to derive many of the same conclusions that our profiling tool's more than 240 questions reveal in one assessment.'

Hearing Grace talk about how the assessment tool would cast light on his being to reveal the shadows or troubled parts of him filled Yoren with dread.

What if this tool reveals too much information about me, things I don't share with anyone? And what if Grace discusses the findings with Jen?

Feeling vulnerable and exposed, Yoren tried to make excuses and continued to push for coaching alone. Not to be deterred and as though she could read his mind, Grace assured him the results would be confidential and only discussed between them. She also let him know that she would only have access to a series of scores indicating the health of his relationship with the Aspects of Being measured, or how he relates to them, and not his response to each question. By this stage, she had decided she would like to work with him and was confident she could support him on the journey and make a difference. In fact, she was looking forward to the challenge. But she knew it was up to him to responsibly choose to embark on that journey.

'Let me tell you a bit more about the assessment itself, Yoren, to help you decide whether or not to proceed,' continued Grace. 'The assessment consists of over 240 strategically designed and optimised questions that are designed to measure your relationship with 31 Aspects of Being. Many people say that completing the assessment and receiving the comprehensive report it provides at the end is an extremely valuable exercise in and of itself as it raises their self-awareness. However, most want to take it further with coaching to explore the results more deeply and transform the shadow parts of themselves that the profile identifies.

'Aside from the tool's accuracy, it also ensures any work we do together is non-judgemental and relatively unbiased. As I said earlier, we human beings can be biased. Without an objective snapshot to use as a benchmark for the discussion, even the best coach can unconsciously apply their own moral framework to assess what they're perceiving about a coachee. And if a coachee is asked questions by a coach they don't yet fully know and trust, they might disguise and filter their responses so they don't look 'bad' or give too much away. So the assessment tool not only saves time but also dramatically increases accuracy and minimises biases in providing answers as well as in analysing the results.

'By going through your profile report first, we'll have a common language to go deeper than the observed behaviours and actions of which you are aware. This often helps to establish an effective channel of communication and generates trust, two elements that are extremely important for effective coaching. We'll speak about your relationship with, for example, courage, responsibility, vulnerability and forgiveness and how the relationships you have with these and other Aspects of Being impact your results and your current experience of life. As I said earlier, the qualities measured by the assessment tool are the ones that, after extensive studies, have been shown to most contribute to effectiveness in the scope of leadership, performance and the fulfilment of one's intentions in life.'

'I see,' said Yoren, feeling somewhat defeated as he couldn't come up with any logical arguments to counter Grace's points in favour of completing the assessment.

Yoren's scepticism reminded Grace of the first time she'd been introduced to the conversation about being and the assessment tool. She remembered how invulnerable she'd been at the time and, in fact, far more sceptical than Yoren was.

Present to his persistent hesitation, Grace continued, 'It's worth pointing out that the assessment isn't static; it offers a reference point and benchmark. If you decide to pursue coaching to transform certain Aspects of Being, you can re-do the assessment at various stages while working with me as your coach to gain visibility of your progress. Over time, you'll have a chronological view of how you're transforming your relationship with those various Aspects of Being. Furthermore, as the saying goes, "what gets measured improves". So it can also be useful for accountability. At the end of the day, it's not so much about the scores on the report but the *possibility* that those scores and each Aspect of Being's distinction create in terms of the conversations they encourage between the coach and the coachee. And there are also the conversations they can generate in your own mind on matters you might otherwise not be aware of.'

'Okay, you certainly make a convincing argument, Grace. What's the next step if I want to complete this assessment?'

'Excellent! I will email you a link to set up a secure account. Then all you need to do is complete the online questionnaire. Allow about an hour to complete it, and don't overthink your responses. Once you've submitted the completed questionnaire, I'll arrange a time with you for your debrief session. That's when I will walk you through your profile report and we work out where to go from there. The debrief takes two hours, which gives us ample time to discuss the results and for you to ask questions. How does that sound?'

Despite his sceptical nature, Yoren found Grace's arguments compelling enough to agree to experience the assessment and the follow-up debrief session. In the relatively short time that he'd been on the phone with her, he'd become more receptive, open and vulnerable, letting the conversation flow, something he was typically not used to doing. While he put up his guard at times, particularly when he felt triggered, something about Grace put him at ease and made him feel like he could trust her. He just couldn't articulate what that was at this stage. But he was keen to learn more.

'Sounds like a plan, Grace. Go ahead and email me the link and the cost involved.'

'That's great, Yoren. You'll receive my email before the close of business.'

'Before we end the call, I am curious about one more thing,' said Yoren. 'What happens after the debrief session?'

'Part of the debrief session will be set aside for you to articulate, at a high level, the areas you most want to focus on. That's determined by what you wish to achieve, your intentions. At the end of the session, we can discuss a potential agreement around a defined timeframe for ongoing coaching to support you in the transformation process. As a certified ontological coach who leverages a framework centred on the being discourse, I have the skills and qualifications to guide you through that process.'

'What do you mean by ontological coaching, Grace?' Yoren asked.

'To clarify, ontological coaching offers ongoing, intentional conversations that raise awareness, empower and contribute to the integrity and effectiveness of an individual or a team to live out their potential to fulfil their intentions and perhaps also benefit others. When someone refers to themselves as an ontological coach, it means they focus on being, not doing. This means they focus on what *drives* behaviours as opposed to the behaviours themselves. However, that does not mean all ontological coaches offer the same benefits. It is important to distinguish the ontological model they use to see a human being.

'In my case, I use a framework that incorporates the 31 Aspects of Being I spoke about because of the clarity and common language it offers around someone's being in the scope of performance and effectiveness. I also use it because it gets to the root causes of any issues and supports us to transform these for sustainable results. Addressing the behaviours alone is like watering the leaves of a tree but paying no attention to its roots. Not all ontological coaches adopt a model and approach that focuses on the deep underlying qualities that drive our behaviours, decisions and actions. That's why I choose to use the framework centred on the being discourse that you've been learning about. Does that answer your question, Yoren?'

'Yes, it does. Thanks, Grace.'

'So, the profile report you receive after completing the questionnaire not only establishes a benchmark to work with but also offers a mutual language for us to use as coach and coachee,' said Grace. 'In this way, it facilitates communication during our coaching conversations while supporting you to shape an authentic conception of various fragments of reality about yourself and how you relate to others and the world.

'As your coach, I would then support you in identifying your intentions and the areas you need to transform to achieve them. I would also use powerful, intentional questions to generate a higher level of awareness and support you in understanding the difference between being, doing and having and that how you are *being* leads to what you do and have in your life.

'My commitment will be to support you to go beneath the surface and become present to the underlying qualities that influence your decisions, behaviours and actions as opposed to aiming to have so-called rapid behavioural changes. I'm not suggesting that the behaviours and actions we can see are not important. On the contrary, they're highly significant as it is through our decisions, behaviours and actions that we live our lives, express ourselves, perform and participate in life and impact the shared reality out there. In other words, they determine our experience of life and our accomplishments. But, as an ontological coach, I focus on what *drives* those decisions, behaviours and actions. Think of it as delving deep beneath the surface to see far more than just the tip of the iceberg.'

'Okay, I get it. The iceberg metaphor is a good way to clarify it. Thanks, Grace!'

'You're welcome, Yoren. Now, if you choose to work with me as your coach, I'll also request that you commit to applying what you learn in our coaching conversations between sessions. My ultimate objective will be to support you to transform so you can grow and fulfil your intentions. Last but not least, I'll hold you to account to ensure you don't give up in the middle of the process, as there will be times when you find the process quite challenging.'

Grace explained the terms of the agreement and they ended the phone call with Yoren's firm commitment to complete the online assessment and book a debrief session. Not wanting to waste any time, he decided to complete the assessment that night. He waited until Mel had gone to bed, making an excuse that he had some reports to complete for work.

Why do I feel so nervous about this? It's only a bunch of rating scale questions. How hard can it be?

One by one, he answered the questions, remembering not to spend too much time on each one, as Grace had suggested. However, he couldn't help but feel confronted by the unique nature of some of the questions being asked. Many of them were unlike anything he had ever been asked or even contemplated before. He found a few of the questions so confronting that he could have easily ended the process and walked away. They required him to look into and reveal his authentic understanding of himself, and this made him feel uncomfortable. But he had made a commitment, and he was determined to meet it.

He recalled what Erik, Jen and Grace had said about the shadow and suddenly understood it in a different light.

Perhaps that's why the world's highest achievers actively seek out their shadow sides and face them head-on: so they can restore the integrity of their being! They know the heavy cost of letting the shadow run the show. It gets in the way of their effectiveness and prevents them from fulfilling their intentions.

With all of this swirling in the back of his mind, Yoren completed the assessment. While it had only taken him just over an hour to complete, he felt mentally exhausted. But at the same time, he felt excited that he'd completed the first step and was looking forward to seeing his results. Despite the scepticism he'd felt earlier, he was now sincerely curious about the next steps and hopeful that the process might support him to overcome the blockages standing in the way of fulfilling his dream of building his own business. He quietly slipped into bed beside Mel and quickly fell into a deep, peaceful sleep.

The Shadows Revealed

Grace de Jong had been coaching full-time for the past six years. Happily married with three children – two daughters and a son – she found deep fulfilment in integrating her career with her family life. Born in South Africa to a Dutch father and a Nigerian mother, she and her younger brother experienced a loving upbringing with parents who refused to be impacted by racial slurs. The family, including the maternal grandparents, immigrated to Australia when Grace was 12 and settled in Sydney's eastern suburbs, where her parents, both early childhood teachers, established their first of what would become five thriving early learning centres. Two years later, the paternal grandparents also joined them from the Netherlands.

Now 38, Grace often looked back fondly at her childhood and admired her parents' resilience and courage. They'd always encouraged both of their children to be well-read and educated. Many evenings were spent discussing various topics around the dinner table, from popular culture, philosophy and current affairs to politics, the economy, art, history and religion. Sometimes her grandparents on both sides would join them for dinner, and the animated conversations would often continue late into the night.

The de Jongs gave their children the freedom to explore whatever they were passionate about and encouraged them to be true to themselves. Curious to learn and explore as much as she could about the world, Grace took full advantage of that freedom. While she made what she later considered to be mistakes along the way, each challenge served to build her resilience, and she knew she could always count on the love and support of her parents whenever things became too challenging for her to handle on her own. She was grateful to both her parents and grandparents for their positive influence, which led her to develop a deeply inquisitive and open mind.

After finishing high school, she completed a psychology degree, graduated with Honours and accepted a position with a high-profile management consulting firm in their human resources division. Working closely with the organisation's emerging and senior leaders, she discovered a passion for supporting leaders when they were challenged to embrace or lead change. During her time there, she became increasingly aware of the dysfunction within the corporate environment, including office politics, and how it often sabotaged the sustained effectiveness of individuals and teams. Over time, she gained a deeper understanding of the significance of leadership and culture-building in organisations and how they could impact human beings' experience of life.

It gradually became clear to Grace that no matter how often she supported leaders to change through measures like technical training, setting KPIs and offering incentives, addressing the behaviour alone failed to produce the desired outcomes. She discovered that while such methods might work for a while, most people would revert to the old behaviours over time. It made her question the behavioural theories she'd been exposed to and realise that the issues were deeper and more complex than behaviour alone. This led Grace to search for a more effective approach, one that regarded people as ever-evolving beings capable of transformation.

As Grace continued her quest to better understand human beings, including herself, she embarked on a Master of Psychology, intending to become a fully qualified psychologist. Upon completing her master's, she worked as a psychologist under supervision for a year. However, despite all her studies and qualifications, she still felt something was missing. So she began to delve into metaphysics, phenomenology and ontology – the study of the reality of human beings and matters in life – to gain a deeper, more congruent understanding of human beings and the world. The more she learned, the more she became obsessed with what it actually means to be a human being and how we perform in life. Her quest to better understand the mechanisms around decision-making and behavioural patterns led her to delve deeper into ontological approaches to coaching and psychology, which focus on being rather than doing. These approaches taught her that tapping into what, who and how we are being dramatically influences how we show up in life and, therefore, impacts the results we achieve.

One evening, she attended a keynote presentation about a new paradigm rooted in ontology and phenomenology. The more she listened, the more hope it gave her that this paradigm offered a framework to clearly articulate the deeper qualities or attributes that all human beings possess but which we relate to differently. It also came with what appeared to be a powerful tool that could measure those qualities or Aspects of Being. She was eager to learn more.

It was during that event that Grace met Jenah Healy. Feeling an instant connection, Grace invited Jen for a coffee after the session. Coffee turned into dinner, and they ended up talking for hours. Before they left, Jen invited her to experience the profiling tool for herself by completing the online assessment. She also offered to conduct the follow-up debrief session with her. Grace accepted without hesitation and completed the assessment the following morning. A week later, she met with Jen for the two-hour debrief session. She found the entire experience eye-opening and well worth her investment of time and money.

Despite the framework's simplicity and apparent lack of sophistication on the surface, it made complete sense to Grace. It was articulated in a way that appeared to allow users to dive deeper into themselves and others than any other tool she'd experienced. Grace was so enthralled by the process and what she learned about herself that she decided to commit to six months of coaching with Jen. Her experience of being coached and undergoing a gradual transformation using this approach led her to realise that her true calling in life was to leave the corporate world and become a coach herself.

Today, Grace is a professional ontological coach working with the same paradigm she experienced with Jen. She focuses on supporting people to understand and transform how they relate to the qualities that lie deep within and therefore change their decisions, behaviours and actions so they can achieve their intentions and express their true selves to the world. She has never been more fulfilled, personally and professionally.

— ∎ —

Grace had just finished preparing for the debrief session with Yoren when the doorbell rang.

'Wow, he's five minutes early. He's either really keen or eager to get this over with,' she smiled to herself.

It had been a week since Yoren had completed the assessment, and he'd found several of the questions unexpectedly confronting. But he was keen to begin the debrief and extremely curious to know how he scored.

Grace greeted him warmly and shook his hand firmly before welcoming him in and showing him to her office, which was situated off the entry to ensure privacy from the rest of the house. She was casually yet smartly dressed, and her dark, naturally curly hair was swept off her face, highlighting her clear blue eyes and generous smile.

Her office was spacious, beautifully presented and overlooked the garden through a large bay window offering abundant natural light and a tranquil outlook. She invited him to sit on one of two beautifully upholstered sofas placed around a solid teak coffee table in the centre of the room and offered him a chilled glass of water. Taking a seat on the adjacent sofa, Grace started by confirming that he was comfortable and his phone was turned off or switched to silent so that they could converse without interruption or distraction. He hastily flicked his phone to flight mode and waited for her to begin.

'So, tell me, Yoren, how did you find the experience of completing the profile questions?'

'To be honest, Grace, I found some of the questions a little odd and also confronting at times. And some seemed to be asking more than one question at once, as though they were measuring more than one thing, making them difficult to answer. It definitely didn't feel like a typical questionnaire to me. I will admit that a few of the questions made me so uncomfortable that I was on the verge of giving up and walking away. However, others gave me some interesting insights into myself, which I didn't expect until the debrief, and so I'm keen to learn more.'

'That's great, Yoren. Can you give me an example of a question you found odd or confronting?' asked Grace.

'I remember there was one question that was more of a statement and required a yes or no response. It was something like: "I never have any worries". My immediate reaction was to select yes, which I did, as that is how I present myself to others. But deep down, I know there are times when I am worried. So, I believe I responded incorrectly. But reflecting on it since, I wonder what my response says about me.'

'I'm not surprised to hear you say that, Yoren. Many people share a similar experience. The questions are strategically designed to support you to dig deeper than you might have done before. Do you have any other questions before we begin?'

'No, I'm keen to get started on the debrief and find out how I went. I really want to see my scores.'

'Before we begin, it's important to understand that this process is not so much about your scores, but about how we can use them as indicators,' said Grace. 'They can help me to facilitate a series of intentional, ongoing conversations: partly in this session and continuing in greater depth if you decide to embark on a coaching program with me. These conversations will open doors for you to gain a deeper insight into yourself and how you relate to the various qualities or Aspects of Being that have been measured. Does that make sense?'

'Yes, I guess so,' responded Yoren. 'I've always been a high achiever, so scoring well on tests is really important to me,' he laughed. 'Seriously though, I'm not at all concerned about my results. I'm confident I scored well, or at least above average.'

What if I didn't score well? I'd never live it down. No, surely that's not going to happen! When have I ever underperformed in anything?

Ignoring Yoren's last remark, Grace continued. 'Let me explain in a bit more detail what we'll be covering over the next two hours and give you some context, so you can see the bigger picture. Is that okay with you, Yoren?'

'Sure.'

'Great. I'm committed to providing you with a debrief today that will enable you to see yourself more clearly than you may have experienced before. At the very least, it will offer you a distinctly new perspective. The questions you answered resulted in scores out of 10, with zero being the lowest and 10 the highest. Those scores indicate the health of your relationship with various Aspects of Being. Overall, the assessment will help to shine a light on your being so that your shadows or troubled sides are revealed. The shadows highlight the areas to work on, so you should be thrilled to discover them.'

Hearing Grace talk about how the profile would reveal his shadows made Yoren feel uneasy.

Sensing his discomfort, Grace said, 'While using the word shadows may come across as though they are dark and troublesome, they actually represent your growth potential. Unless there is something to own, to be responsible for, there is nothing to address and transform. If someone perceives themselves as already perfect at the start of this process, it will get in the way of their growth and transformation. I'd also like you to remember that this is not a personality assessment. So it's not based on the notion that you're the sum of a series of fixed traits, as in a typical psychometric test. We're here to look into your relationships with various human qualities within the scope of performance, leadership and effectiveness.'

Yoren was sceptical. 'The way I understand it, a psychometric test is objective, but what you're describing sounds rather subjective to me,' he said.

'I understand where you might be coming from, Yoren. I've studied and experienced many different types of profiles. While they all have merit, I've found they lack the balance between objectivity and subjectivity. The framework we're using here is unique in this regard. It offers a mutual language and model through which we can first objectively see an individual as a member of the class 'human being' and then subjectively assess that individual's relationships with a series of shared human qualities. By subjectively, I mean how an individual is *being* by examining how they relate to those qualities.'

Noticing Yoren's confused expression, Grace continued, 'Let me clarify. The ontological model is designed to objectively map out the qualities relevant to all human beings within the scope of performance, leadership and effectiveness. The objective model can then be leveraged in directing you where to look into the subjective self and work out how you relate to and act upon each of the 31 Aspects of Being. So, the model is objective, meaning it relates to all human beings. And when it's used to understand how you, as a unique individual, are subjectively being in relation to the Aspects of Being, it helps you to understand yourself more effectively.

'Why has it been designed like this? Because as individuals, we all relate to each of the qualities differently. For example, everyone relates to fear, but not everyone relates to fear in the same way. So while there are several commonalities in terms of nature, and we correspond in character and kind because we are the same species, we are different in terms of *how* we relate to those commonalities, which influences the way we act upon them. So the model is designed to allow you to gradually develop a lens to see deeper and know where to look. Then you can see how you relate to each quality. This is how the model enables you to get to know yourself and how you are being.'

'Don't other assessments also look at human beings objectively and subjectively?' asked Yoren.

'Many other schools of thought choose to ignore either the objective or the subjective side,' responded Grace. 'Some focus purely on the essence of human beings, deconstructing what it is to be a human being and completely ignoring our subjective sides. In doing so, they are essentially downgrading human beings to nothing more than fixed and predefined objects. Other models focus purely on the subjective sides of human beings and ignore the objective side – the things we all share – to the extent that they essentially make human beings unstudiable or overly mutable. This approach became popular in the 19th century with the rise of existentialism and was later favoured – and even radically extended – by some post-structuralist philosophers. Hmm, I could speak on this topic for hours. But let's not get too philosophical here. After all, we only have limited time,' laughed Grace.

Yoren couldn't help but be impressed by Grace's apparent knowledge of the subject.

> *Wow, there's far more to this than I thought! Clearly, a lot of work has gone on behind the scenes to ensure this paradigm and assessment deliver detailed and valuable information.*

'Well, perhaps that can be the topic of discussion for another time,' said Yoren. Still curious to learn more, he asked, 'So tell me, how do you know the questions in the assessment strike the right mix of objectivity and subjectivity?'

'The questions are designed to assess *what* you know about your objective human qualities as well as *how* you subjectively relate to those qualities or Aspects of Being, for example, how you relate to responsibility or assertiveness,' responded Grace. 'Then the assessment goes even deeper and asks questions that indicate how you *act upon them* in various aspects of your daily life, such as your work and career, your relationships and your family. Again, this will differ from person to person and is therefore subjective.'

'That all makes sense in relation to human beings as a species. But how does it measure *my* relationships with those Aspects of Being?' asked Yoren.

'Good question, Yoren. *How* you are being is how you, as a unique individual, *relate to* the qualities relevant to all human beings. Let me explain by walking you through the ontological model and your results for some of the Aspects of Being.

'Before we start, it's very important to understand that the profile is entirely non-judgemental and independent of morality,' she continued. 'There's no right or wrong, good or bad. The scores simply represent a snapshot of your being based on your responses; it's like being given x-ray vision that enables you to see deep within yourself to the underlying qualities you can't normally see or have access to. Remember, each score represents how you *relate* to that particular quality. A lower score will reveal the shadow. It will indicate a less-than-optimal or relatively unhealthy relationship with that quality. A higher score, on the other hand, will indicate a relatively healthy relationship with that quality.

'As we examine your relationship with each Aspect of Being, I'd like to encourage you to link your result to the distinction of the Aspect of Being and relate it to your life. If there's anything you don't understand or that raises questions for you, we can have an open conversation about it. Feel free to interrupt me at any time, as this process is designed to be interactive. Any questions before we begin?'

'No, I'm ready to get started,' said Yoren as he put on his reading glasses.

Grace opened his report and began to walk him through it.

'Let's begin with a high-level overview of the model for context. We find going from general to specific is the most effective way to go through the report.'

Yoren nodded.

'As I said earlier, the ontological model represents the qualities relevant to all of us in the scope of performance, effectiveness and leadership,' said Grace. 'It's used as a benchmark to measure how you, as an individual, relate to each of those Aspects of Being from a subjective point of view. To use a simple analogy, everyone has a level of iron in their blood, but how much iron we have differs from one person to the next. Too much or too little can have serious consequences. For optimal health, wellbeing and functionality, there is an agreed benchmark for how much iron we should have. The same is true for the Aspects of Being.

'If we zoom out, your scores represent the breakdown of your being into smaller pieces called Aspects of Being. For example, you can be aware or unaware, responsible or irresponsible, authentic or inauthentic, assertive or non-assertive, and so on. Naturally, there are degrees in between, but I'm sure you get the gist. Any questions so far?'

'So far, so good,' responded Yoren.

Grace continued, 'The model is broken down into four layers: Meta Factors, Moods, Primary Ways of Being and Secondary Ways of Being. The Meta Factors are the three highest-level factors that influence one's performance and ability to be an influential leader. They are awareness, integrity and effectiveness.'

Grace revealed Yoren's results for the three Meta Factors and they discussed each of them briefly. When Yoren expressed concern over his lower-than-expected scores for all three Meta Factors, Grace reiterated what they represented.

'Remember, each Aspect of Being is scored from zero to 10, where zero is the lowest and 10 is the highest,' she said. Scores of zero or 10 are almost unheard of. In fact, it is extremely rare to achieve either the highest (9, 10) or the lowest (zero, one) scores for any Aspect of Being. This aligns with reality in that very few people sit at the edge of the spectrum. These are health scores. For example, if someone scores 8 out of 10 for anxiety and fear, that doesn't mean they are an anxious and fearful person. On the contrary, it means they have a relatively healthy relationship with anxiety and fear. They can step forward despite the presence of anxiety or fear. Does that make sense?'

'Yes, got it,' said Yoren.

As they conversed, Grace asked a series of relevant questions. Yoren's responses revealed glimpses into how he relates to certain things in his life and reacts or responds to various situations. The more they talked, the more he offered snippets of his life and, importantly, the challenges he experienced around his intention to start a business. Grace reinforced her commitment to make the being discourse relevant to his life rather than consider it from a theoretical or intellectual perspective, explaining that today's session was more high-level than any subsequent coaching would be.

'The next layer after the Meta Factors is the Moods: vulnerability, care, anxiety and fear,' said Grace. 'Then we have the Primary Ways of Being. These are the underlying qualities that influence our decisions, behaviours and actions. As you can see, there are 16 Primary Ways of Being in our model: authenticity, responsibility, freedom, courage, commitment, gratitude, higher purpose, empowerment, presence, peace of mind, compassion, love, contribution, partnership, forgiveness and self-expression. Last but not least, we have the Secondary Ways of Being. These represent the bridge between the underlying Primary Ways of Being and the decisions, behaviours and actions we can see on the surface. There are eight of them: assertiveness, proactivity, confidence, persistence, resourcefulness, resilience, accountability and reliability.'

Yoren stared at the model, trying to find a way to find fault with it as Grace walked him through it. However, he couldn't help but be impressed.

'Going back to your question about how the profile measures *your* relationships with those Aspects of Being, let's break it down further,' continued Grace. 'If we consider *what* you are, we can agree that you are a human being with the same core qualities that all human beings share. Now, *how* you are is determined by how you *relate* to being a human being with all those constituent parts or Aspects of Being in place. For example, when it comes to responsibility – one of the Primary Ways of Being – one person may relate to this Aspect of Being as if they have full control over life, that they have absolute autonomy. Others may relate to it as though life is just happening around them and they have little influence over it, meaning that they relate to their autonomy in a more passive way. Both extremes are unrealistic and indicate an unhealthy relationship with responsibility.

'The benchmark that is considered realistic, authentic and congruent with reality when it comes to responsibility is having the power to influence the circumstances you find yourself in or cause. It means you respond rather than react to matters and accept ownership of the outcomes and consequences of your actions. This benchmark indicates a healthy relationship with responsibility. So, a person with a healthy relationship with responsibility is neither a passive victim who believes life is occurring to them and they have absolutely no say in it nor someone who lives life from the viewpoint that they have god-like autonomy. Instead, they are an active agent in life. Would you like to look into your relationship with responsibility, Yoren?'

'Yes, that would be great,' he responded.

Grace and Yoren talked about his marginally unhealthy score for responsibility in relation to its distinction.

Responsibility

Responsibility is being the primary cause of the matters in your life, regardless of their source. It is the extent to which you choose to respond rather than react to them. *Responsibility* is distinguished by how you honour the autonomy that you have as a human being and is considered the power to influence the affairs, outcomes and consequences you are faced with. *Responsibility* is not about blaming or determining whose fault it is. Instead, it is to intentionally choose, own, cause and bring about outcomes that matter, work and produce results while also being answerable for the impact and consequences.

A healthy relationship with *responsibility* indicates that you have the power to influence the circumstances you find yourself in and/or cause. Others may consider you capable of appropriately responding to matters, which is a prerequisite to producing and bringing to fruition effective results. You fully accept ownership of both outcomes and consequences and have the capacity to make informed, uncoerced decisions. You are unquestionably the active agent in your life.

An unhealthy relationship with *responsibility* indicates that you may often be stuck, experience a loss of power, and are a victim of circumstances. You frequently experience being disarmed, as though you have no choice in influencing outcomes and there is an inevitability about your future. You may be inclined to self-sabotage and make repetitive complaints without seeking, putting forward and implementing solutions. You frequently make excuses for your lack of accomplishments while abdicating or avoiding consequences. You may be considered ineffective in consistently fulfilling the promises you make and producing intended results. You are a passive victim in your life. Alternatively, you may live life from the viewpoint of being the sole cause of matters and exert your will onto your surroundings and others or be over-responsible and attempt to control all matters all the time. You may also expect that matters should always go your way.

After reading the distinction, Yoren said, 'I must say, the way responsibility is described here is very different from how I've always seen it in myself and others. I've always considered responsibility as one's duties and obligations and to be at fault or to blame for something.'

'Yes, many people find that when they read the distinctions around what the profile measures,' said Grace. 'Notice I used the word distinction rather than definition. We leave definitions to dictionaries. We use distinctions so that primacy is given to the *meaning*, not the word. Referring back to responsibility, the profile measures it as the quality of being an autonomous being or an active agent rather than being either a passive victim in life or a control freak who tries to exert or impose their will on everything and everyone. The word 'responsibility' has been chosen to refer to that meaning. That's why we use distinctions to describe what that is. While your understanding of responsibility isn't incorrect, all I ask is that you consider that it is not what is measured here.

'You will find the same with some of the other Aspects of Being, such as integrity. Many people only see integrity as the quality of being honest and having strong morals. However, we measure integrity as the state of being whole or complete and in optimal condition. So that's the meaning it refers to. Let's now look into the distinction of integrity.'

Integrity

Integrity is the state of being whole, complete, unbroken, sound and in optimal condition. *Integrity* encompasses all primal Aspects of Being in the same way that the various limbs and organs are the constituent parts of your body. *Integrity* is the prerequisite to being effective and operating at the optimal level of performance and is fundamental to generating trust and workability. *Integrity* brings about ease and flow and is considered 'being well', 'well put together' or the wellness of your being.

A healthy relationship with *integrity* indicates that you know
yourself to be sufficient and mostly experience flow and
workability in life. Ease, trust and consistency are present for both
you and those around you. You actively address and maintain
whatever may impair your *integrity*, particularly qualities that are
diminished, misplaced or require refinement or transformation.

An unhealthy relationship with *integrity* indicates that you mostly
experience frustration and dysfunction, with recurring problems
and unresolved issues. There are many areas in your life you feel
the need to fix. Others may experience an absence of workability
and consistency around you, hence trust and *effectiveness* are
often compromised and brought into question. Alternatively,
you may be obsessed with perfection and struggle to be with
shortcomings or incompletion. You may avoid pursuing matters
unless success is ensured.

'Notice how the distinction has three parts,' continued Grace. 'That's
the case for all 31 Aspects of Being. The first part briefly describes the
Aspect of Being. In this case, it describes the meaning for integrity in
this framework. The second part describes what it looks like to have a
healthy relationship with integrity, while the third part describes the
indications of an unhealthy relationship.'

They discussed Yoren's result for integrity at a deeper level and Grace
explained how all Moods and Primary Ways of Being feed into it as
constituent parts of the 'whole'.

'The distinctions are designed to clearly depict a vivid picture of
how it is to be X or Y: for example, what it looks like to be courageous, committed, authentic, present, vulnerable and so on,' Grace
explained. 'They're intended to create *relevance* so that you can
relate them back to you and your life as opposed to being abstract or
theoretical. Remember, we're not only talking about *what* you are as
a human being from an objective point of view but also *how* you, as
an individual, are *being*. The distinctions build the bridge between
the ontological aspect – what is real about human beings – and the

phenomenological aspect – your experiences as an individual in relation to these qualities. Does this make sense, Yoren?'

'Yes, it does. I must say, I'm impressed with the depth this goes into. I've never seen myself in this way before.'

Grace smiled and said, 'Yes, most people feel like that when they're first exposed to this way of seeing themselves. It also gives them an insight into how useful this model can be to support them in seeing others too. It can make an enormous difference when selecting people to partner with, hiring and even choosing the right person to be in an intimate relationship with.'

'Hmm, yes, I can see how that could be very beneficial,' said Yoren, thinking about Mel and some of the challenges they'd been experiencing in their relationship of late. Quickly pushing that away, he returned to the conversation at hand, saying, 'You've explained the what and the how. But what we haven't covered yet is how this profile works out who I am as a unique individual.'

'Excellent question, Yoren. It shows that you are thinking deeply about all of this. Now, when it comes to *who* you are as a unique individual, nothing, including this profile, can claim to measure that because it is far too mysterious and subjective to measure. However, we do attach significant importance to it. We call it your unique being. And the overarching objective of polishing and transforming your Aspects of Being through coaching is that the process supports you to tap into and authentically express your unique being to the world. You could say it's the unique piece of the puzzle of existence that only you can fill. What we know is that you can't become aware of, tap into and fully actualise this potential unless who you are being is as congruent with reality as possible. The more authentic your understanding, the higher the probability that you will be effective in fulfilling your intentions and projecting your unique being and unique contribution to the world. Are there any other Aspects of Being you would like to discuss in terms of how you relate to them based on your profile result, Yoren?'

Examining the insights delivered by the report, Yoren couldn't help but be triggered by his scores for vulnerability, authenticity, assertiveness and confidence, as they indicated his relationships with those Aspects of Being were on the unhealthy side. So he asked Grace if she could spend some time explaining those qualities and why he might have scored the way he did.

'I'm glad you asked, Yoren. Let's start with vulnerability, a Mood that's often misunderstood as a weakness when it's actually a strength, a quality to be leveraged, not hidden. It's closely related to authenticity. If I were to briefly describe someone who is both vulnerable and authentic, I would say they were transparent and open, someone who owns their vulnerabilities and doesn't attempt to hide them. People who have a relatively healthy relationship with vulnerability and authenticity also ask for what they need and are willing to expose how they feel and express themselves freely without putting their walls up or pretending to be someone they're not.

'Vulnerability is a critical quality to have a healthy relationship with if you want to build a business, a team, a community, an audience, or even to find the right person to partner with in business and in life. Your score indicates the shadow side of this Mood; in other words, this is an area you struggle with to a degree. Let's read through the distinction of vulnerability together and see if you can relate the unhealthy side to what's going on for you right now. Remember, there's no judgement here. Remember also that whenever a shadow is revealed, you should see it as a positive because it highlights an area that you can work on to transform. Without this knowledge, you might not have been aware of it as an issue. And who knows how much it could be blocking you from achieving your goals.'

'By saying I need to be more vulnerable, are you suggesting that I should be weak, Grace?' The tone in his voice made it clear that Grace's words had hit a nerve.

'No, on the contrary, Yoren. Being vulnerable isn't being weak. It's being authentic in terms of how you are being. Consider that we're *all* vulnerable from the moment we're born. While we gain independence when we grow up, we remain vulnerable to the circumstances and events of life. Some people acknowledge this and live their lives from this viewpoint. In fact, often their effective decisions stem from this acknowledgement, which leads them to make more effective decisions and own them with full responsibility. Others live in pretence and suffer the consequences. Now, I'm not suggesting that's how you are. However, your profile suggests that vulnerability is a troubling area for you, and if you decide you'd like to continue this work, it would be highly beneficial to look into how you relate to your vulnerability, as I can see it's vital in the context of your report and life in general. Let's read through the distinction of vulnerability together. Better still, could you please read it to me?'

Vulnerability

Vulnerability impacts how you relate to the concerns you have with respect to how you are being perceived or thought of in different situations. It is how you are being when confronted or exposed to perceived threats, ridicule, attacks or harm (emotional or physical). *Vulnerability* is not being weak, agreeable or submissive. It is when you embrace your imperfections. It is considered the quality of being with your authentic self without obsessive concern over the impression you make.

A healthy relationship with *vulnerability* indicates that you are open as opposed to guarded or closed in receiving unfamiliar knowledge and feedback. You are willing to reveal your authentic self to others, regardless of what they may think of you or the prevailing circumstances. You may often leverage the power of being vulnerable to generate trust and build relationships. You acknowledge and embrace your imperfections to support your growth and influence. Rather than letting other people's opinions of you hold you back, you learn from them to propel you to wholeness (*integrity*) and fulfilment.

An unhealthy relationship with *vulnerability* indicates that you are
likely to defer or avoid taking action or making decisions when
you feel they may impair your reputation. You may also avoid or
put your guard up in situations where you could expose yourself
to ridicule or look foolish. You are more concerned with being
seen to do the right things, looking good or impressing others
than actually doing the things you know to be right. You may
be inclined to sacrifice your authentic self or image to project a
fake persona that you consider more acceptable and impressive
to others. You tend to take criticism personally. Alternatively,
you may attempt to create unrealistic boundaries to maintain a
'safe' distance, avoiding the unknown and refusing to explore
new territories. You may be overly controlling of others or your
environment.

As he read the distinction, Yoren felt deeply confronted. All his
life, he'd believed he shouldn't be vulnerable as he considered it a
weakness and a surefire way to be taken advantage of. He would never
allow himself to be humiliated in that way, which is why he worked
so hard to create and maintain his over-confident persona, professionally and personally. No matter how much hesitation and doubt he
felt, he would conceal those emotions behind a mask. Now, reading
the difference between what a healthy and an unhealthy relationship
with vulnerability looked like made him reflect on how he was being
at work, in social situations and even at home.

It was much the same situation with assertiveness and confidence,
both Secondary Ways of Being he asked to look into. Grace would
normally have preferred to discuss some of the Primary Ways of
Being before any Secondary Way of Being, given their role – together
with the Moods and Meta Factors – in contributing to how one relates
to a Secondary Way of Being. However, she intentionally gave him
the freedom to choose and could see that his relatively low scores
for assertiveness and confidence were troubling him. For context
and clarity, she explained how we project Secondary Ways of Being,
like assertiveness and confidence through our decisions, actions and

body language, and that they're more familiar to us than the deeper underlying qualities, which is why people often want to address them immediately. She then explained that multiple relationships exist between our Aspects of Being and that our Secondary Ways of Being emerge from the deeper Primary Ways of Being and Moods, which is why it's critical in a coaching scenario to address them first.

Yoren acknowledged Grace's explanation but persisted in wanting to at least look into assertiveness and confidence from a high level first. He'd always considered himself to be extremely assertive and confident. However, when it came to assertiveness, the distinction supported him to realise that he often relied on manipulation and domination to get his way without considering the opinions or feelings of others. As for confidence, he'd never regarded it as how one relates to certainties, uncertainties, doubt and hesitation before. He always thought it was more akin to bravado and ego. He suddenly realised that the confidence he thought he possessed in abundance was largely a front to his lack of faith in his own abilities and qualities.

Could these be the reasons I'm blocked in moving forward with my business idea?

Sensing his mood, Grace said gently, 'Unless we become aware of the Aspects of Being and have situational awareness around the matters in life, we can't move forward or address what's not working for us and what's preventing us from fulfilling our intentions. With this in mind, let's go back to awareness, one of the Meta Factors.'

They read through the awareness distinction together and she could see it had an impact on him.

'At the end of the day, as human beings, we can't be intentionally effective at anything we're not aware of,' said Grace. 'That's why your relationship with awareness plays a major role in how you are being and your results. We always go from a degree of awareness to a degree of effectiveness, and this is a continuous life-long process and pursuit, not a one-off objective to be ticked off a to-do list.'

Yoren was so thoughtfully engaged in the conversation that Grace smiled and said, 'I can see your interest in this topic, Yoren, and I'd love to continue it with you at a deeper level in due course. However, I'm aware that we both have commitments and need to be mindful of time. But just before we wrap things up today, could you tell me what you were hoping to achieve from this exercise? Do you have a specific intention or goal you wish to fulfil?'

Without a moment's hesitation, he replied, 'Yes, I've always wanted to start a business of my own. I have plenty of ideas, but something keeps preventing me from moving forward. After attending the info session and talking to Jen, I wondered if this exercise might shed some light on why I can't seem to take the next step.'

There, I said it! It's been in the back of my mind the whole session, but I didn't know if it was appropriate to tell her. In fact, this is what's been bugging me for such a long time. I kept pushing the thought away and keeping it hidden from everyone except Mel, in case they judged me for not having done anything about it yet.

'Great. Thank you for sharing that, Yoren. I'm confident that if you decide to work with me as your coach, I can support you in transforming the areas that might be blocking your way. Now, in relation to your profile report and what we've discussed today, what are you present to right now?'

After contemplating the question for a moment, Yoren said, 'I'm present to the gaps and curious to learn what would happen if I close them. It makes me wonder what a 10 out of 10 could look like in all of these aspects and how that would impact my results and my ability to move forward with my dream of starting a business.'

'Fantastic! If it's okay with you, I'd like to offer my recommendation for the next steps,' said Grace.

'Sure, fire away.'

'Based on the areas you identified in your debrief session and your willingness to work on the shadow parts that might be getting in the way of you starting a business, I'd like to offer to work with you and look at ways to shift those areas and transform your relationship with them. I can offer you two options, both involving a combination of training and coaching: fortnightly sessions over 12 months or weekly sessions over six months. Most people choose to give themselves more time, especially as we combine elements of practical learning and training, and extend it over 12 months. However, if you're committed and have the time and dedication to give it what it takes, I currently have space in my diary to offer the weekly option. Do you have a preference, Yoren, now that you're clear on your intention?' asked Grace.

'If I decide to go ahead, I'd definitely want to commit to weekly sessions and have it over and done with in half the time,' he responded with a hint of sarcasm. 'I'm intrigued about the philosophy behind this too, so the combination of training and coaching sounds good to me.'

Grace smiled. 'We can be flexible in how we allocate the time between training and coaching, depending on your needs. We'll discuss and agree on that at our first session if you decide to proceed. You don't need to give me a definitive answer today. As we've covered a lot of ground, I recommend you give yourself time to go through the report and read through each distinction carefully. You'll have access to the full report via the website. It's totally secure and private. All you need to do is log in using the credentials you established when you completed the assessment.

'All the distinctions and their references are available on your profile,' she continued. 'So, as you take the time to read through the full report, ask yourself, where is that present for me and where is it not? Which Aspects of Being can I be with and which do I struggle to be with? Be honest with yourself. Then consider if you can see any relationships between some of those Aspects of Being. Don't worry if you can't see the relationships yourself. We'll dive deeply into those during our coaching sessions if you decide to proceed. I'll also send you a proposal outlining the fees involved and further details about the next steps, the coaching process and the level of commitment and time you'll need to be prepared to put in. How does that sound, Yoren?'

'That sounds fine, Grace. I'll give it some thought,' said Yoren, poker-faced.

Although he felt excited at the prospect of coaching to support him in breaking through the blockages to finally realise his dream of building a startup, he refused to let Grace see it. He thanked her for the debrief and left feeling more hopeful than he had in a long time.

CHAPTER 7

A Glimmer of Hope

It was midnight. Willing sleep to come behind tightly closed eyelids, Yoren was wide awake and vividly present to his earlier conversation with Grace and to the dream he'd always concealed and neglected to acknowledge, let alone take any steps towards actualising. The images in his mind were so sharp and crystal clear that it was as though a beam of light was slicing through the pitch-blackness of the bedroom to cast a spotlight on his thoughts and bring them to life.

He knew those images could not be unseen, no matter how tightly he shut his eyes and despite the darkness of the bedroom with its heavy drapes that blocked any outside light. He'd always known he wanted to build a business, but the fear and anxiety of dealing with the tremendous uncertainty this could bring kept getting in his way. The ideology his father had tried so hard to instil throughout his childhood had almost made him believe that the wealthy were greedy and accumulated their wealth by stealing from and exploiting others and that money was the root of all evil. It wasn't until he was a young adult that he realised his father was a self-identified neo-Marxist social scientist with an almost obsessive interest in economics and power within social structures and organisations. Most of the academic papers he wrote were centred around power dynamics, inequality and the relationship between the private and public sectors. He often adopted a moral high ground on the subject of economics and power, which frequently caused major disagreements with his own father, Samuel, who had an entirely different view of and approach to wealth and power.

Yoren had always looked up to his grandfather and felt their views were more closely aligned. However, having been raised under his father's roof, he couldn't help but feel torn at times between his father's teachings and values about economics, and his personal yearning for financial growth and fulfilling his dream of making a difference through entrepreneurship. Deep down, he knew that building a business was as much about self-expression and contribution as it was about wealth accumulation. These were views he'd learned from his grandfather and through personal experience. He'd been exposed to various workplace cultures and office politics within the corporate world throughout his career, giving him a clear indication of what worked and what didn't. He was inspired to build the kind of business that would entice the best talent to want to work there.

While he'd never had an issue with being an employee and was well-remunerated and respected for what he did, his vision was to create jobs and opportunities for others as opposed to just occupying a role within someone else's organisation. In part, owning a business was also about making a good impression, as he'd always regarded company owners and directors as having a higher social status than employees, a view his father vehemently disagreed with. Overall though, he couldn't quite put his finger on why leaving a well-paid career to take such an enormous risk was so important to him. He just knew he wanted more. He longed to play a bigger game, not just for the money, but also to challenge himself at this stage in his life and actualise the potential he knew he possessed. But how to tap into that potential? It was as though something was always blocking his way.

Now, after completing his debrief session with Grace and reading through some of the distinctions, his attention was drawn to the likely cause of his blockage. It wasn't just that he had lots to learn about the technicalities of building a business from scratch. He now realised some deeper, underlying qualities were getting in his way, even to the point where they prevented him from looking into the technicalities and processes associated with creating and building a startup. Until now, he had always found some vague excuse as to why he couldn't do it, from being too busy to concern over what others might think, including his father and even Mel.

As he lay there in the dark, he recalled the insights shared by Erik during the information session and his conversations with Jen and Grace. Now, he felt he could finally articulate that vagueness. It suddenly dawned on him that he'd always needed a definitive answer to any problem he faced before he felt comfortable enough to move forward. The thought of delving into the unknown had always filled him with dread. While he knew he could have convinced himself to ignore or neglect what he was now present to, which is what he would have done before receiving all this new information, he now understood that it would be inauthentic of him to look away from something he could see so vividly. His newfound awareness of the likely root causes of his blockages was a true moment of reception for him.

Despite his clarity, Yoren still wavered and hesitated in deciding whether to commit to coaching with Grace. This was a typical response for him whenever he faced a dilemma or had to make a significant decision. He often concealed his lack of confidence in making decisions at work by outsourcing the decision-making to others on his team. Then, as is the case in many organisations, he would happily take credit for a decision made by a subordinate that proved to be right. However, he was quick to point the finger if a decision proved to be less than favourable. There were also times when he would present his boss with various options provided to him by one of the technicians on his team and ask him to decide. When this happened, the decision-making would sometimes be delegated up the line till it reached the CEO. The more layers of management, the more the options and ideas would be diluted to the point where the CEO might have just a couple of options to select from. Ironically, the CEO would often ask for advice from the technician who came up with the options in the first place due to their more advanced technical knowledge of the matter at hand. And so, a decision would sometimes be left to a non-executive member of the organisation.

Thrown into this turbulent mix was the anxiety of dealing with tremendous uncertainty, including concern about what his father would think if he decided to become an entrepreneur. He knew his father had written several papers – which he always emphasised had been 'peer-reviewed' – that leaned heavily towards his preferred ideology. In those papers, he would tap into the knowledge of a handful of carefully selected philosophers and conclude that most people in a neo-liberalistic society were either entrepreneurs or consumers and how problematic he found this so-called 'conversion of citizen to consumer'. He was also deeply concerned about what Mel would think of him leaving his well-paid, high-status and relatively safe job with one of the top consulting firms in the world for a potentially risky career as an entrepreneur. His father had constantly lectured him on the more than 90% failure rate among startups and how that well-researched and validated statistic meant it would be madness for him to pursue such a pipe dream. In his mind, Mel had agreed to become engaged to an associate solutions specialist, not a man with a dream.

It was a hot, humid night. Unable to sleep, he got up, flicked on the air conditioner and quietly poured himself a glass of water from the jug on the nightstand by the window. He opened the drapes just enough to catch a glimpse of the view, hoping it wouldn't disturb Mel. It was a full moon, and he stood momentarily mesmerised by its golden reflection on the ocean extending almost to the horizon. He redirected his gaze from the reflection to the moon itself, observing that it was exceptionally bright. The longer he looked, the more his breathing slowed, and a sense of peace and calmness began to wash over him. As he stood there, focused on the moon's golden glow, it suddenly dawned on him that there was no need for him to have all the answers right now. While he'd always been accustomed to intellectualising the world and rationalising every decision and action, he suddenly realised that he was overthinking things and worrying too much about the what-ifs.

Nobody's asked me to make a decision about leaving my job and starting a business now. There's no need to decide that right now. All I've been invited to consider at this point is whether or not I wish to accept Grace's coaching proposal. It's a simple yes or no decision. And if I say yes to the coaching, it might not even significantly influence the business decision. I'm making a mountain out of a molehill!

In the past, it had never occurred to Yoren that he might be over–analysing something. He'd always taken great pride in the precision of his analysis and would often brag about how he was always the one making the 'right', well-informed and data-driven decisions. But this time was different. He was beginning to see things through a new lens. He decided to pay attention to what his gut was telling him, something else he was unaccustomed to doing as he'd never considered intuition valid before.

Do I trust Jen? Do I believe Grace is trustworthy? Did I find them competent enough to give it a go?

Suddenly, the answers were crystal clear, making his decision easy. His gut told him to say yes to the coaching experience. At the start, he'd been merely intrigued. But now, his newfound clarity made him sincerely curious to discover what the coaching could uncover for him. Oddly, he found he was enjoying this newly discovered awareness of the matters in his life. He smiled as he remembered Jen seeking sincere curiosity when she asked him if he wanted her to reveal the fourth mood during his recent visit.

I want to start my own business. And if I discover through this coaching experience that there are certain matters getting in the way, then I'm committed to addressing them.

Still gazing at the moon, he could see a glimmer of hope. It was enough to convince him to take a step forward and not let his fear and anxiety of dealing with so much uncertainty get in his way.

Closing the drapes, he climbed back into bed and put his arms around Mel, hugging her tightly. Feeling calm, courageous and, to an extent, confident and hopeful, he quickly fell into a deep sleep.

— ∎ —

The next morning, Yoren emailed Grace to advise her of his decision to accept her proposal. He then paid the required deposit to firm up his commitment to the six-month coaching journey with her. To Yoren, making this payment made the process ahead of him real and confirmed that he was committed to seeing it through. In the past, it was not uncommon for him to overanalyse matters to the point where opportunities slipped through his fingers. He recalled the time when he got cold feet and pulled out of a property deal at the last minute, only to discover later that it would have been a highly lucrative investment. Knowing fear and anxiety often got in his way, he was relieved to make the payment and close the back door. Grace called him later that day to schedule their first weekly session. They agreed to start the following Saturday.

In the meantime, Yoren decided it was time to tell Mel about his decision. Over dinner, he revealed how much he had been impacted by the information session and the conversation with Jen, despite his initial resistance. He also told her about his experience completing the assessment and the follow-up debrief session with Grace, albeit without revealing too much information about her. The last thing he wanted was for Mel to look Grace up online and see how attractive she was. He walked Mel through parts of the report and read through some of the distinctions, taking great pains to conceal his results as he hoped to reveal them later when some of them were higher.

The only time Mel could recall seeing Yoren this enthusiastic and animated was when he told her about his dream to start a business.

She was also delighted to see him being so unusually open and vulnerable. She didn't even mind that he wasn't ready to reveal his results. Just talking about it was a big step for him. At the same time, Yoren was amazed at how receptive and open his fiancé was about everything he shared. He was even more surprised when she expressed no concern about his commitment to a six-month coaching journey with a woman she didn't know.

I should never have assumed Mel would expect me to maintain this corporate role and that she was opposed to the idea of me taking a risk on something new. She's being so amazingly supportive about all of this!

The week flew by, and before he knew it, the morning of his first coaching session with Grace arrived. As he drove to her office, Yoren wasn't sure if he was excited or nervous. A mixture of emotions swirled around in his mind and heart. He wound down the window, revelling in the refreshing sea breeze, and put on his favourite playlist for the rest of the drive.

On arrival, Grace greeted him warmly and ushered him into her spacious office, inviting him to take a seat on the sofa. As she poured them both a glass of water, Yoren's eyes swept the room as though seeing it for the first time. Aside from a large, colourful African landscape on the wall, a few flourishing indoor plants and a large whiteboard, the room's decor was relatively minimalistic, yet impressive and classic in design.

'The purpose of this first session, Yoren, is to explain how the coaching process works and align our expectations, create the trajectory for the next six months and establish the relationship between coach and coachee,' said Grace. 'I'll also explain the tools and concepts required to facilitate the coaching component and the coaching itself. Then we'll begin the coaching. Finally, we'll discuss your commitment for the week and consider the agenda for the next session. Any questions before we begin?'

'No, that sounds good.'

Yoren actually had several questions running through his mind but decided to withhold them rather than eat into his billable time. He'd always been frugal with money and wasn't about to stop now.

'The most important expectation I have of you is to be willing,' said Grace. 'That means rather than coming to each session through a sense of obligation or with an intention to just learn something from me, I want you to commit to being open and willing to engage in a two-way coaching conversation. Now, let's establish the outcomes you wish to achieve from our coaching journey to ensure we're both on the same page. This will determine the overall coaching contract. Then, at the start of each session, we'll agree on a contract for the work we want to do in that session.'

'Why do we need a contract? I don't feel the need to sign one. I have complete faith in you, Grace.'

Hearing Yoren express his complete faith in her made Grace smile. She knew his intention was in the right place but that it was inauthentic for anyone to express complete faith in someone they barely knew.

'I appreciate your faith in me, Yoren. But I'm not referring to a legal contract. In coaching, we use the word 'contract' to refer to the setting of expectations between the coach and coachee. That way we know we're both on the same page. It also minimises misunderstanding around what's to be achieved during the entire coaching period and in each session. That's why we need a contract for the six months and one for each session. Does that clarify it for you?'

Feeling a bit sheepish, Yoren nodded.

'Great. So what outcomes do you aim to achieve over the next six months?'

'The main outcome I want to achieve is to overcome my internal barriers to starting my business. Something keeps making me hesitate and stops me from just going for it.'

'I understand. Let me just document that,' said Grace, typing into her laptop.

'Just to clarify, Yoren, it's important to understand that coaching is not an exact science. It's not a case of achieving a given output based on certain inputs. While many psychologists or coaches will have their clients believe they can deliver predictable outcomes, there's considerable subjectivity associated with this process. By that, I don't mean we're going to just sit here and talk. We'll be tapping into a framework, methodology, processes and practices. However, the value you gain from this process will depend on the level of focus and commitment you're prepared to put into it. How you are being is key to its success.

'Ironically, the more polished your being, the more likely you are to benefit from each of the sessions. Consider this as an iterative process where you'll loop through the three stages of awareness – reception, perception and conception – and then move to the application stage where you act upon your best comprehension of the Aspect of Being you're working on. Don't worry if this doesn't make sense to you right now, Yoren. I'll walk you through the full Transformation Methodology in our next session, but we'll touch on it a little later today as well.

'Simply put, the more polished your relationship with different Aspects of Being, the more likely your commitment, care, courage, vulnerability, openness and so on will lead you to experience exponential growth. So I encourage you to be as authentic and open as possible and don't withhold internal conversations. You're here to do the work, and I'm here to facilitate the process, encourage action and commitment from you and foster accountability. Are you comfortable with that? Any questions at this point?'

'That all makes sense, Grace. But yes, I do have one question. My understanding from your proposal is that the coaching won't be centred on how to build a business but on what's getting in the way of doing so. Have I understood that correctly?'

'Yes, that's correct,' she replied. 'I'm glad you raised that because it's very important to confirm from the outset that this is not business coaching. That's a separate type of coaching altogether. It's also important for you to be aware that this is coaching and not therapy. So it's not a substitute for health treatment. The purpose of this coaching, as outlined in my proposal and based on our conversation during the debrief session, is to address the blockages preventing you from taking proactive steps to start your business. So I want to be very clear that I won't be offering you any business advice or health treatment. In fact, I won't be offering advice at all, unless requested. Again, my role as your coach is to facilitate the enquiries into what it will take to transform the Aspects of Being standing in your way of effectiveness, performance and fulfilling your intention. And for most of us, the very thing standing in our way is ourselves, our very being. Over the next six months, I'll support you to remove what's getting in your way.

'You might recall how Erik introduced the key prerequisites to fulfilling our intentions and priorities in the info session you attended. In your case, one of those priorities, or perhaps the most important one in your life right now, is to start your own business. Our intentions change throughout our lives, but right now, transitioning from employee to entrepreneur is your primary focus. Is that right?'

'Yes, correct,' responded Yoren.

'Okay, so you have an intention you care deeply about. So our priority over the next six months is to work out which qualities or Aspects of Being you need to address and transform your relationship with so there's no mismatch between your intention and your values. Unless we focus on the key Aspects of Being that align with your intention of starting a business, you won't achieve the outcome you're seeking. Any questions, Yoren?'

'What did you mean when you said transforming my relationship with certain Aspects of Being?' asked Yoren. 'Are you suggesting I undergo some weird process of transformation?'

Observing the concerned look on his face, Grace smiled and said, 'Before I answer your question on transformation – and don't worry, Yoren, it's not as mystical as it might sound – would you mind if I introduce a few of the tools and concepts we'll be using over the next six months?'

'Sure, go ahead,' responded Yoren.

'Okay, great,' said Grace. 'We'll be using the ontological model as a tool to support you in objectively understanding the constituent parts of a human being, the qualities we all share that either contribute to or detract from our effectiveness and performance in life. So far, we've used the model's assessment tool to support you to see how you relate to each of the qualities or Aspects of Being in the model, which to a great extent also explains how you act upon them. Consider this the starting point for coaching.

'Your profile report maps out and articulates what we call your 'as-is model'. This is your current overall state of being. It provides a holistic view while also breaking down your overall being into tangible and more readily identifiable and digestible parts that are able to be assessed, polished and transformed. These constituent parts are the qualities we call Aspects of Being. Any questions?'

'No, that's all clear to me,' he replied.

'Excellent,' Grace continued. 'So, we have your as-is model and we're both clear on your intention of starting a business. Now, the next step before we commence work on the process of transformation is to identify the 'hot spots'. These are the shadow parts of you that we determine are the most important troubled areas to work on in the context of unblocking whatever is holding you back from starting your business. You'll recall that the assessment metaphorically casts light on your being. Whenever light is cast, a shadow is revealed, which represents your troubled parts. The aim over the next six months is not to address all the troubled areas identified in the report. It's not about becoming the 'perfect human being'. Instead, we'll address and transform the shadow parts that might impact your ability to fulfil your intention. That's why we call them hot spots. They're the relationships that, when addressed and integrated, will contribute to your overall integrity, thereby considerably increasing the probability of you fulfilling your intention. Does that make sense, Yoren?'

It took considerable effort for Yoren to keep his views about the shadow conversation to himself. Unaccustomed to metaphorical descriptions, he still found the subject too mystical, fanciful and intangible for his liking. But he kept his mouth shut and simply nodded.

'Now, returning to the fulfilment conversation for a moment,' continued Grace. 'For anyone to fulfil their intention, they need to be effective in their endeavours. That means they need to make effective decisions and take effective actions to ensure their efforts are put to good use and not wasted. We cannot intentionally become effective at anything we're unaware of or have misconceptions about.

'For you, Yoren, it means you can't be effective without awareness and clarity around your intentions and awareness of the constituent parts that are compromising your integrity and getting in the way of your ability and/or willingness to move forward with your plans. You also need an authentic and congruent awareness of what it takes to build a business, such as understanding others and knowing how the economy works. You need to know how to hire the right people, shape a go-to-market strategy and implement an effective financial structure and revenue model, as well as how to build commercial partnerships and shape an authentic and distinctive brand. You need to know how to establish and maintain your business accounts and how the taxation system works. You need to become aware of your legal obligations as a director, and the list goes on. In order for you to gradually come to know enough about all these things to make effective decisions, you have to start by addressing your relationship with awareness itself.

'While I'm not going to teach you all those business-building skills, we're here to establish a workable foundation so you're ready to receive, perceive and conceive this new knowledge and act upon it in the most effective way possible. With this in mind, we'll start by working through the Meta Factors: awareness, integrity and effectiveness, specifically, how you relate to each of them. Any questions?'

Yoren sat in silence, appearing to quietly digest the information. However, his inner voice was anything but silent.

What's this about addressing my relationship with awareness itself? I haven't come this far in my life by living in a vacuum or burying my head in the sand. I'm more than aware of everything that's going on, including my relationship with awareness!

Recognising that Yoren wasn't ready to be vulnerable, Grace decided to move on, knowing his relationship with vulnerability would be explored later.

'Okay, so now that we've established the ground rules and fundamentals, I'd like to walk you through what we refer to as the 'exposure triangle' to help explain what the process of transformation looks like and why it's so effective. Would that be okay with you, Yoren?'

'Sure, go ahead.'

'The term 'exposure triangle' was inspired by photography. A photographer relies on their camera's aperture, ISO and shutter speed – among other factors – to take photos that accurately reflect the reality of the subject they're photographing. In the same way, our ability to check the accuracy, congruence and clarity of our perceptions relies on the health of our relationship with three Aspects of Being: awareness, which is one of the Meta Factors, vulnerability, which is one of the Moods and authenticity, which is a Primary Way of Being. These three Aspects of Being form the 'exposure triangle'. How you relate to them shapes your conception of various fragments of reality.

'Just like a camera, we human beings are constantly taking snapshots of reality. Using a metaphor, consider light as authentic knowledge about various fragments of reality. The amount of light being let into the lens of the camera is your awareness. The amount of time the camera's shutter stays open and allows light into the sensor is a reflection of your vulnerability. And how sensitive the camera's sensor is to light is your authenticity. The quality and accuracy of the snapshots we take depend on our relationship with awareness (or intentional consciousness), authenticity (or congruence) and vulnerability: our openness and willingness to learn about matters we either haven't been exposed to or have misconceptions about. The healthier our relationship with these three Aspects of Being, the more vivid our vision – or ability to see or see through something – and the more discerning we become when making a decision or choosing from various options available to us. Then the convergence of these decisions influences our behaviours and actions. Consequently, they largely determine the outcomes we enjoy or the consequences we face.'

Clearly triggered, Yoren exclaimed, 'It seems you're implying that the environment, the economy, other people and basically all external factors are insignificant in all of this!'

'No, Yoren, that's not what I mean,' said Grace quietly, but firmly. 'All I'm saying is that the more congruent your conception of reality, including those external factors, the greater the likelihood that you'll make effective decisions and actually consider those elements. So your acknowledgement that those factors exist and have an impact, combined with your ability to discern a more effective and healthy way to relate to them, increases the likelihood of you being effective in your decisions and endeavours. Let's take a moment to revisit your results for awareness, vulnerability and authenticity, and consider them in the context of starting a business and what we just discussed. Okay?'

'Sure, go ahead,' replied Yoren, still unconvinced.

Grace pulled up Yoren's report on her laptop and they looked at his result for each one, all of which indicated a relationship on the unhealthy side.

'Now that we're clear on the exposure triangle and why awareness, vulnerability and authenticity are critical to overcome the blockages to actualising your intention, I propose we start with those in our coaching and continue to explore other Aspects of Being that are important to you as they come up. The reason I propose we start with the exposure triangle is that our experience and empirical data show that addressing those three Aspects of Being first supports people to relate to the other Aspects of Being in a more accurate and healthy way. As I said though, it's ultimately your decision. Would you like to start with awareness, authenticity and vulnerability? Or would you prefer to start with another Aspect of Being?'

'You're the expert, Grace, so I'm happy to start with the three you suggested.'

'Great. But before we do, I'd like to return to your question about transformation and explain how I'll support you to transform your relationship with the Aspects of Being that are critical to unlocking your ability to move forward with your intention. Do you have any further questions or queries about the exposure triangle before we move on?'

'No, please go ahead. I'm keen to know how this so-called 'process of transformation' works,' said Yoren.

Grace observed how Yoren slouched back in his seat, arms folded, and was present to his renewed cynicism and scepticism.

'As your coach, my role is to support you to become receptive and present by drawing your attention to some of your blindspots or misconceptions around how you relate to certain Aspects of Being. I use the word 'support' because I won't give you the answers. You're going to find them yourself through my questions. So, finding the blindspots or misconceptions is step one. That's what we call the 'reception stage'. Remember that reception is when your attention is drawn to a matter you were neglecting or wasn't on your radar, and it suddenly becomes a priority, making it the focal point of your care and attention.

'Then I'll ask you to contrast your current perception of an Aspect of Being – like your current understanding of responsibility, for instance – with various other perceptions of the same word, phrase or idea. We call this the 'perception stage'. Let me explain. There are various ways an individual can perceive the same thing, be it a word, a phrase, an idea, a matter, or whatever it may be. So far, you've been presented with one perception of each of the Aspects of Being as explained in the model's distinctions. These are based on objective, discovered knowledge. As part of our contract for this coaching process, it's important that we're in agreement that whenever we refer to an Aspect of Being, we're using the perception proposed by the distinction, since this is what the profile measures. I'm not suggesting that your or any other perceptions are incorrect. It's just that we're giving primacy to the concept in the distinction, not the word itself, and we want to avoid confusion.

'Finally, I'll support you to link your fresh perception of the Aspect of Being in question to the context of your life and what's important to you. In your case, and for this coaching journey, the context is you unblocking whatever is getting in your way of starting your own business. We call this the 'conception stage'. Any questions at this point?'

Yoren shook his head and, while Grace could see that he was beginning to relax and become more present, he still looked somewhat unclear.

'You probably feel like I'm bombarding you with information,' she laughed. 'Don't worry; all of this will come together for you as we go. We have plenty of time. Now, before we move on, I just need to reiterate and emphasise that the real work will be done between the coaching sessions. As your coach, my role is to facilitate the enquiry and discovery by supporting you to see the cost and dysfunction of how you are being in the context of each of the Aspects of Being we are working on. So reception and perception will occur during each session while conception will begin in the session and then be solidified between sessions. Are you okay with completing certain challenges in your own time, Yoren?'

'Sure, I expected there'd be work to do,' he responded.

'Okay, great. So, on that note, there's a simple but very effective tool called the conception worksheet that we use to support the process of transforming one's relationship with an Aspect of Being between sessions. It aligns with the conception stage we just talked about, where you relate your congruent perception of an Aspect of Being in the context of what we're here to address.'

Grace opened a document on her laptop to show Yoren what the worksheet looked like as she talked him through it.

'The conception worksheet supports you to become more aware of your relationship with an Aspect of Being between sessions by reflecting on real events and circumstances in your life. The exercise facilitates intentional reflection, which helps you to refine your conception of the Aspect of Being you're working on over time. Notice it has four columns: Instance, Consequences, Alternative and Outcomes. So if we take the example of authenticity, you start by considering some instances when you were not being authentic and the consequences of that. And then you'll reflect on an alternative – such as being authentic in that situation – and the outcomes of that. Any questions?'

'Does the transformation only occur at the awareness level? How about the execution?' asked Yoren.

'That's a good question, and you're right; there is another stage of the Transformation Methodology that's focused on execution. We'll discuss that in our next session as I don't want to get too bogged down in details today. For now, let's stick to setting the trajectory for the six-month coaching journey. If you agree, let's start with awareness. Are you happy with that?'

'Yes, that's all good, Grace. Please proceed.'

'Great. So we're beginning with awareness because it's the first Meta Factor, alongside integrity and effectiveness, and it also combines with vulnerability and authenticity to form the exposure triangle.

Together, these three Aspects of Being establish your relationship with the reality of matters and develop your ability to see and discern between various options when making decisions. Consider also that you can't intentionally become effective in something you're unaware of. Now, as we dive more deeply into awareness as an Aspect of Being, I'm going to pose a few questions for you to consider.'

Some of the questions Grace posed during their conversation included: Are you often blindsided or shocked by someone's actions or words? Do you often get surprised by how others react to your decisions or how they treat you based on the way you communicate with them? Are there times when you or others don't live up to your standards and expectations? If so, do you find that frustrating? The questions resulted in an animated and meaningful conversation. It was clear to Grace from Yoren's thoughtful responses that he was paying close attention and carefully considering each question before responding.

Bringing the conversation back to Yoren's intention, Grace asked, 'Thinking about your vision of starting your own business, can you tell me exactly what you believe is getting in your way of fulfilling that intention?'

'Yes of course. As I've already mentioned, I think I have a tremendous level of uncertainty around business-building in general. For starters, there are so many unknowns. I don't even know how to register a business, let alone how to build one. I don't know where to begin.'

'Of course. That's the case for anything new at the start. How can we know something we haven't been exposed to before? Consider that a person with a healthy relationship with awareness would be able to *be with* uncertainties. They live life from the viewpoint that they cannot be knowledgeable about everything. They acknowledge that no one can know it all and they're okay with not knowing. Because they can be with that level of uncertainty, they don't let it get in their way and don't allow it to suppress how they express themselves and contribute to outcomes in their life. They seek to learn what they know they don't know.

'People with a healthy relationship with awareness are present to the fact that there will also be things they don't even know they don't know. I realise this sounds odd; it simply means they are aware they have blindspots: things they need to know but are not yet aware of. So, rather than relying on themselves to work it all out, they know the value of tapping into the knowledge other people have already accessed through reading, study and consulting with subject matter experts so they can learn what they need to achieve their goals.

'Such people also understand the value of being coached or mentored, or of seeking the guidance of someone with experience in the matter to support them in their quest to fulfil their intentions and also hold them accountable for their commitments. They don't live life in isolation, intellectually or mentally, and they don't waste time reinventing the wheel. Furthermore, they're clear that being human means they'll have inauthenticities or misconceptions at times. They know they have access to limited perspectives on matters relating to their intentions and are open to other points of view to help them shape a more comprehensive and complete understanding. This all leads them to develop authentic awareness rather than succumbing to whatever society, their culture and family expect of them. This is how awareness, vulnerability and authenticity combine to support them to be effective in their decision-making. How does all this sit with you, Yoren? What do you relate to here?'

'I'm aware that there are many things I don't know, but I push them away in the 'too hard basket'. I probably do this with a lot of things I'm uncertain about as I often procrastinate or try to push decision-making onto someone else on my team,' he responded.

'Which Moods do you think set the scene for your procrastination?' asked Grace.

'I think all of them, to a certain extent. But I can really see how vulnerability, and particularly my concern over how others might judge me, plays a major role in why I'm so closed and guarded. I can also see how it leads to pretence, or inauthenticities, as you call them.

I'm afraid of failing or looking foolish to others and would feel humiliated if I didn't succeed. I'm also a bit concerned about the potential consequences of my actions.'

'Spot on, Yoren. So tell me, how does that make you feel?'

'It makes me feel irresponsible, but I never let that show. I'm also afraid that by expressing my ideas about my business, someone might steal them from me or I might be judged.'

'What exactly are you afraid of or anxious about in that context?' asked Grace.

'I am anxious about what my fiancé Mel and my father might think of me. I'm also afraid of damaging my reputation because I'm known as someone who always makes the right decisions and does everything right. Nobody ever sees me fail at anything.'

'Does this lead you to act as if you're not afraid or anxious, even to yourself?'

'I guess so.'

'I'd like to challenge you to consider whether the things you fear and are anxious about are grounded in reality. For example, will your accountant steal your ideas when you share them? Do you really think Mel will leave you if you start a business? Have you even discussed it with her? And does it really matter whether or not your father approves?'

> *How am I supposed to determine what's real or 'grounded in reality', as she puts it, and what's not?*

Grace was present to Yoren's confusion as she continued, 'These questions are designed to make you aware that how you relate to awareness, knowledge and understanding – your preferred epistemological approach for examining reality – massively influences what you know to be real or not. Later, we'll see that how you relate to and act upon authenticity will largely determine the accuracy of your understanding and the level of precision you'll be satisfied with regarding what's real or not, what works and what doesn't. Let's re-read the distinction of awareness so you can see what I mean.'

She opened the distinction on her laptop and asked Yoren to read the first part aloud.

> *Awareness* is the state of being intentionally conscious of your consciousness. It is how you relate to what you know and understand as well as what you don't know and don't understand. *Awareness* is always intentional and directed at something. It is to know and understand yourself, others and the world around you, in particular the impact of the world and others on you and the impact you have on the world and others. *Awareness* is your access to knowing and understanding and is required to fulfil your intentions.

'I've read a lot of books on consciousness and awareness, so I consider myself quite knowledgeable on the subject,' said Yoren. 'To me, awareness is relative. I'm knowledgeable about some matters, but not about others.'

'Just to clarify, with awareness, you weren't being assessed on your knowledge,' said Grace. 'You were being assessed on how you *relate to awareness itself*. It's about how you choose to relate to the matters you currently know and understand as well as how you choose to come to know something unfamiliar to you. It's important for both of us to be on the same page here. It's also about becoming aware of your relationships with various Aspects of Being, such as the Moods and how they impact your relationships with the Primary Ways of Being. The awareness conversation will always be there because we always go from a degree of awareness to a degree of effectiveness as we move through the coaching and transformation process.'

Grace then asked Yoren to read the next part describing what it looks like to have a healthy relationship with awareness.

> A healthy relationship with *awareness* indicates that you have a clear understanding of your impact on others and on the world

around you. You are not easily misled, coerced and/or manipulated. You are both self-aware and aware of how you are perceived by others. You are attentive, alert and rarely surprised or caught off guard. You can find your way forward despite uncertainty or not knowing, and are available to consider feedback, guidance and critique.

'What do you read in this, Yoren? Does any particular part catch your attention? And what does this say about your intention to start a business and the things that are holding you back?'

Yoren admitted that he was often caught off guard and struggled to move forward whenever he was uncertain or hesitant. He also acknowledged that he could be better at accepting feedback and guidance from others, using the excuse that everyone looked to him for all the answers. Grace could clearly see how his relationship with awareness and authenticity influenced how he related to and acted upon confidence, particularly when faced with dilemmas and doubt. She could also see how this would suppress or weaken his self-expression and ability to move forward in starting a business.

Finally, Grace asked him to read the paragraph describing an unhealthy relationship with awareness.

> An unhealthy relationship with *awareness* indicates that you may choose to ignore or be oblivious to matters and the impact you have on others and the world around you and vice versa. You may often be confused and shocked by matters and how others respond to you and blindsided when they fail to live up to your expectations. You may deliberately choose to ignore what there is to see. Alternatively, you may freeze or find it difficult to progress in the face of uncertainty or not knowing as you are compelled to know everything before making decisions or taking action.

'Can you tell me what you're present to now that you've read the full distinction, Yoren?'

'I actually found I was confused reading through this. I've never thought about awareness this way. But now it makes sense why people respond the way they do at times. Sometimes I'm surprised at how people react when I share my ideas. I always expect them to be cynical, so it's surprising when they aren't.'

Grace picked up on some inconsistencies in how Yoren was interpreting and articulating his experiences, thoughts and beliefs. It gave her an insight into why he remained stuck, despite wanting to be an entrepreneur for so long. She could see they would need to work on his awareness as well as fear, anxiety, vulnerability, authenticity, confidence, assertiveness and even care. While she knew he cared deeply about starting a business, he lacked the focus to see it through, a key part of care.

After reflecting for a while, Yoren suddenly looked Grace in the eye and said with excitement, 'Wow, now I get it! All this time, I thought I needed to learn more when I might have been able to trust other people more and consider their feedback and guidance.'

'Great! Now that you've realised this, what are you committed to doing?' asked Grace.

'I think I should brush up on awareness for starters. I'm curious to understand it better. Any suggested readings?'

Grace smiled at his enthusiasm. 'Sure, I have some source material I can give you access to.' She handed him a book and other materials that delved into the framework.

'Thank you. That would be great. What else do you suggest I do before our next session?' he asked.

'Your challenges for this week are to keep a journal documenting how you feel each day, especially in relation to the four Moods: vulnerability, care, fear and anxiety. I also want you to complete a conception worksheet on awareness, particularly noticing any time you're shocked or surprised by how you're treated or how your expectation of others plays out.'

Before he left, they established a high-level trajectory for the six-month coaching journey that Yoren was happy with. Grace then suggested they focus on authenticity in the next session, as well as vulnerability after Yoren expressed interest in exploring that Aspect of Being further. She assured him that nothing was set in stone and he could always change his mind if he felt the urge to explore another Aspect of Being first.

'After this session, your awareness of how you're being is likely to be heightened,' said Grace. 'So, as you complete the conception worksheet and journal, and as you go through your day-to-day life at work and at home, you might find other questions arising. That's why we create a new contract at the beginning of each session, to ensure we work on what is most relevant to you at the time. This process is flexible and fluid. Our view is that coaching should be aligned with emerging phenomenological situations and experiences rather than being rigid or trying to meet a predefined set of criteria.'

Yoren left the session feeling slightly overwhelmed but also excited and hopeful. Thinking back to the information session he initially attended to appease Jen, he realised he was no longer the same person who'd listened halfheartedly to the conversation and with a great deal of scepticism. Back then, he never imagined what had been initiated in that session would lead to something so profound. He was sincerely curious about what was to come.

CHAPTER 8

Resisting the Light

Although Yoren left his first session with Grace full of enthusiasm, hope for the future and eagerness to get stuck into his challenges for the week, his mood had shifted significantly by the evening. Staring at the empty page in his journal and the blank conception worksheet, which he planned to tick off his to-do list that night, his mind was a whirl of emotions and thoughts. On the one hand, he was both nervous and excited at the prospect of finally getting to the bottom of why it was taking him so long to start his business. On the other, he was beginning to question how the session had gone. He was even starting to question whether or not Grace was the right coach to support him. On reflection, while much of what she had said made sense, there were also times during the session when he felt she was undermining his intelligence and capabilities with her questions. The more he looked at the conception worksheet headed 'Awareness' on his desk, the more uncomfortable and confronted he felt.

He recalled what he had agreed to do: think of a situation when you lacked awareness and identify the consequence of that. What could you have done differently in that situation and how would the outcome have been different?

This is ridiculous! How naive does she think I am? In all my adult life, there hasn't been a single instance when I've lacked awareness. I wouldn't be where I am today without a high level of awareness. If my profile report suggested I have a problem with awareness, then there must be something wrong with the assessment! I don't need Grace's or anybody else's help to 'relate to awareness in a healthier way'. I wonder if she was just patronising me to see how I'd react.

Ironically, it didn't occur to Yoren that he could have been documenting his thoughts and feelings in his journal, which is precisely what he'd agreed to do. Grace had explained that there was no right or wrong, good or bad in this judgement-free process and that he could document whatever was on his mind to reflect on and discuss later. But he refused to put pen to paper. He was determined to only document positive thoughts and feelings, and right now, none were forthcoming. So the journal page remained untouched.

Yoren wasn't generally open to receiving feedback or advice, especially unpaid advice. And even when he paid for advice from a reputable professional, he typically distrusted it, despite often paying top dollar to see someone who came highly recommended. Sitting at his desk, he recalled the time when he was in the market to purchase his first investment property. One of his friends had suggested he speak with a financial planner due to the complex nature of the off-the-plan development he was considering. It was one of the rare occasions that he took advice on board, albeit reluctantly, as he felt quietly confident in the extensive research he'd done on the developers himself. He eventually paid a significant fee to see one of Australia's top property investment advisors, only to ignore his advice to proceed with the purchase and pull out at the last minute, forfeiting his deposit.

Five years later, he regretted that decision when he learned the property was valued 50% higher than the price he would have paid and the rental return had skyrocketed. Despite those facts, Yoren continued to defend his actions, even to himself. Like many people with an unhealthy relationship with vulnerability, his walls would go up whenever he felt his effectiveness might be questioned, potentially damaging his reputation. Only in his solitude would he occasionally query his decisions and regret his actions. But he avoided owning up to those instances, even to Mel.

Bringing his thoughts back to the coaching experience with Grace, Yoren couldn't help comparing the two situations. He was paying good money to see her as she'd come highly recommended, but now he was questioning her 'advice' just as he had with the financial planner. And he was ignoring the fact that she had explicitly said she wouldn't provide advice, as she explained the differences between coaching, mentoring and advisory services. He wanted her to validate his reason for being there and, at the very least, to acknowledge some of his positive attributes.

Yoren couldn't see that he actually wanted advice, but only if he agreed with it. He failed to recognise that his need for advice that aligned with his point of view meant he was actually limiting the contribution of others. And since he typically resisted input from others unless it was communicated in his preferred learning style, he prevented many competent people from contributing their unique insights to him. Furthermore, he tended to switch off if he felt someone was undermining him or invalidating his opinions. And if he didn't like how something was said, he would either ignore it, get offended or blame the messenger, which is how the first coaching session had mostly unfolded, apart from those momentary glimpses of awareness.

Picking up his pen for the umpteenth time, Yoren re-read the instructions for the exercises Grace had given him: the conception worksheet for awareness and the daily journaling exercise. The latter required him to be present to how the care, fear, anxiety and vulnerability Moods play out in his day-to-day life, setting the scene and creating a context for his decisions, behaviours and actions. Over the next two hours, he jumped from one task to the other before finally deciding to focus on the awareness exercise. He pushed the journal aside and stared at the worksheet, pen poised to begin writing. But no matter how hard he tried, he struggled to identify any situation impacted by his supposedly unhealthy relationship with awareness. More than an hour later, the page was still blank. After sitting at his desk unproductively for another hour, he concluded that he wasn't personally responsible for his inability to move forward with his goal of starting a business. He laid the blame squarely on issues well beyond his control.

Why am I to blame? None of it's my fault! Any dysfunction is due to systematic issues in our neo-liberalistic society, the capitalist economy and the way greedy corporates influence politicians to lobby for what they want, leading to further systematic dysfunctions. I'm not one of those lucky rich kids who receive money from their parents and inherit a trust fund at the end! With no seed capital to start a business, how foolish am I to think I can create one? I'm smart enough to see that only a tiny minority of elites own and control the means of production. The problem isn't me: it's capitalism and the monopolies that already exist out there. I'd be crazy to start a business when there are so many giant corporations – like the one I work for now – that are so well-established and rooted in the system that new small businesses don't stand a chance.

Yoren felt justified in pushing the awareness exercise away. In reality, his self-described 'lightbulb moment' was the outcome of delusional thinking and nothing more than indulging in his own narrative. It was the kind of story he would often fabricate to justify his decisions and actions. The fact that he was unaware of this pointed to how much he needed to complete the exercise. But instead, his inner voice continued ranting.

At least I'm clever enough to know it'd be foolish to jump into a game I can't win, a game designed to make people like me the middle-class losers. And why would I engage in the madness of entrepreneurship when the statistics clearly show that more than 90% of startups fail in the first year or two of operation? It was obviously irrational on my part to even consider starting a business in light of the current economic situation. The solution to the system should be radical. Capitalism festers like cancer! The only solution is to change the system.

Suddenly aware of his inner rambling, Yoren shook his head and shoulders as though physically shrugging off the jumble of erratic and irrational thoughts swirling around in his head. He felt a tinge of shame as he pulled himself together.

In entertaining these thoughts, he was not only doubting his original intention and its importance but also failing to prioritise the coaching he was investing in to help him address the roadblocks in his way. Given his unwillingness to be responsible, it wasn't surprising that he couldn't find a single instance where he had been the problem, let alone acknowledge where he could have responded more appropriately to change course. Tossing the blank conception worksheet in the bin, Yoren got up, stretched his arms and back – which were stiff after sitting for so long – and lay on the sofa in his office so he wouldn't disturb Mel at such a late hour.

Although weary, he stared at the ceiling for what felt like hours, his mind consumed with thoughts of self-righteousness intermingled with self-doubt, guilt and glimpses of awareness when he occasionally noticed his thoughts. In these brief insights, Yoren toyed with the idea that perhaps Grace was on his side. Although she wasn't there to give advice, she could support him to break through to the next level and be more effective in his endeavours towards starting a business. While he still had doubts, he knew Grace wasn't making him wrong like many others tried to do, especially his father, during their many heated arguments. Working with Grace was different. Deep down, he knew she wasn't the tyrant he made her out to be. However, while her language was neither offensive nor provocative, he noticed he felt triggered by her observations because he thought he was being judged. Casting her as the enemy fitted his agenda better than seeing her as an ally.

Am I being too open and transparent with her? Perhaps I'm revealing too much about myself.

Yoren wasn't used to being open. He'd always seen vulnerability as a weakness that could be used against him. This seed was sown from a young age when he was bullied in primary school. The experience led him to develop a 'strong' persona, which he learned to successfully sell to others by the time he started high school. His actions were validated when other kids at school began to look up to him, and before long, he was hanging with the popular crowd and attracting the attention of the 'best-looking' girls. His high school experience taught him the benefit of adopting a fake persona whenever he wanted to portray himself as influential and powerful.

By the time Yoren started his career, he was an expert at donning his 'mask of intimidation' to get his way in meetings. He quickly developed a reputation as someone who didn't care about others' opinions and who commanded respect at any cost. And so he learned that inauthenticity, lies and hidden agendas worked in his favour and helped him climb the corporate ladder by allowing him to present a charismatic persona while making it challenging for others to figure out his next move. In reality, however, he was obsessed with what others thought of him. So he always felt enormous pressure to ensure he appeared successful.

Now, all the effort he put into developing and maintaining his so-called 'powerful persona' was being shattered into tiny pieces. There were moments during that night when he even considered coming up with an excuse to pull out of the coaching contract. He didn't want his life to be 'fixed' by anyone, including Grace, and would only be satisfied if he came up with the solutions himself. He wanted to ensure that others – particularly his father and Mel – regarded him as someone who had it all: the winner, an invulnerable hero who could take care of everything by himself. At that moment, he regretted telling Mel that he was starting coaching as it would make it hard to back out.

I wonder what she thinks of me now? How can she rely on me as the man in her life, knowing I need coaching? In opening up to her about that, I was signalling that I'm stuck and don't know what to do. Now she thinks I need a 'self-help guru' to tell me what to do!

In reality, Mel didn't feel that way about Yoren at all. In her heart, she sincerely believed he was strong and knew what he wanted. Having seen him step up and show leadership in times of crisis, she knew he was the kind of person who rarely succumbed to critical challenges and could resolve almost anything, qualities that she had always found attractive. However, she also knew he tended to exaggerate, not from a malicious harmful intention, but because he wanted her to admire him as a strong masculine figure. He didn't realise she could see straight through him, including the authenticity he was hiding – unlike at work, where managing the impression he made seemed to work in his favour.

He was suddenly overcome by intense anxiety as a barrage of what-ifs flooded his mind, causing his pulse to race and his breathing to become rapid and shallow. He was filled with despair and disappointment that the spark of hope he could see at the end of the tunnel seemed to be fading, making him question the value of attending the next session. But deep down, he knew he would never raise his concerns with Grace, meaning there was no way out; he had to attend. He also knew he'd never live it down with Mel and Jen if he pulled out now. His reputation would be ruined.

Yoren's anxiety about his reputation and his unhealthy relationship with vulnerability compromised his ability to see the options available. This meant he wasn't even responsible and empowered enough to remove himself from the situation, although he had every right to do so if he wished. Feeling cornered and against his better judgement, he reluctantly decided he would continue with the coaching. But his commitment lacked grace, and he harboured resentment that the coaching contract was yet another burden he was forced to shoulder. Consumed by a combination of self-hatred and victimisation, he tossed and turned before finally falling into a fitful sleep just before dawn.

Yoren managed to avoid thinking about his coaching commitments for the remainder of the week and focused on his work, his 'impression management mask' firmly affixed the entire time. The day before his coaching session arrived and he still hadn't started his challenges. However, a week away from looking inward had restored his self-confidence and he was once again finding fault in the being discourse and those who embraced it. He also used this position to justify his lack of action, believing that he could see through the rhetoric of liberation, empowerment and growth espoused by Erik, Jen and Grace. He found their focus on being powerful, free, integrous, effective, authentic, and becoming receptive and awakened etc., irritating. In his mind, it wasn't much different from how bourgeoisie market capitalists identify a series of reasonably universal pain points and sell a self-aggrandising mixture of the market's own potency, agency and victimhood in exchange for money. This is how they live off society instead of serving it. Ironically, he was oblivious to how much his inner musings were influenced by his father, with whom he had clashed so much growing up due to their dramatically opposing beliefs and opinions. Fuelled by self-righteousness and Stewart's influence, Yoren's inner rant continued.

This is a classic example of coercion, control and manipulation. The very people who tell you to wake up and stand on your own two feet are the ones who lure you in and then cripple you until you're dependent on them! Once you subscribe to their narrative, you're halfway to becoming brainwashed.

Stewart Healy often argued that those who say we can free ourselves from ideologies are merely promoting another ideology. He was known as being so far to the left in his political leaning that Yoren's marginally left-winged views could have easily been considered to the 'right'. Stewart had been negatively impacted by what he rashly interpreted as his father's 'orthodox right-wing' views. Unlike his brother Igor, who had decided to toe the line and play the lobbying game in pursuit of his political career, Stewart had allowed his opposing views to significantly shape his academic persona and social identity. Ironically, while Stewart often protested against issues like inequality, injustice and a lack of freedom, Igor shared his views on such matters but had a radically different conception of them.

Growing up, Yoren was often confused to see his father and uncle arguing over concepts they both held as core values. He sometimes felt like a curious bystander. Observing the radically opposing pathways his father and uncle pursued in academia and politics inspired him to choose a different path altogether: entrepreneurship. Watching and listening to his father and uncle had made him realise that the pathways they had chosen, and which each wanted him to pursue, were far too limiting for his free-spirited and liberal nature. He decided business was a far better choice. But he lacked the courage to start his own business, instead pursuing a corporate career.

While Yoren deeply admired and respected his grandfather and all he had achieved, he dreamed of running a business with purpose and meaning, something more worthwhile than just creating a purely profit-generating venture as he believed Samuel had. He vividly remembered how his grandfather always tried to persuade him to build a 'money-making venture', but misunderstood what he meant at the time. Not getting any younger, Samuel desperately wanted someone to whom he could pass on the wealth and legacy he'd worked so hard to build. He often engaged in lengthy conversations with his grandson about his future. However, Yoren sometimes misinterpreted his intent. His perception of business was vastly different from his grandfather's and, living under his father's roof, Yoren was naturally more influenced by Stewart than Samuel.

Stewart believed that making money from business was akin to living off society, while Samuel fully supported the idea of generating revenue and profit from a business that serves humanity and solves a burning pain. As a successful businessman and investor, Samuel knew that capital, the right people, and an effective financial structure were critical for all business ventures, even the most charitable. However,

Yoren would misconstrue his grandfather's constant references to these vital factors as efforts to subvert his 'fanciful ambition' into nothing more than a greedy 'money-making venture'. To Yoren, becoming the kind of entrepreneur who solves serious problems for humanity was a calling he could no longer deny or ignore, which is why he decided to pursue coaching. It wasn't until much later in life that he realised his grandfather had simply been trying to encourage him to be less dreamy and more realistic about all the factors needed to get a business off the ground so he could serve people in the most effective way possible.

Despite experiencing a range of emotions, self-judgement, mood fluctuations and even elements of regret and self-sabotage, Yoren found himself responding differently to the deep conversations he was having with himself. Normally, when negative thoughts entered his mind, he pushed them aside and moved on, leaving whatever had been bothering him incomplete until it inevitably triggered him again. However, this time was different. Now he noticed he was prepared to be with the pain. While the feelings he was experiencing were uncomfortable, it was more like the muscle pain one experiences after working out in the gym, the kind that leads to growth and strength instead of strain or injury. Although a big part of him still believed his vision of entrepreneurship was nothing more than a pipe dream for reasons beyond his control, the sensations he was feeling were enough to give him a tiny glimmer of hope that it might be possible to live a life that was authentic and congruent with his intention after all.

— ∎ —

The next morning, Yoren arrived at Grace's office prepared with excuses for why he hadn't met his commitments. She greeted him with a beaming smile and was brimming with energy as she showed him into her office. Yoren took a seat on the sofa while she pulled back the curtain, allowing the sun to stream in.

'Gorgeous morning, isn't it,' she said with enthusiasm as she poured them both a glass of water.

Yoren nodded and took a sip, hoping she wouldn't see straight through him.

Observing his silence, Grace looked him in the eye and asked, 'So, how was your week? And how did you go with the awareness exercise using the conception worksheet and the journaling to document your Moods and how they play a part in setting the scene for your thoughts, feelings, decisions and behaviours?'

Without directly meeting her gaze, Yoren said, 'I had a few urgent deadlines to meet at work this week and a couple of my team members were off sick, so I didn't have time to complete those exercises. But at least I'm here and keen to see what you've got in store for me today.'

His sense of unease and unwillingness to reveal what was going on beneath the facade didn't go unnoticed by Grace.

'Is there something you feel like expressing, Yoren?' she asked. 'I encourage you to share whatever's on your mind so you can be fully present as we begin today's session.'

He shook his head, but berated himself inwardly.

Why don't I just tell her what's been on my mind? Isn't that what I'm here for? Isn't it her role to coach me into a better headspace?

As if reading his thoughts, Grace asked again, 'Are you sure there's nothing you feel like expressing, Yoren? I'm concerned that we'll waste our time and your money if you're unwilling to be open and honest with me …'

Before she could finish, Yoren burst into a rant about how he couldn't find a single example of a time when he had an unhealthy relationship with awareness. He then continued with a barrage of empty complaints covering everything from the system being at fault for his inability to fulfil his dream of entrepreneurship to his mistrust of the coaching process and doubt that it would solve any of his problems.

Grace sat back and listened attentively, giving him the time and space to express himself. Once he was finished, she said calmly, 'I understand and acknowledge how you're feeling, Yoren. Beginning the process of looking deep within yourself isn't easy if you've never done it before. I can assure you that many people struggle in the beginning. The fact that you're going through this reflection process and openly expressing yourself is a great start. Before we move on, is there anything else you'd like to get off your chest?'

Yoren shook his head, eyes downcast. He was surprised that Grace wasn't reacting to his rant.

'At the end of our last session, we agreed that we would mainly work on authenticity and also vulnerability after you expressed interest in exploring it further,' said Grace. 'Are you still thinking these will be good for today's session or do you have other areas you'd prefer to address today?'

'No, that all sounds fine,' he responded.

She pulled up the awareness distinction on her laptop and turned the screen so Yoren could read it.

'Let me ask you a question, Yoren. Looking into the distinction of awareness, can you see that what you've been dealing with – for example, not being able to distinguish instances when you lacked awareness – may, in fact, be an indication of your unhealthy relationship with this Aspect of Being?'

'No, I don't see that at all,' he replied, arms crossed.

'There are a few other areas we could explore, such as your judgement of this process, the assessment, the ontological framework and even yourself to an extent,' said Grace. 'These judgements might suggest that you've been interpreting your recent experiences and creating your own narrative or stories about them.'

Triggered, Yoren responded, 'What do you mean, creating stories? These aren't stories; they represent how it is! It's reality.'

'How do they represent reality to you, Yoren?'

He frowned and looked away.

'I'm not suggesting you're wrong, Yoren,' Grace continued. 'After all, what we experience is what we experience and is valid. However, I encourage you to be vulnerable and consider that your experiences are only part of reality. Let me explain. Many people automatically take whatever they receive through their senses as gospel, be it reading an opinion piece, watching the news, listening to a podcast and so on. They consider it the totality of the truth about the matter in question without also considering that there are multiple other perspectives and ways to perceive them. Consider that your narrative is your creation and how empowering it is to acknowledge that you have the autonomy to create your own narrative. Consider also that the conversation we're having right now is expanding your narrative.

'Although you'll never have direct access to the totality of the truth of any matter, no matter how well-equipped you are, leveraging the tools and materials at your disposal during our coaching together and beyond will exponentially increase the authenticity and congruence of whatever you're assessing. Doing so will ensure you see beyond your 'personal experience' to also consider other information sources and perspectives. Does that make sense?'

Yoren looked thoughtful as he considered Grace's response.

'I think I need some time to reflect on this, Grace', he said.

After a few moments, she asked, 'When you view your narrative as reality and the only way, where does the power sit?'

'In the narrative,' replied Yoren.

'What if you could choose to recreate and reinterpret the narrative?'

'Then I would feel more empowered and that I have the autonomy to challenge my narrative by considering other perspectives and even create one that serves me to achieve what I want,' Yoren responded thoughtfully.

'Great. Would you agree that this comes with a tremendous level of responsibility and power to influence your interpretation of reality and, therefore, your experience of life?'

Yoren gave a slight nod as he pondered her words.

Grace continued, 'If we live life from the viewpoint that we're all capable of responding to the matters and events that life brings us, regardless of the source, then we would also be aware that our response influences the circumstances. Acknowledging this ensures we take a more active role in our lives. What if you had chosen to be open and allowed your reality to be influenced by others over the past week?'

'I wouldn't have spent the last few days feeling stuck. I could've thought things through differently and probably would've taken different actions,' Yoren replied.

Grace smiled. 'Exactly. This attitude leads us to thrive. Without our imperfections, blindspots and vulnerabilities, there would be nothing to address to change course, have the potential to grow or the ability to expand your conception of reality for yourself and influence the shared reality for others.'

Yoren was silent, but Grace suspected from his demeanour and body language that he was considering his newfound realisation, suggesting he experienced a moment of reception. She found it remarkable how present Yoren was to a perception of awareness that he'd never been exposed to before. In her experience as a coach, it usually took coachees more time to comprehend it. She paused to give him space to be with his thoughts. Then she brought up an image of the exposure triangle on her laptop, referring to the model to remind him of the relationship between awareness, authenticity and vulnerability, linking it to his recent narrative and the inner turmoil he was feeling.

They talked about awareness and how he related to knowing and understanding. They discussed authenticity and to what extent he was either lenient or rigorous regarding the validity and congruence of his perceptions. And they explored vulnerability and his willingness to be open to new information rather than putting up his guard and blocking it out. They also talked about the benefits of emptying his cup so that new knowledge and perceptions could be poured in, allowing him to take a sip and see how he liked it.

'Just to clarify, Grace, are you saying there are certain things we're genuinely oblivious to and other things we're aware of but simply don't want to acknowledge?' he asked.

'Correct. However, consider also that you might have been somewhat lenient and fickle in shaping a conception of certain matters, leading to a misconception,' Grace replied. 'And there might also be some matters you understand well but may have deliberately chosen to ignore, perhaps because you believe they could get in the way of your immediate interests. Does this resonate with you, Yoren?'

'Yes, it does,' he admitted.

'When we refuse to acknowledge certain fragments of reality and choose to be guarded, it may indicate an unhealthy relationship with vulnerability,' said Grace. 'And when we have our guard up, we intentionally filter certain things, demonstrating an unhealthy relationship with authenticity as well. How does this land with you, Yoren?'

Yoren's face broke into a knowing grin, and he excitedly said, 'So when I deliberately choose not to look at some things, it may point to the health of my relationship with the qualities that make up the exposure triangle. I'm starting to see the threads and connections now between awareness, authenticity and vulnerability! So vulnerability would be a dominant influence behind authenticity?'

'Spot on, Yoren.'

As the conversation continued, Grace noticed Yoren was increasingly connecting with the information she presented. For Yoren, the discussion helped him dig deeper and discover new things about himself and how he interpreted the reality of what was going on in his life. He was doing most of the talking in response to her probing and thoughtful questions. Learning how much his interpretation of reality differed from actual reality was humbling. He was also becoming increasingly present to how so much of what he was articulating to himself was his own creation. Observing that Yoren seemed to now understand what was meant by awareness in the context of being, Grace thought it would be useful to recap the stages of awareness.

'So remember, there are three stages of awareness: reception, perception and conception. Let's say you have a particular blindspot, meaning you're not giving a specific matter or Aspect of Being the attention it deserves. This will have consequences. Through our coaching, I'm supporting you by bringing those blindspots to your attention so that you become aware of them. We describe this as the 'reception stage'; it's where you're becoming informed. Please bear in mind that some of the things we'll be discussing might not imme-diately make complete sense to you because it all depends on your current way of thinking. We're here to cause a paradigm shift. This will require you to think beyond the here and now and be willing to delay gratification if you want significant and sustainable results. All of this requires patience.'

Grace paused to give Yoren time to consider her words.

'Any questions, Yoren?'

'No, that all makes sense to me,' he replied.

'When we're working with the ontological model, I'll typically introduce a preferred perception of the Aspect of Being in question by reading its ontological distinction together and identifying a relatable example,' said Grace. 'This allows us to get on the same page in terms of the meaning I'm referring to when I reference each Aspect of Being. We call this shared knowledge the 'perception stage'. Put simply, there may be several different perceptions of the same quality. Take responsibility, for example. One perception of this quality is that it's an obligation or duty. Another is to be at fault for something. Yet another is the ability to respond to matters and circumstances in life. This last one is the ontological distinction of responsibility in our framework and that's the perception we refer to in this coaching process. So whenever I present you with a perception, it creates a mutual language and understanding between us. Any questions?'

Yoren shook his head.

'Once you have been through reception and perception, then you can start to relate everything you've learned about the Aspect of Being in question to your life and what's important to you,' continued Grace. 'We refer to this as the 'conception stage'. It's when you're beginning to develop wisdom or practical knowledge.

'Unlike perception, which is often a rapid process because you come to know and understand something through your sensory abilities, conception is an iterative, longer-term mental process achieved through analysis, reflection, contemplation, retrospective thinking, comparison, reasoning and so on. We'll be touching on this in each session, but you'll also focus on it in your challenges between sessions. The conception stage highlights why it's so important to approach our coaching with sincerity and not just curiosity. Without sincerity, this whole experience would lose relevance for you, Yoren. It would become more theoretical and philosophical than practical and relevant. Can you see how our conversation took us from reception to perception and then conception in this session, Yoren?'

'Yes, I can see that,' said Yoren, a new twinkle in his eye.

Grace then asked Yoren to recap the conversation and was delighted to hear how he articulated it. It was clear that her explanations had landed well for him.

Leaning forward in his seat, Yoren said, 'So, I can now see how to develop a more congruent conception of a matter if I first become receptive to something that may not have been on my radar. And then, the perception stage is where we refer to the ontological model to present a perception of authenticity, awareness, vulnerability or any other Aspect of Being so we're both clear on what we're talking about. And then, the conception stage is when I relate the meaning of that Aspect of Being to my life, and particularly to my intention of starting a business. Have I summed it up alright?' he asked, looking triumphant.

'Indeed you have. That's a brilliant recap! I couldn't have said it better myself,' she laughed.

'Thanks, Grace. And you were going to tell me what happens after the conception stage. So how do we apply or execute this awareness?'

'Yes, absolutely. For the remainder of our coaching together, and particularly during the time in between sessions, I'll be encouraging you to apply the learnings through analysis, comparison, reflection, contemplation and assessment of how you're being in relation to the Aspect of Being we're working on using a series of processes and principles called the Transformation Methodology,' said Grace, bringing a diagram up on her laptop.

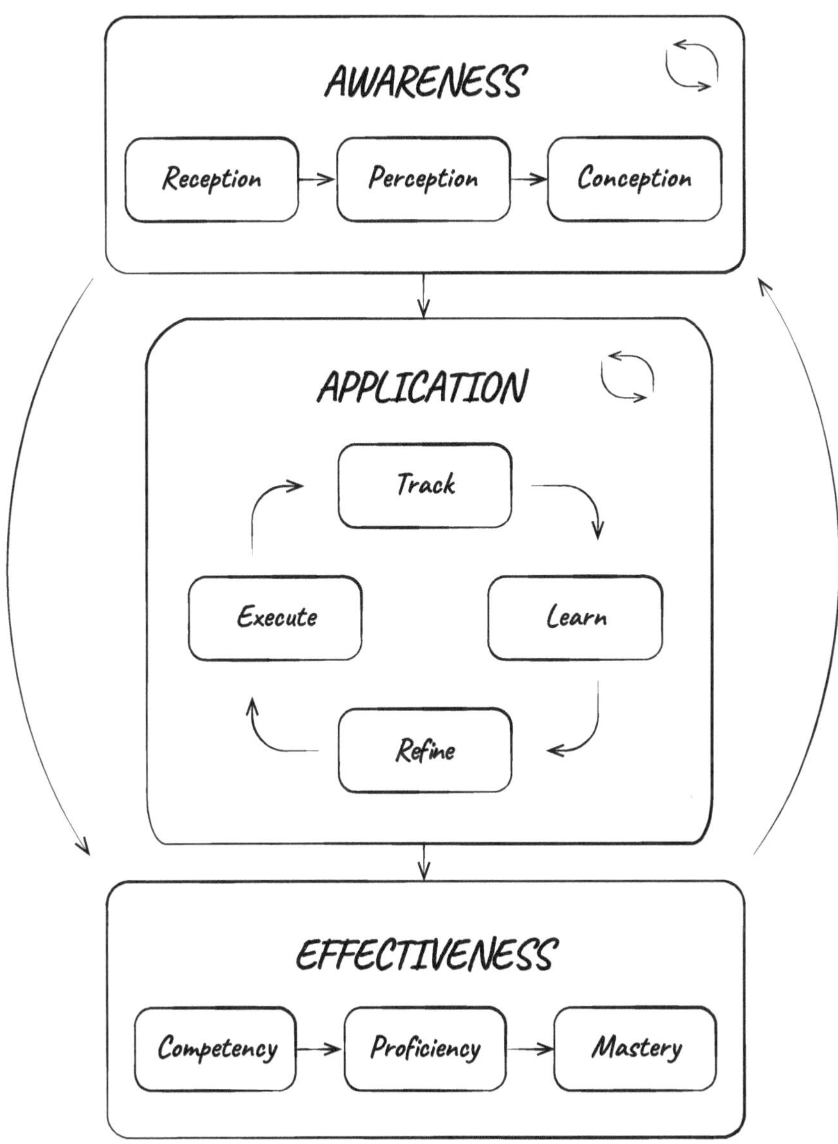

'You may recall that we started talking about the process of transformation in our first coaching session together, and I promised to discuss it further with you in this session,' she continued.

'Yes, I do remember. That's when you walked me through the conception worksheet. Could you please refresh my mind about this process?' asked Yoren.

'Sure. As human beings, we are not fixed objects destined to stay the same forever. We all have the ability to transform. Simply put, transformation occurs the moment you travel from a degree of awareness to a degree of effectiveness. If you're interested in looking into transformation more deeply, I suggest you read chapter five of the book I gave you in our first session together and then come back to me with any questions.'

Yoren made himself a note to look into chapter five.

'Now the Transformation Methodology is a series of processes that lead you on a journey of change from where you are now to where you want to be,' continued Grace. 'It begins with the awareness phase, which, as we discussed, takes you from reception to perception and then conception. We always begin with awareness because it's impossible to intentionally become effective in something you're unaware of or have misconceptions about. To go from a degree of awareness to a degree of effectiveness, you need to work through an application phase. This is the practical part of the Transformation Methodology. The tool we use to work through this phase is the conception worksheet, which you're familiar with. As you can see from the diagram, it's a cyclical, iterative process of executing, tracking, learning, refining and then executing again. Importantly, each cycle always has a specific commitment, such as being more assertive in meetings or more authentic with your team and so on.'

'Why does it begin with execution? Shouldn't the learning come first?' asked Yoren.

'That's a great question, Yoren. You execute first because you start by acting on your current conception of an Aspect of Being and then track how that plays out for you. Then you learn from that experience, refine it and execute again based on your more refined conception. The idea is to repeat, tweak and make progress with each cycle, ultimately transforming your relationship with the Aspect of Being you're working on. Does that answer your question?'

'Yes, understood. It's a lot like testing and refining new software before it's released to the market.'

'Yes, I guess you could say that,' smiled Grace. 'In a nutshell, this process will enable you to gradually shape a more authentic conception of each Aspect of Being by relating it back to why you're here: to remove the roadblocks preventing you from starting your business.

'I don't want us to get too bogged down in the Transformation Methodology at this point. We'll revisit this in future sessions, and you'll have ample opportunity to apply it when completing your challenges. For this particular session, we agreed to focus on authenticity and vulnerability, both of which are closely related. However, it was important that I explained the tools, practices and processes we'll be working with upfront as part of the training. Now that we've established this foundation and you understand how it all works, we can focus primarily on the coaching process. Do you have any questions about that?'

'No, everything's clear so far. I'm ready to move on,' said Yoren. After a long pause, he added, 'So since we're starting with authenticity, my score suggests I have a less-than-healthy relationship with this Aspect of Being. I'm curious to learn more about it and why I scored the way I did.'

'Sure, let's look at the distinction,' said Grace, pulling it up on the screen.

Authenticity

Authenticity is how you relate to the reality of matters in life. It is the extent to which you are accurate and rigorous in perceiving what is real and what is not. It is also how sensitive and diligent you are to the validity of the knowledge you perceive. *Authenticity* is paramount for you to carefully consider that your conception of reality – including your beliefs and opinions – is congruent with how things are. When you are being authentic, you are compelled

to express your unique being – what is there for you to express –
while being consistent with who you say you are for others and
who you say you are for yourself. It is the congruence or alignment
of your self-image – who you know yourself to be – and your
persona – who you choose to project to others.

A healthy relationship with *authenticity* indicates that you take the
time to thoughtfully consider your beliefs and opinions, as the
validity and accuracy of your conception of matters is important to
you. You mostly experience yourself as being true to yourself and
others. Others may consider you genuine, distinct and trustworthy,
and that your actions are consistent with who and how you are
and what you communicate.

An unhealthy relationship with *authenticity* indicates that there
may be no solid foundation for your beliefs and opinions and how
you choose to examine reality, and you are often lenient and fickle
with how you express your views and the truth. You may consider
yourself to be fake or an imposter and often question your own
abilities. Others may consider you to be someone who lacks
sincerity and often acts inconsistently with who you say you are.
You are frequently uncomfortable with being yourself and being
with yourself. Alternatively, you may be righteous, opinionated,
biased or prejudiced, considering your 'truth' to be the only truth,
and may be unwilling to give up being 'right'.

'What stands out to you here?' asked Grace.

'That there seem to be two parts to authenticity,' he replied. 'I'm more
accustomed to the part about how we perceive ourselves and how we
project ourselves to others. This is about my self-image and how I
show up for others, which is something I strive to do … keeping an
image that's respected and aligns with my role at work. But I don't
really get the other part. I haven't thought about it in this way before.'

'Sure. Let me explain it further,' said Grace. 'The aspect of authenticity
that you're struggling with is how we relate to various parts of reality.
For your conception of any matter to be congruent with reality, it's

paramount to be authentic in your awareness and understanding of it. It's where you ask yourself: Are my beliefs and opinions on this matter congruent with how it actually is? The matter itself could be anything from the economy, money or politics to your family or, in the case of you starting a business, being authentically aware of what it takes to start and grow a successful startup. It relates to what I explained to you earlier about considering other perspectives and not just relying on the first thing you see or hear as the whole truth about a matter.'

She pulled up a model called the 'authenticity quadrant' on her screen and they discussed it at length, focusing mainly on self-image and persona, and exploring why Yoren felt the need to constantly manage the impression he made with others by projecting a fake persona both at work and in social settings.

Self-image	**Persona**
Conversations you have with yourself about yourself	*Conversations you have with the world about yourself*
Beliefs	**Opinions**
Conversations you have with yourself about the world	*Conversations you have with the world about the world*

'You mentioned you wanted to explore the self-image and persona aspect of authenticity, Yoren. But before we do, I want to reiterate that this process is intended to be free from moral judgement, so we're not seeing anything from the perspective of it being 'right' or 'wrong', 'good' or 'bad',' said Grace.

'Got it, thanks,' he responded.

'You indicated before that you have a tendency to exaggerate the truth about yourself when introducing yourself to someone you've just met,' said Grace. 'And you also mentioned that you sometimes choose not to reveal everything you know or don't know to others rather than ensuring they have access to the most accurate and complete information so they can make better-informed decisions.'

Immediately triggered, Yoren exclaimed, 'I most certainly do not exaggerate the truth about myself! I'm like an open book; people can choose to like me or not. And in relation to not revealing everything I do or don't know, yes, sure, at times I hold things back. But as a team leader, I'm expected to be on top of everything; my team relies on me. So, naturally, I'd never let on if I don't have an answer. I'd just delegate anything I'm unsure about like any good leader would.'

'I appreciate you may have been triggered by my questions about your relationship with authenticity, Yoren. But let's pause here and take a moment to notice the connection between your reaction and vulnerability. Let's take a moment to revisit the distinction,' she said, pulling it up on her screen.

Grace paused to give Yoren time to re-read the distinction of vulnerability.

After a few minutes, she asked, 'What are you present to?'

'Well, I understand that having one's guard up indicates an unhealthy relationship with this Mood,' said Yoren. 'And, as I read earlier, authenticity and vulnerability are closely linked. When you asked me to read the distinction of vulnerability during our debrief session and see if I recognised myself in any of it, I found it confronting. I also didn't really get the link between vulnerability and authenticity when we talked about the exposure triangle in the last session. But now I can see it clearly; although I'll admit, it's a bit uncomfortable, and I don't particularly like it.'

They discussed authenticity and vulnerability at length, including how and why they're connected and how they might be holding Yoren back from moving forward with his business idea. He could see that Grace kept bringing the discussion back to that intention with her questions. As they conversed, Grace noticed Yoren's walls were slowly beginning to come down. Yoren sensed it too. He was coming to terms with his discomfort. He now realised that his habit of constantly denying he was causing some of the problems he was dealing with and ignoring his ability to respond to matters, even when he wasn't the source, indicated the shadow side of awareness and vulnerability. He could also now see how this impacted his authenticity and why he was so easily triggered.

Grace also referred back to the exposure triangle, reminding Yoren how awareness, authenticity and vulnerability are critical in shaping our conception of reality and how they can easily distort it if we have an unhealthy relationship with one or more of those key Aspects of Being. Grace was pleased to see Yoren so engaged in the conversation and asking lots of relevant questions. As they approached the conclusion of the session, she recapped what they'd covered before outlining his challenge for the week.

'Okay, so now to your challenge. Remember, most of the learning and paradigm shifts happen between sessions, so what you get from our coaching is largely up to you. You can start by working on authenticity this week using the conception worksheet. I'd also like you to start journaling your Moods, with a particular focus on vulnerability. I suggest you nominate a time each evening to reflect on the day and use the worksheet to document situations when you weren't being authentic, either with your beliefs and opinions or with your self-image and persona. Document the outcome of that incident and then consider how the outcome might have differed if you'd been more authentic. Any questions?'

'No, that seems clear enough.'

'Are you prepared to make a commitment to execute on this challenge, Yoren?'

'Yes. In fact, I'm happy to shake on it,' he said, leaning over to shake her hand.

As Grace saw him out, she was present to Yoren's sense of overwhelm beneath his external bravado. It reminded her of her own coaching and transformation journey many years ago under Jen's guidance and how deeply challenging she'd found it, especially in the beginning. But she knew the immense rewards of persevering and was confident Yoren would benefit enormously from the exercise if he chose to meet his commitment. While she could tell from his expression that he also felt uncomfortable, she sensed a new measure of humility in him. So she was confident he would follow through this time.

CHAPTER 9

From the Roots Up

Samuel Healy was known for being very determined, but never more so than as a young man. His resilience in the face of challenging circumstances made him come across as hard and lacking compassion. Having grown up in poverty and hardship, he was laser-focused on pursuing financial prosperity in such a way that, from an outsider's perspective, he prioritised money over everything else, even his family. But he knew in his heart that his wife and three children were everything to him, which is why it was so important to him that they always be well provided for. While his journey in life was far from conventional or common, it would eventually have an immense impact on his entire family.

Samuel focused on business and investment as vehicles to fulfil his purpose of creating a safe environment and wealth so his family wouldn't suffer the way he had. From the day he knew Uriel would be his wife and the mother of his children, he promised himself that he would never let his family experience scarcity. Samuel had detested being poor in his youth. So once he confirmed that Uriel shared his vision for financial success, he knew she was the one. Having survived the horrors of World War II as a young Jewish girl, Uriel found immense comfort in Samuel's vision. She met him in Israel soon after losing her beloved father and was immediately drawn to the young Irish-born Israeli's strength and resolve to create a prosperous life despite the enormous post-war challenges they faced. Samuel reminded her a lot of her own father in that way, so his commitment was what she had come to expect from a husband.

While Uriel happily stayed home to look after the household and the couple's growing family, Samuel worked feverishly to build his business portfolio in Israel, creating several iterations along the way, many of them unsuccessful. Often, his attempts to develop the right products and services to meet the market's needs failed. Other times, he chose unstable and unreliable business partners. He also repeatedly fell victim to fraud and struggled with Israel's socialist-leaning economy at the time. But he refused to give up. Even when walking away might have been the best option, he stubbornly dug in his heels and pushed on to the point where he developed a reputation as someone who would leap into dangerous, unchartered waters without a life jacket, despite not knowing how to swim.

Samuel's overconfidence and bravado often led him to take uncalculated risks and ego-centric business decisions, resulting in more losses than wins. With a wife and young children to support, he knew his ineffectiveness had ramifications beyond himself. Still, he refused to let go of his business goals and get a regular job. By this stage, he was an employer, so his staff also suffered the consequences of his actions. But somehow, he always managed to get back on track.

Eventually, Samuel took the opportunity to emigrate to Australia with Uriel and their three children and try his luck there. However, it would be several more years of blood, sweat and tears before he achieved the level of financial security he so desperately wanted for his family. His ultimate success was only made possible after he developed a more congruent conception of business and an authentic awareness of how things really were. That was when he realised that business was not just a vehicle to accumulate wealth for himself and his family, but a way to find meaning and purpose by addressing burning needs and problems in the market.

It was a eureka moment for Samuel when he realised he'd been looking at business in limited ways for so many years, both in Israel and Australia. He recognised he'd been seeing business from a selfish, what's-in-it-for-me-right-now perspective and that there was far more to building and running a business than just accumulating money and immediate, ad-hoc financial wins. It wasn't about him and his goals at all. It was about going beyond himself and forgoing instant gratification to focus on serving the needs of the market. This significant paradigm shift unlocked the door for him to maximise his business's profitability and take it to the next level. He learned that money is a medium for exchanging value, which requires the business owner to care about their customers and give rather than take. He gradually realised that unless he began to care about the problems afflicting human beings, there wouldn't be a market to sell his products and services. And so, over time, he developed a more altruistic, compassionate and service-oriented mindset, devoting more of his time and resources to serving others through his businesses, charities and microfinancing or mentoring social entrepreneurs.

Throughout their turbulent journey, Uriel stuck by her husband with steadfast loyalty and unwavering support, doing her best to manage the household so that the family's financial struggles had minimal impact on the children. However, as the eldest child and an observant, sensitive soul who was very close to his mother, Stewart saw through the facade. He sensed her loneliness and could tell when she'd been crying, although she did her best to hide it. Uprooted from his home while still young, Stewart developed resilience beyond his years. But while he could cope with a move to the other side of the world, the loss of friendships, loneliness, frequent outbursts from his father and financial challenges without a word of complaint, he couldn't bear to hear his mother cry at night when she thought her children were fast asleep.

Stewart was so present to the suffering that his father's venture-building journey had on the family, especially his mother, that he refused to consider business as a potential career. As he evolved from child to teenager, he grew to despise the risk-taking associated with entrepreneurship and to value stability and security above all else. A deep thinker and intelligent beyond his years, he developed a passion for reading, especially books on philosophy, and would consume content he could barely understand. He was only 13 when he started to fill his solitude and loneliness by reading the works of Karl Marx and other philosophers and thinkers like Paul Lafargue, Simone de Beauvoir, Jean-Paul Sartre, Theodor Adorno, Herbert Marcuse and Erich Fromm. His interpretation of those works supported him to gradually shape his worldview and later influenced him to become an academic. The narrative he created from a young age was that his family had suffered because his father was a 'greedy neo-liberal capitalist'. This perception turned him against capitalism, neo-liberalism and any other 'ism' he believed his father favoured.

It was a different story for Stewart's younger siblings, Jen and Igor. As a child, Igor was impressed by his father's perseverance compared to other fathers he knew, as he saw Samuel push through no matter how hard the path. But in later years, he realised there was more to becoming successful in business than just hard work and persistence. Eventually, Igor came to believe that his father's moral compass was the main reason he failed multiple times, hence the suffering endured by the family. He also saw his father as naive and gullible in trusting people too easily after misinterpreting their intentions. Despite knowing Samuel eventually broke through and succeeded in his objectives, Igor continued to believe his father was far too 'nice' and 'moral' for the business world. Igor believed this was why Samuel had often been taken advantage of by 'the elites who rule the world'.

From a young age, Igor longed to be part of what he called 'high society' so that he could have a greater influence than he believed his father ever could. To Igor, 'real deals' were unachievable for anyone adopting Samuel's approach. His deep yearning led him to build relationships with politicians and society's most influential and wealthy people. He also learned the importance of having the media on your side to make the impression you want instead of highlighting who you authentically are, and he became highly proficient in public relations and marketing himself.

Igor developed a keen interest in politics towards the end of high school, and the materials he read and people he followed heavily influenced his views and political leaning. To this day, he maintains that the economy and banking system were designed to keep people in debt and that all inflationary fluctuations are either planned by the reserve banks and those who influence them or result from government inefficiencies. But instead of protesting or challenging the status quo, he decided to join them at their own game and reap the benefits. Samuel held similar views to Igor about the banking system and inflation, but the way he acted upon his beliefs differed from his son. Where Samuel tried his best to avoid participating in what he called 'the madness', Igor – who constantly criticised his father for his views – believed it was critical to leverage and capitalise on the system as much as possible.

After completing high school, Igor studied economics and public relations at university with the ambition of a political career. On achieving his dream and entering parliament a few years later, he worked hard to develop relationships with members of his preferred political party and the most influential politicians. He also became a vocal lobbyist for multiple causes, believing that lobbying is a legitimate democratic pursuit. As a lobbyist for some time before entering parliament, he initially represented the interests and causes of third-party corporations. Later, after becoming an MP himself, he created a coalition of other politicians who aligned with his preferred policies – ones that benefited those who funded him. Entering parliament reconfirmed Igor's perception that it takes more than just hard work and good intentions to excel in life, particularly when it comes to status and wealth: it takes strategic thinking and astute relationship-building first and foremost.

Samuel and Uriel's middle child and only daughter, Jen, was the most free-spirited of their children. As a dreamer who spent much of her childhood in her bedroom immersed in fairy tales, fantasy novels and the magical world of her imagination, Jen was relatively oblivious to the challenges within the household and, therefore, the least impacted by them. She was so fascinated by the beauty and diversity of life that, as a joyful and curious girl, she longed for the day when she would finally be old enough to have the freedom to explore the world. Her parents and brothers always seemed to be so consumed with the ups and downs of everyday life that she was mostly left to her own devices, which is exactly how she liked it.

When Jen was old enough to leave the nest, her adventurous nature and free spirit led her to travel the world on a shoestring budget and explore her options rather than pursue a defined pathway like her brothers. She eventually spent years travelling, meeting people from all walks of life and engaging in diverse experiences with the intention of finding herself before she was ready to come home and settle into a career. Jen's travels opened her mind to different lifestyles, trends and cultures, and she became fascinated with how people behave and what drives their behaviour. By the time she came home to study at university and begin her career, she felt like she'd come full circle but with a wealth of unforgettable memories and experiences along the way. Her adventures matured her and gave her a broader perspective on life. In part, this unique background led her to be attracted to the idea of coaching to support others on their journey.

— ∎ —

Seven weeks had passed since Yoren's debrief session with Grace. The debrief was followed by their first coaching session, which established the agreement, introduced him to some of the principles, practices and tools they would utilise during their time together and set the trajectory for the next six months of weekly coaching and training sessions. After realising what was expected of him between sessions, Yoren experienced uncertainty and doubt, coming close to quitting. To his credit, he raised his concerns with Grace, and her response and their subsequent conversation helped him regain his confidence to continue the coaching journey.

They agreed to begin by focusing on the constituent parts of the exposure triangle: awareness, authenticity and vulnerability, and then spent subsequent sessions delving into integrity, effectiveness, care, fear and anxiety. They talked at length about how our Moods create the context for our decisions and actions, and allow us to attune ourselves to life and how we interact with others. Grace also supported Yoren to understand the importance of considering each way of being in the context of Moods rather than assessing it in isolation. They explored how Yoren's relationship with vulnerability, for example, directly impacts his authenticity and how his relationship with care impacts his commitment and how focused he is when choosing to fulfil a particular intention. Grace also encouraged Yoren to avoid intellectualising and to link the content back to his life, particularly to his intention of building a business.

— ∎ —

Driving to Grace's for his next session, Yoren selected his favourite Baroque collection as he found that style of music helped him think more clearly. Inching his way through the Saturday morning traffic, he reflected on their last few meetings. In particular, he wondered how Grace always managed to get him to open up about what's been happening and how he was being in the previous week, despite him doing everything he could to politely avoid her probing questions. After all, his avoidance tactics were quite effective with Mel and his colleagues at the office. So why did he blurt out everything without a filter with Grace? What was her secret? Deep in thought, he found the time passed quickly, despite the traffic, and before he knew it, he had arrived at Grace's place.

Once seated inside the office, Grace looked Yoren in the eye and asked, 'How are you?'

'Fine, thanks. And you?'

Holding his gaze while smiling broadly, she said warmly but firmly, 'Yoren, I didn't ask that question out of courtesy. That was the first question of our coaching session today. We've covered a lot about Moods, and you've done your journaling and completed your conception worksheets. So, let's try again and see how in tune you are with your Moods today. How are you? Can you tell me what your dominant Moods are right now?'

'Oh, okay, I get it,' replied Yoren. 'I think the main one is care. I notice I'm no longer engaging at a superficial level and regarding this coaching journey as an intellectual exercise. It's much more than that. I also recognise that I care a lot more about what I can take from each session in addressing the blockages that have been getting in my way of establishing my business. I think I'm far more open now because I'm less concerned about you judging me or how my words or actions may land to you. I'm also less concerned about how I may judge myself as I now prioritise addressing what isn't in place or, as you say, what I don't have a healthy relationship with. I realise it's in my favour to be more vulnerable or open and to care more about what might work without being so easily offended. So I'm conscious of being more vulnerable, and that's helping me prioritise stepping towards my intention far more than worrying about how I might be seen.'

'Great! So, are you ready to create our contract for today?' asked Grace

'I am.'

'Okay, so is there any in particular that you'd like to address in today's session?'

Without hesitation, Yoren replied, 'Well, I'm quite concerned about how I can possibly build a consulting business when there are so many well-established corporations with far more resources and talent out there.'

Grace would be horrified if I told her that these concerns have been circling around in my mind night after night to the point where I now can't believe I even dared dream of such a grand plan! How can I start to build a business from scratch when there are so many unknowns and uncertainties to deal with?

Grace listened attentively as Yoren expressed his views on all the reasons why he shouldn't start a business, everything from capitalism and neo-liberalism to the current state of the economy. But she also suspected that he was holding back on sharing his deepest fears.

Why would an intelligent, rational adult like me start a venture that could ruin my corporate career, humiliate me, threaten to put me in debt and jeopardise my future with Mel, all for some ridiculous pipe dream that, based on the statistics, is highly likely to fail?

'Thank you for sharing what's on your mind, Yoren,' said Grace, knowing what he'd shared might only be the tip of the iceberg. 'Is there anything else coming up for you?'

Yoren fidgeted uncomfortably. 'To be honest, Grace, sometimes I feel foolish and incompetent. I'm also afraid that my lack of confidence might be obvious to others, especially with all the what-ifs and doubts I have …' Realising he'd shared far more than intended, he stopped abruptly.

Grace paused to see if he had more to say. When nothing more was forthcoming, she said, 'Thank you, Yoren. It's normal to feel apprehensive at the start of any new journey, especially as an amateur. When you cast your mind back to other firsts in your life, like when you first entered the workforce or went on your first date, what were those experiences like for you?'

Yoren sat back and frowned, looking up as though he was trying to catch sight of his own thoughts while Grace waited patiently for his response. Reflecting on his first 'real' date as a teenager made him realise that similar feelings came up every time he embarked on something new, especially anything he really cared about. He also reflected on the previous work he and Grace had done together and couldn't help but notice the connection. Knowing he was also stepping into unfamiliar territory this time made him feel more at ease about his fears and concerns.

How arrogant of me to think I might not have any gaps in my knowledge or skills! We all have many areas of incompetence, and to become effective in those areas can require considerable time, dedication and perseverance.

After several more moments of reflection, he exclaimed, 'Ah, now I get it! That's why having a healthy relationship with awareness, all four Moods, and authenticity is so important. These Aspects of Being will help me relate to matters and circumstances as they are, so it's okay to feel apprehensive and unsure.'

Grace could see from his expression and hear in his voice that he was beginning to resonate with how it feels to start something new and unfamiliar. However, she could tell he still resisted fully opening up to her.

'Can you tell me how knowing that it's normal to feel apprehensive and unsure is making you feel right now?' she asked.

Yoren paused while he processed Grace's question. Again, she gave him ample time to think.

Eventually, he looked up and said, 'It eases the burden on me and encourages me to set the right expectations of myself as a fledgling business-builder.'

'Great!' Grace smiled, observing Yoren's more relaxed posture. She was used to seeing him seated upright at the edge of the sofa, not leaning comfortably back against the cushions as he was now. It looked to Grace like the mask he was so accustomed to wearing was finally beginning to fall away, giving her a glimpse of the authentic Yoren Healy. The thoughtful expression in his eyes suggested he was deeply absorbing this new perception and it was all gradually falling into place.

Making the most of Yoren's receptivity, Grace asked, 'Okay, Yoren, so which ways of being do you think are most relevant to what we just discussed?'

'I would say confidence plays the most significant role. So could we focus on that today?' he asked.

'Let's explore the question a little further, Yoren. We know it's normal to go through doubts and hesitation in life. But let's consider that someone with a relatively healthy relationship with confidence wouldn't stay in doubt for long. However, as you'd recall, confidence is a Secondary Way of Being, and while it's perfectly fine to start looking into Secondary Ways of Being, where do you think we could look to begin addressing the shadows around it? For example, which of the more subtle and deeper Aspects of Being do you think might be contributing to your lack of confidence?'

Yoren responded thoughtfully, 'I know we've talked about the difference between Secondary Ways of Being and other Aspects of Being in previous sessions. But I'll admit I'm still a bit confused about the differences. So would you mind recreating it for me briefly? I'd like to understand it better, especially the relationship between them. I'm still unsure why we can't just dive straight into confidence as I'm convinced that's what's holding me back more than anything else.'

'Sure. Let's explore this together,' replied Grace. 'You'll recall that Secondary Ways of Being are behavioural factors that are readily observable, which makes them familiar to us. You could say they're the link between our primal qualities, which we call Primary Ways of Being, and our decisions, behaviours and actions. In other words, they bridge the gap between how we relate to the more subtle Aspects of Being and how we ultimately act upon them. Some of the Secondary Ways of Being include confidence, assertiveness, reliability, accountability and proactivity. For example, it might be easier to tell if someone is being assertive by observing their behaviour than it is to gauge their awareness, authenticity or vulnerability. Does that make sense?'

'Yes. But all of our Secondary Ways of Being can still be polished and transformed, can't they?' he asked, looking slightly puzzled.

'Absolutely,' replied Grace. 'You can definitely transform your relationship with any Secondary Way of Being, including confidence. However, let's consider that it may not be the most effective place to start. While it's not uncommon for people to ask for coaching on Secondary Ways of Being first, looking into them is one thing – directly transforming your relationship with them is another. To transform your relationship with any Secondary Way of Being, it's far more effective to address the more subtle, deeper qualities first, such as the Primary Ways of Being that impact your relationship with confidence. Does that make sense?'

Yoren nodded. 'I think I'm beginning to understand. But, just to be sure, could we explore which qualities might be contributing to my confidence, Grace?'

'Sure,' said Grace. She drew a circle in the centre of a blank sheet of paper and wrote 'confidence' inside it.

'Several primal qualities can impact how we relate to and act upon confidence. Can you tell me what you think they might be in your case, Yoren?'

'Based on the work we've done, I would say awareness and authenticity are two Aspects of Being that impact how confident I am or how I deal with doubts, dilemmas and uncertainties,' said Yoren.

'Okay, let's consider that,' she responded, writing awareness and authenticity on the page and drawing arrows pointing to the confidence circle in the centre to indicate how they feed into it. 'Can you think of any others?'

Yoren opened his profile assessment report and examined the distinctions for various Aspects of Being. After a few moments, he replied, 'I would say freedom because you need a healthy relationship with freedom to see the options available. I'm pretty sure another would be responsibility because being responsible allows you to live life as an active agent who can choose how to respond to things, even if they're beyond your control. I think having a healthy relationship with both of those Aspects of Being would make you more likely to be confident.'

'Okay, let's add those,' said Grace, adding freedom and responsibility to the page. 'Any others come to mind?'

'Maybe courage?' suggested Yoren.

'Sure, that makes sense. We all need courage to step forward despite the presence of fear, anxiety or discomfort. I would also suggest adding empowerment because when you're empowered, you can take action towards fulfilling your intentions with confidence. It's about telling yourself "I can" and ignoring that voice in your head that says, "I can't". Would you like me to add courage and empowerment?'

Yoren nodded, and Grace added them to the page.

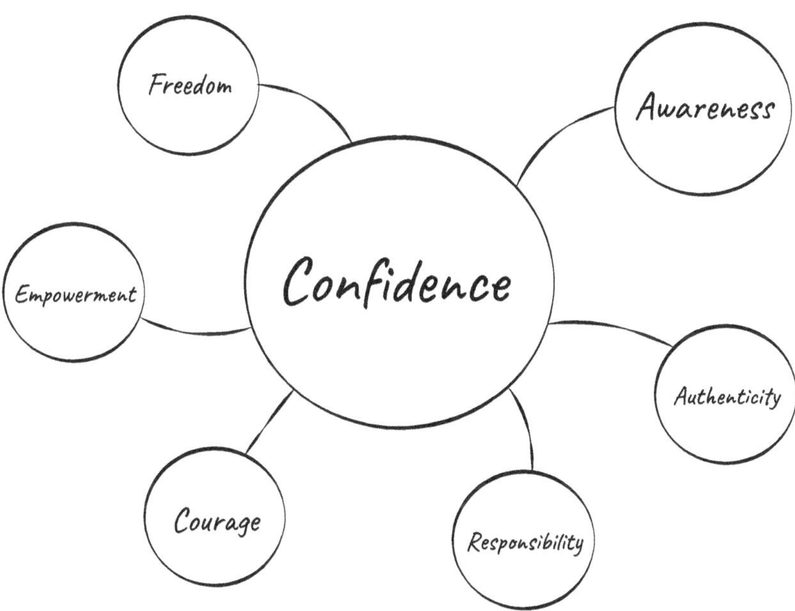

'Let's consider that all of these Aspects of Being feed into your confidence,' said Grace. 'Consequently, having a relatively unhealthy relationship with them would compromise your relationship with confidence and, ultimately, your overall integrity and effectiveness. So we could start by exploring courage and then look into the others you suggested to see how your relationship with those qualities impacts your confidence and other Secondary Ways of Being. Once we've established that, we can spend some time zooming in on confidence. How does that sound?'

Yoren welcomed Grace's suggestion and they spent some time looking into the diagram they created together, discussing the patterns it conveyed. Then they listed all the Aspects of Being that related to confidence and agreed to explore them further over the next few sessions. In wrapping up, Grace tasked Yoren with noticing and journaling how he related to confidence each day over the coming week. She also suggested he read the chapter on courage in the book she had recommended and highlight the areas that stood out to him.

— ∎ —

The week flew by, and before Yoren knew it, he was once again seated on the sofa in Grace's office. While he had completed his challenge for the week, he hoped she wouldn't ask if he'd read the book chapter on courage.

'Okay, so last week, we agreed to focus on courage in today's session,' began Grace. This is a self-generating Primary Way of Being, which means it's generated by itself rather than by an external force. It's also a fundamental starting point for any new endeavour in life. While courage is not dependent on other things, we all need courage just to dare to *be* first and foremost,' said Grace. 'So just to confirm, are you still happy to focus on courage today, Yoren?'

'Yep, sounds good,' he responded, thankful that she hadn't asked him to provide his feedback on that chapter.

'Great. Now, let me ask you a question. How does courage show up for you?'

Yoren considered the question for a moment and then said, 'I know it'll take great courage to dare to start a business when all the statistics tell me it's madness because the odds are stacked against me. With such a high failure rate, I'd be much better off sticking with my corporate job, at least financially. If only I was fearless and never got anxious.'

'Is this how you relate to courage, Yoren? Being fearless and free from anxiety?' asked Grace, suspecting from his response that he hadn't read the chapter on courage but keeping that thought to herself.

'Yes, without fear and anxiety, I'd have far fewer concerns and would be less worried about the risks,' said Yoren.

'It's true there may be risks associated with doing anything new, and your response partly addresses when you need courage. But, considering our distinction in the context of starting your own business, can you describe how courage shows up for you, including what it feels like?'

Grace pulled the distinction of courage up on her laptop screen.

Courage

Courage is the state of being that gives rise to the ability to make decisions, move forward and take action when you are uncomfortable, frightened, worried or concerned for your safety and/or the safety of others. *Courage* is not the absence of *fear*; on the contrary, *courage* shows up when *fear* or discomfort is present. *Courage* enables you to continue to be of service and pursue objectives, even when circumstances appear insurmountable, unpleasant or dangerous.

A healthy relationship with *courage* indicates that you are likely to look for ways to move forward, make decisions and take action, even when you are afraid, feel threatened or are challenged. Others may consider you brave-hearted, daring and spirited, and someone who stands up for their values and in defence of others when challenged.

An unhealthy relationship with *courage* indicates you may freeze, shut down or withdraw in the face of difficult circumstances or when you are challenged or frightened. You may be inclined to avoid confrontation and be hesitant to express and assert yourself or deal powerfully with uncomfortable situations while tolerating

unwanted circumstances. You may avoid confronting and looking
into the reality of matters if they challenge or frighten you.
Alternatively, you may be reckless in dealing with dangerous or
high-risk situations and be unable to predict the consequences of
your bravado. You may also underplay and diminish the impact of
how you are being and your actions.

'Well, I'd say signing up for coaching with you proved I'm actively looking for ways to move forward with my intention,' said Yoren. 'According to the distinction, that indicates a healthy relationship with courage. I'm also someone who stands up for their values when challenged, but, if I'm perfectly honest, not so much in defence of others. I just want to be successful, and I'm afraid that if I fail, others will look down on me, including Mel.'

'Great. Thanks for sharing that, Yoren. Courage is often mistaken for being fearless or heroic. But there's no such thing as being fearless. Fear is a Mood that we all experience. In fact, courage, fear and anxiety go hand in hand. Courage is the way of being that enables us to step forward despite the presence of fear, anxiety and discomfort. In your case, Yoren, it's about daring to take the first step to start a business, despite the risks.'

Courage is stepping forward despite the presence of fear, anxiety and discomfort. I've never thought of courage in that way before. This changes everything.

Grace could see the light switch on in Yoren's eyes and smiled as she witnessed his moment of reception. It was moments like these that she loved most about being a coach.

'Yoren, why do you think you need a healthy relationship with courage to start your business?'

'To dare to take the risks required, to say what I need to say, to be successful and to be open about it all with Mel.'

'Absolutely,' said Grace. 'I'd like you to also consider that when we're born, we enter existence as vulnerable beings, which naturally makes us anxious about the what-ifs. So we need the courage to dare to be as a prelude to daring to be successful, expressive, honest, confident and so on. That's why courage is a self-generating quality. However, being courageous doesn't mean being reckless or full of bravado. Being reckless when dealing with high-risk situations or diving into a new endeavour without understanding the risks and how to mitigate them indicates a shadow side of courage.'

'I see. Well, I know I'd never just jump into business ownership recklessly. But I can relate to not wanting to take action until I know I'll be successful. What's wrong with that?' asked Yoren.

'Well, considering we're all vulnerable to the perils and circumstances of life, it's logical to assume that we'll face many fear-generating situations throughout our lives,' said Grace. 'We largely express ourselves through the Moods of vulnerability, anxiety, fear and care. When it comes to what to care about, especially when we're bombarded with many things at once, it's easy to become overwhelmed, which can lead to paralysis. So we either do nothing and stay in our comfort zone or determine what we value most and prioritise.

'Care supports us in prioritising what to focus on,' she continued. 'And it's closely connected to courage, because when we have clarity around our priorities, we're more likely to have the courage to step forward and act upon them. The care-courage relationship can manifest in more behavioural factors such as confidence, assertiveness, proactivity, resourcefulness, reliability and so on. For example, some people exude confidence, but that doesn't necessarily mean they're courageous if their confidence is inauthentic. How does courage make you feel with this new understanding in mind, Yoren?'

'I've never looked at courage this way before,' he responded. 'This new perspective makes me feel better about being somewhat afraid to take action on my business idea because I now see that fear is healthy and normal. It's refreshing to think that fear, anxiety and discomfort are normal human experiences and that courage is stepping forward despite those feelings. I've always experienced self-judgement and self-sabotage over this. I thought being strong meant having no fear and always being on top of things. If I'm realistic about the fact that the path will be rocky and even treacherous at times, then I can move beyond my fear and step forward anyway because I care about my business idea so much.'

They continued to explore how the relationship between courage and the Moods is particularly significant and how humans have evolved beyond the primal fight or flight instinct to step forward with courage when we care deeply about something. Grace explained that's because the care factor allows us to take action despite our anxiety about the what-ifs and concern over what others might think.

In wrapping up their conversation, Grace suggested Yoren complete a conception worksheet focusing on courage during the week. She also asked him to continue journaling his Moods and to consider how courage is connected to responsibility, reminding him that, as autonomous beings, we can respond in ways that make things work to our advantage. As Yoren re-read the distinction of responsibility, his invulnerability once again got the better of him.

'What?!' he exclaimed. 'Are you suggesting I'm the source of all my problems and lack of accomplishments? How about things beyond my control? Do you think I have control over climate change and everyone's carbon footprint, or how the value of the money I'm paid fluctuates and ultimately depreciates? Are you kidding?'

Grace listened patiently, allowing him to express himself without interruption. When he'd finished, she paused as he gathered his thoughts before letting him know there was more to the conversation and asked if he was open to hearing it. He agreed, albeit reluctantly.

'Our distinction of responsibility doesn't suggest that you are the ultimate source of the problems you face,' said Grace. 'It simply indicates that you can live life from the viewpoint that you are the primary cause of the matters in your life and that, regardless of the source, you can choose to respond to them as they come. This perspective empowers you to influence an outcome or reduce unwanted consequences so you actively steer your course rather than simply let life happen.

'For example, imagine wandering the streets late at night in an area of town known for crime, wearing a Rolex watch and extravagant clothing, and you get robbed. Naturally, the thief is 100% to blame and should be required to deal with the legal consequences of their actions. However, in that situation, you should ask yourself if you made a wise decision and whether or not your decision and its outcome were founded on an authentic awareness of the reality. A person with a more congruent conception of reality would be better equipped to consider multiple factors when making decisions. Can you see how taking a safer route and not waving your Rolex in the air would have demonstrated a healthier relationship with awareness, authenticity, vulnerability and responsibility?'

Yoren nodded.

'Some people might fantasise that they're living in a utopian world,' Grace continued. 'But that's far from reality. An authentically aware person sees and acknowledges things as they actually are rather than how they want them to be. Their authentic awareness enables them to respond effectively, which can lead to their unique contribution and, ultimately, their ability to influence and expand the shared reality. Herein lies our true power. In contrast, people who choose to be victims or who live life as if they are solely responsible for everything are not only inauthentic and have an unhealthy relationship with responsibility, they're also delusional. Let me give you a simple analogy. If I ask you to raise one leg while standing, could you do it?'

'Yes.'

'Now, if I ask you to lift the other leg at the same time, could you do that?'

'Of course not!'

'This example demonstrates that we all have autonomy, but only to a degree, because other forces and laws restrict our freedom. However, failing to acknowledge and surrender to that fact will result in a lack of workability and unfulfilled dreams.'

At the end of the session, they agreed to explore responsibility next, including its shadow sides and how we act upon it through Secondary Ways of Being like confidence, proactivity, accountability and reliability, which are all critical to entrepreneurship.

— ∎ —

Arriving at Grace's the following Saturday, Yoren felt quite excited and was ready to discuss responsibility. After listening to him share what he'd noticed during the week and reading through his conception worksheet on courage, Grace wasted no time getting into the next topic.

'Tell me, Yoren, how do you relate to responsibility?' she asked.

'I relate to it as being responsible for doing something, in the sense of it being one's duty or obligation,' Yoren replied. 'I also see it as being to blame for something going wrong. For instance, whenever a problem occurs in my team, it's usually up to me to find out who's responsible or whose fault it is.'

Although Yoren had read the ontological distinction for responsibility more than once, Grace wasn't surprised that he still related to it as a sense of duty or needing someone to blame for something. In her experience, it was quite common for coachees to take a while to let go of previously held perceptions around some Aspects of Being. However, based on his response, she decided to continue the line of enquiry.

'In the context of starting your business, what do you blame others, the world or yourself for?'

'I blame the system for making it so hard to start a business. I blame my father for always trying to talk me out of entrepreneurship. And

I blame myself for letting external factors and others hold me back from fulfilling my dream,' he answered.

'Does blaming yourself, the system and others make you feel powerless?' asked Grace.

He pondered her question for a moment and responded thoughtfully, 'Yes. I feel stuck and unfulfilled in a job I don't particularly enjoy anymore.'

'So if we consider responsibility as being the primary cause of matters in your life, regardless of the source, and choosing to respond rather than react, can you tell me how your relationship with responsibility might be holding you back from moving forward with your business venture?' asked Grace.

Yoren skimmed over the distinction again, reviewing the descriptions for a healthy and unhealthy relationship with responsibility.

'Looking at the distinction, it seems I've been regarding myself as a victim of circumstance rather than someone who has the power to influence them and be an active agent rather than a passive one,' he said.

'Absolutely,' said Grace. 'Being responsible means you demonstrate autonomy in response to things in life, regardless of who or what caused them.'

'Yes, I see,' said Yoren. 'So instead of laying blame, I could respond appropriately to matters, including things I can't control. From this, I can assume that even though the failure rate for startups is incredibly high, the small number that succeed must, to a great extent, be the result of a founder who has a healthy relationship with responsibility. They choose how they respond and steer the ship in the direction they want to go rather than letting circumstances beyond their control dictate their outcomes.'

'Spot on, Yoren. It's up to each and every one of us to choose how we respond to things as they arise. So, even when things go wrong, your response matters. How you handle the situation determines the outcome, at least to an extent. It's about *being* responsible as opposed to *taking* responsibility. Does that make sense?'

Yoren nodded thoughtfully.

'I'd now like to bring your attention to the two shadow sides of responsibility,' said Grace

'What do you mean, two shadow sides? Isn't there only one shadow?' asked Yoren.

'For every Aspect of Being, the shadow generally manifests itself in passive and active ways,' responded Grace. 'If we zoom in on the part of the distinction describing an unhealthy relationship with responsibility, you can see that, on the one hand, it describes someone who sees themselves as a victim of circumstance with little to no power to influence an outcome. That's one shadow side of responsibility. The other shadow side is when we live life as if we're the sole cause of matters and we try to control everything all the time, as though there are no limitations to our will and autonomy. Someone whose shadow manifests itself on this active side typically expects everything to always go their way, which is completely unrealistic and inauthentic. Can you see yourself in either of these descriptions, Yoren?'

'Is it possible to have a little of both shadow sides, Grace? I know I can be controlling at times, especially at work, because that's where I feel most confident. But if I get stuck on something, I'm so laser-focused on sorting it out that my persistence works in my favour.'

'Yes, but consider what might happen if your persistence turns into unreasonable insistence or stubbornness?' she asked.

Yoren chuckled and said, 'Yes, if you asked Mel, I'm sure she'd tell you I can be both insistent and stubborn at times!'

'An unhealthy relationship with responsibility certainly can impact one's relationship with persistence, which is a Secondary Way of Being. We can definitely explore persistence later if you like. For now, though, I encourage you to zoom out and focus on responsibility itself,' suggested Grace.

'Sure,' agreed Yoren. 'I can definitely see signs of an unhealthy relationship with responsibility in me, especially if I consider both the active and passive sides. I've started to notice that while I tend to expect things to go my way, I've been making excuses for not taking even the first step towards starting my business. Instead, I've blamed the economy, the policies, the policymakers, the larger monopoly corporations and many other factors. But now I'm beginning to understand that I can relate to responsibility as a very powerful way of being. It's much more empowering when I relate to it as more than just duty or an obligation or even being to blame for something. I love what you said about relating to it as being 'response-able', Grace: having the capacity to respond appropriately and proactively to circumstances and other people's decisions and actions. I'm going to remember that one!'

'Great, Yoren. Your self-reflection aligns with why you've been feeling blocked from moving forward with your business idea. So it's good to hear that you have a new understanding of what it means to be responsible from an ontological perspective. Before we move on, I'd like to explain the difference between reacting and responding in more detail. This can assist you in developing a more congruent conception of what we mean by 'responsibility'. Reacting immediately to things is so primal to us as human beings. We react to how others behave, from other drivers on the road to our team members or intimate partner. We react to what we see and hear on the news, and so on. But, in most cases, reacting is not as effective as responding. When we respond, we give ourselves time to consider multiple perspectives and perceptions of an idea.

'As a critical thinker, Yoren, I'm sure you consider it of utmost importance to be authentic in your awareness of matters. When you are authentically aware, you resist the urge to react by making ill-considered decisions. Instead, you pass all the information you have through a relatively objective filter and your Moods until you have clarity and can respond appropriately. When you respond in this way, you increase the effectiveness of your decisions and behaviours, which helps you to fulfil your intentions. Operating in this way sets you free to project your unique being to the world, regardless of the circumstances or what others might think. You can authentically and intentionally communicate your beliefs, values, feelings and emotions. This is true self-expression, which we will explore later in your coaching. I just wanted to touch on this as it's relevant to responsibility.'

They discussed the two shadow sides in more detail, briefly looking at other examples, and Grace also explained the close relationship between responsibility and other Aspects of Being, most notably awareness, authenticity, freedom and vulnerability. Time seemed to fly faster than usual, and before Yoren knew it, the session was over. Before he left, they agreed they'd covered responsibility well, particularly as he'd also been working to develop a deeper conception of it between sessions. Setting the trajectory for the next two sessions, they decided to work on freedom, followed by empowerment and confidence, the latter enabling Grace to address Yoren's earlier request to understand which of the deeper qualities feed into this Secondary Way of Being.

— ■ —

On his way to Grace's house a week later, Yoren found it hard to believe he was halfway through his coaching journey. As he drove, he reflected on the last 11 weeks and marvelled at how much he'd learned and how far he'd come. But he still didn't feel anywhere near as close as he hoped he would be by now to taking the first steps towards becoming an entrepreneur. He knew they'd be working on freedom in today's session but was unclear why. He'd simply agreed on freedom because he didn't want to appear foolish or naive to Grace by asking why, especially after coming this far.

We live in a so-called democratic society, yet I don't feel at all free to do whatever I please without restriction or constraint! Building a business is a classic example. I definitely don't feel free to exercise my rights in any way I choose. I feel trapped and suppressed, forced to fit in with other people's agendas. I see so many people protest over their pay or push so hard to get a promotion so they can get paid more. Yet anyone can choose to start a business or become self-employed. So why aren't more people tapping into their autonomy and doing all they can to take charge of their lives instead of complaining or expecting others to play their game?

Ushering Yoren into her office, Grace could see he was deep in thought and more apprehensive and subdued than usual. After discussing his week and reviewing his conception worksheet on responsibility, she introduced the subject of freedom, another Primary Way of Being. Together, they explored where he felt constrained, what he would do if he was free to do anything, where he saw possibilities in relation to the business he wanted to build and what freedom might look like. She could tell from his responses that he was seeing freedom through a different lens. Walking him through the distinction, Grace supported him to understand why freedom as a way of being mattered and how it related to his intention.

Freedom

Freedom is living life from the viewpoint that you always have options. It is your capacity to choose to be, do, say, feel and think whatever you wish without being controlled, coerced, constrained or limited by unwanted external forces while simultaneously accepting any subsequent consequences of your words or actions. You acknowledge that you have the choice to act despite constraints imposed on you while accepting that there are limitations associated with the reality of being a human being.

A healthy relationship with *freedom* indicates that you see options and possibilities available to you and can create opportunities when the need arises. When you are being free, you are not at the mercy of manipulative or distorting forces. Others may experience you as someone who chooses not to be restrained by situations or challenges imposed on them and communicates openly without constraint. You may actively consider self-discipline and self-imposed restrictions to prioritise what you most care about. When you have a healthy relationship with *freedom*, you refuse to succumb easily to the manipulation or domination of others.

An unhealthy relationship with *freedom* indicates that you often experience being held back and suppressed in the face of circumstances in your life due to a lack of options and may feel trapped or coerced. Others may experience that you withhold and are limited in what you can accomplish, contribute and communicate. You may wait for opportunities to be created and offered to you by others or miraculously land in your lap. You may often feel resigned and disarmed and frequently give in to others or external forces. You may feel imprisoned, stuck or frozen by your inner desires, shackled by dysfunctional habits. Alternatively, you may see and consider too many options, which often leads to paralysis. Avoiding self-imposed routines and disciplines may cause you to lack the momentum required to make progress.

'Can you see from the distinction, Yoren, how freedom is not something you set out to achieve or attain? It's a state of being you intentionally choose for yourself. So, while responsibility is the extent to which you choose to respond to circumstances, freedom is living life as though you always have options. Where others see constraints and limitations, people with a healthy relationship with freedom see possibilities and options, and then take action to leverage them. Does this make sense?'

'Yes, it does. But to me, that seems like empowerment. I think of myself as empowered if I'm seizing opportunities.'

'Responsibility, freedom, courage and empowerment are closely connected,' said Grace. 'Awareness and authenticity play critical roles here too. More specifically, we can make empowered choices when we're authentically aware of the options and possibilities. That's true freedom. Empowerment is living life from the viewpoint that you can fulfil your intentions while enabling others to fulfil theirs. It's about tapping into your power and knowing when to authentically say "I can" instead of "I can't". Like courage, empowerment is an active, self-generating quality, meaning it comes from within. Nobody can empower you. Power isn't something to be received. It's only possible to inspire and support others to empower themselves. The relationships between freedom, courage, responsibility and empowerment can feed into and manifest as proactivity and resourcefulness, two Secondary Ways of Being. Empowerment also commonly manifests through confidence, so it's a great one to explore before we deep-dive into confidence.'

They read the distinction for empowerment together and explored issues that dug deep into Yoren's core through questions like: When or where are you powerful? Where do you experience being disempowered? In what situations do you find yourself disarmed, perhaps even to the point where you feel yourself sinking into despair? Where do you go to become empowered? What's possible from a state of empowerment?

Empowerment

Empowerment is living life from the viewpoint of being able to fulfil your intentions while enabling and inspiring others to fulfil theirs. *Empowerment* is how you relate to your power, capabilities and real or perceived limitations.

A healthy relationship with *empowerment* indicates that you mostly experience being able to take powerful actions towards fulfilling your intentions, purpose and goals while encouraging and inspiring others to fulfil theirs. Others may experience you as someone who takes actions that produce meaningful results in many areas of life and you may inspire them to follow you as your actions also make a significant difference to them.

Grace listened attentively to Yoren's responses, giving him ample time to think and reflect. Many of his responses sparked further conversations and led to some profound insights. Some questions struck a nerve, as Yoren had always considered himself to be powerful. However, after reading the distinction, he could see that he'd been fooling himself because his relationship with empowerment was described almost to the letter on the unhealthy side. They also triggered him around his subtle and well-obscured insecurities and rubbed salt on some of his open wounds and vulnerabilities, bringing his doubts and hesitations about his self-esteem to the surface.

As they conversed, Grace encouraged him to look at empowerment through the ontological lens of being. This new perspective enabled him to see that empowerment is actively gaining freedom and power for oneself rather than passively waiting for others to empower us and knowing you can take decisive actions towards achieving your intentions rather than seeing nothing but limitations and excuses. It also made him realise he had a habit of hiding behind his forged persona. Deep down, he knew this had become a pattern that stopped him from moving forward with his startup.

Grace continued to ask more questions throughout the session, actively listening and deepening her questions where appropriate and in line with Yoren's responses. They discussed what it looked like to be powerful and empowered and how this leads to being confident, proactive, assertive and resourceful in action, all Secondary Ways of Being. By the end of the session, Yoren felt he had a newfound awareness of how his invulnerability, inauthenticity and insecurities caused him to be stuck or disempowered.

The completion of empowerment was a perfect segue into confidence. They devoted two full sessions to this topic, exploring where he got his confidence from, what confidence looked like for him and the kinds of situations where he tended to second-guess or doubt himself and why. Grace then pulled up the distinction on her laptop, and they discussed it at length, considering all the Primary Ways of Being and Moods they had explored so far and their connections to his relationship with confidence.

Confidence

Confidence is how you relate to certainties, uncertainties, doubts and hesitation. It is the belief or understanding that you can rely on or have faith in someone or something, including your own abilities and qualities. Being confident supports you in gaining credibility and making good first impressions while dealing with pressure and meeting life head on.

A healthy relationship with *confidence* indicates you are predominantly able to forego your doubts and uncertainties and don't allow them to stop your progress. Others may experience you as self-assured or at ease, even in challenging situations. You leverage and effectively utilise available resources to move forward despite your hesitations. You are aware of and trust your strengths and abilities and back yourself fully. You can move forward in difficult circumstances, even though you know your limitations and the risks involved and are not reckless. This may encourage others to trust you when you say you can do something, and they expect you to follow through.

An unhealthy relationship with *confidence* indicates that you may be overconfident, inappropriately confident or unreasonably hesitant. You may ruminate, get stuck or be weighed down by your doubts. You may question your abilities and doubt yourself or others, even in familiar circumstances or situations. You can frequently waver in challenging situations and may experience last-minute doubts or panic you are unable to overcome. Alternatively, you may be reckless, dogmatic, display bravado or undertake excessively risky behaviour with little or no regard for the impact or outcome. Others may feel the need to check if you are okay and may have concerns about your ability to see a task through. You may often worry that you or others will disappoint, let people down or not live up to expectations. You may defer making decisions or taking action unless all uncertainties are resolved.

After almost four months of coaching and training, Yoren could see that he had considerably transformed his relationship with a number of Aspects of Being, including confidence, which had been high on his agenda for the past several weeks. He could now see the benefit in waiting and exploring the deeper qualities first.

Finishing their last session on confidence, Grace briefly recapped where they were at and explained how the puzzle pieces came together.

'Once you are authentically aware of the matters that might impact your decision to move forward with your business, your healthy relationship with freedom will enable you to see the options available, including the problems to be solved and the gaps to be filled. Then your healthy relationship with responsibility will encourage you to choose your next steps wisely. Being empowered, you'll tell yourself "I can" and mean it with all your heart. This will lead you to be confident and proactive, acting upon your decisions and steering the course rather than passively letting life happen as though you have no control.

'As you progress, you'll inevitably encounter problems and road-blocks as well as opportunities. And you'll have to respond quickly to overcome the challenges and optimise the opportunities. You'll need to tap into resourcefulness, another Secondary Way of Being, to get the most out of anything by applying solutions with whatever resources are available. Ultimately, this leads to reliability, an essential quality in anything from a product and service to a partner, employee and so on. This is a brief example of how all of these Aspects of Being connect and why the health of your relationship with them matters greatly. In your case, Yoren, your healthy relationship with all of these Aspects of Being will support you to break through the roadblocks that have been holding you back all these years.'

On his way home, Yoren reflected on how his relationship with awareness, authenticity and vulnerability had shifted through a process of enquiry and self-discovery guided by Grace's coaching and the application of the assessment and framework. He thought about the session he'd just had and how Grace had supported him in pulling out a sub-model from the complete ontological model, highlighting what might have compromised the health of his relationship with confidence. This insight helped him realise that those Aspects of Being should be addressed first.

It had taken months to go through all that preparation, but he could now see how addressing those more subtle qualities would contribute to transforming his relationship with confidence. He couldn't help but acknowledge how effectively this ontological model, combined with Grace's coaching and training, enabled him to identify the patterns compromising his confidence to act, especially in relation to his entrepreneurial dream. He was hopeful that this fresh way of relating to confidence would manifest through his future decisions and actions towards establishing the business. Feeling like a heavy weight had been lifted off his shoulders, he couldn't wait to get home to take the first concrete step in his business journey: registering the company.

CHAPTER 10

Transcending Beyond Self

Yoren couldn't believe he'd finally taken one of the initial critical steps of building his business by registering his company. After over an hour of surfing the web to learn how to do it, he was pleasantly surprised when it ended up being a straightforward process that only took around 25 minutes to complete. His eyes welled with tears as he sat back and stared at the company registration certificate on the laptop display, his vision beginning to blur. But rather than fight back the tears, he allowed them to build up until the first drops landed on the keyboard. He took a long, deep breath and allowed himself to be filled with joy while at the same time wondering why he'd taken so long to take that one simple step, one he could have done any time he chose. But he'd never dared look into the process before, let alone take action. He recalled with vivid clarity how his inauthentic awareness, invulnerability and lack of courage and confidence had led him to devise every excuse under the sun to avoid setting the wheels of his entrepreneurial journey in motion.

He was so consumed by his thoughts and emotions that he didn't hear Mel enter the room. She'd been at the gym and looked fresh and youthful in her activewear, her face devoid of make-up, her long, dark hair swept up in a high ponytail. She smiled broadly as she approached him with a mug of steaming hot coffee in each hand. He quickly pulled himself together, turning his face away slightly as he wiped his eyes with his shirt sleeve in a childlike manner.

'How was this morning's session with Grace, my love?' asked Mel, handing him a coffee and taking a sip from hers.

'It went really well. I'm actually feeling so good that it's almost like the fog has lifted and I'm seeing clearly for the very first time. I haven't experienced this level of joy and satisfaction in a long time.'

Mel's smile as she looked into his eyes was so serene and beautiful that he could feel the tears of happiness begin to build again. She could see he'd been crying from the moment she entered the room, but she chose not to question him on it as his demeanour suggested they weren't tears of sadness. Touching him on the arm, she gently wiped a stray tear with her free hand. She sensed an air of vulnerability in him that she'd never felt before.

'Tell me about it, Yoren,' she suggested quietly.

Clearing his throat, he drew her closer toward him and turned to face her. Taking her hands in his, he said excitedly, 'Guess what; I've just registered the company. It's called KeyTech International. What do you think? Do you like the name?'

'Wow, great! Hmm, it's an interesting option. Well done on taking this first step, Yoren! I'm so happy for you. I know how much this business means to you.'

Mel was about to suggest they toss around some alternatives as she'd come up with some ideas of her own, but held back as she didn't want to spoil the moment. His childlike enthusiasm was infectious. The difference she could see in her fiancé was beyond her expectations. She realised that the little spark of hope she'd been patiently holding onto for some time was finally being ignited.

Time seemed to stand still as they sat on the sofa and chatted animatedly. They talked about shared memories, from how they met to the places they'd explored in their travels and where they wanted to go next. They enthusiastically discussed what this company could mean for their future together and dreamed of a more prosperous life full of new opportunities. Mel had never seen Yoren so animated in a discussion before and relished every moment.

Looking at Yoren wistfully, Mel whispered, 'Imagine what our kids will be like.'

With the smile still fixed firmly on his face, Yoren felt the familiar fear and anxiety rising at the thought of starting a family. It wasn't that he didn't want to have children with Mel; he just hadn't expected the subject to come up so soon. The uncertainty around prioritising everything now that he was making serious plans to leave his job and focus on the business made him feel a little overwhelmed. Interestingly though, he was nowhere near as fearful and anxious as he used to be about the possibility of becoming a father. Even the fact that Mel mentioned 'kids', suggesting more than one child, wasn't freaking him out like it would have not long ago. The relative comfort he now felt around the idea of building a family with kids in the equation was unfamiliar. At that moment, he realised he no longer related to himself and his life with Mel in the way he used to.

It really does feel like I'm undergoing some kind of transformation, just as Grace said I would. I'm somehow different, not only in myself but also with Mel.

Observing Yoren's momentary mood change, Mel gave him space to be with his thoughts but remained close by his side in comfortable silence. She was present to the changes in him and incredibly proud of how far he'd come. He had just dared to take the first step in creating the company he'd always wanted; he was being receptive to what she had to communicate without attempting to avoid it; he was being expressive, even showing his emotions. The 'old Yoren' would never have allowed her to see him cry, so that alone was remarkable.

Yoren was silent for a few minutes before carrying on the conversation where they'd left off, even joking about their future children and who they might take after. Once the banter and laughter had settled, he expressed that, despite feeling out of his comfort zone, he now felt free and empowered to be with this discomfort and encouraged her to raise the subject of starting a family with him whenever she wanted to.

The changes in Yoren had an immediate impact on Mel too. She felt comfortable being more open and expressive with him and could feel the authentic and vulnerable atmosphere in the room. They were so intimately engaged in their conversation that neither noticed more than three hours had passed. It was the longest time they'd spent together without any external distractions since when they were first dating. Swept up in the mood and overcome by his love for the woman beside him, Yoren felt like he was seeing her for the first time. The sunset to the west cast a golden glow over the ocean, enveloping Mel in a halo of light through the window. She'd never looked more beautiful. He gently cupped her face in his hands and kissed her passionately. Locked in his embrace, she led him to the bedroom.

It was the most incredible night of Yoren's life. The evening had quickly turned to night, and they eventually fell asleep in each other's arms. Waking at five, Yoren had a strong sense that nothing could ever surpass the rapture of this awakening. He left the bed quietly and padded towards the window. It was still dark, but the light cast from the setting moon gave the ocean an ethereal glow and made the swell lines appear to dance. He opened the large sliding window. A gust of wind extinguished the candle still burning on the nightstand and filled his nostrils with a scent so fresh and sweet he could almost taste it. He turned back to look at Mel, still sleeping peacefully, and, at that moment, saw all the beauty in the world embodied in a single human form.

How could I have been so blind to all these blessings in my life?

Mel half opened her eyes in slumber, and the smile on her face made it look to Yoren like she'd been granted a glimpse of Heaven. Looking back towards the window, the first signs of dawn appeared on the horizon, and the changing colours in the sky were captivating.

— ▪ —

Driving to Grace's the following week for his coaching session, Yoren paid close attention to how he was feeling. He was present to a heightened sense of anxiety, but struggled to discern if it was due to nervousness or excitement, which might suggest a relatively healthy relationship with the Mood. He knew one thing: he couldn't wait to tell her he'd finally registered his company. Noticing his stomach rumbling, he remembered he hadn't eaten breakfast and pulled into a drive-through to order a coffee and savoury muffin. Used to healthier choices, he knew there was nothing else on the way, so he happily tucked in without guilt while driving, listening to classical music to clear his mind in readiness for the session.

'Hi Yoren, how are you?' asked Grace once they were seated.

After four months of weekly coaching, he was well and truly accustomed to Grace expecting a genuine, authentic and thoughtful response. So he did his best to express himself openly, focusing mainly on his emotions and Moods.

'I'm feeling joyful, caring, enthusiastic, vulnerable and open, hopeful and even a little anxious, but in an excited way.' The adjectives poured out of him.

'That's great, Yoren! Tell me more about why you're feeling this way. What else do you feel like expressing?'

'Well, for starters, I finally registered my company after last week's session. I did it as soon as I got home. Not only that, Grace, but Mel and I have been getting on better than ever; not that we didn't get along before, but it's like I'm finally seeing and appreciating her for who she really is. I think a lot of that has to do with me changing from who I was before starting this journey with you. I can feel that some radical transformation is happening. I can't quite articulate it, but it's like I can no longer relate to the person I used to be. I'm more open, vulnerable, confident and courageous. I can be with uncertainty. Not only have I taken the first step of my business journey, but I've also discussed the future with Mel.'

Grace sat back and smiled, listening attentively as Yoren continued.

'The conversations we've had this past week were on the big topics I used to do my best to avoid, like starting a family. The 'old me' would've freaked out discussing the idea of quitting my job and closing the door on my reliable income so that I could focus on building the business, all while planning our wedding and considering kids in the mix. Doing all of this simultaneously seems crazy and illogical. Still, while being somewhat nervous and anxious about dealing with all the what-ifs, I find I'm more at ease with them now,' he laughed. 'At least I think I can be with them on an intellectual level, which I guess is a good start!'

'Welcome to the club, Yoren,' replied Grace with a laugh. 'That's how it is for anyone working towards creating something extraordinary, so you'd better get used to it.'

Yoren suddenly went quiet and looked down as the significance of how far he'd come hit home. Observing his emotional state, Grace nudged the box of tissues on the coffee table towards him.

'Would you like to share with me what's on your mind now, Yoren?' she probed gently.

He took a sip of water and cleared his throat. 'Mel and I were intimate for the first time in ages. It happened after I registered the company and a long conversation we shared. As I sit here and reflect on that now, I can't believe how blind I was to many of the blessings in my life. Just having Mel in my life is a massive blessing in itself. But I'm ashamed to admit that I took her presence for granted for a long time. I was so obsessed with my own thoughts that I couldn't – or perhaps wouldn't – share them with her. It felt good to finally open up and let her in.'

He paused to collect his thoughts before continuing, 'You know, now that I'm sharing all this with you, Grace, I think I might chat with her again later today and ask her to tell me how she's feeling. I genuinely want to hear her concerns, uncertainties and fears. I don't want her to hold anything back.'

'This is so great, Yoren. You cannot imagine how happy I am for you. I'm sure you've been experiencing rounds of transformations. And, as someone who's conducted thousands of hours of coaching, I know how significant these experiences are for everyone who goes through them. They're vital in building thriving relationships and have a huge impact on one's overall quality of life, far beyond materialistic accomplishments. I'm really proud of you.'

'Thanks, Grace, that means a lot.' Yoren was visibly chuffed.

Ironically, now that Yoren was present to the importance of open communication, he suddenly expected Mel to express herself openly with him too. And yet that's precisely what she'd wanted for so long: to feel free to open up to him and for him to do the same with her. His heightened awareness of how challenging it is to be with someone who doesn't express themselves openly made him feel compassion towards his fiancé for what she'd put up with for so long.

Grace leaned forward in her seat and her tone became more assertive, signalling it was time to move on. 'Okay. Let's establish our contract for today's session and set the trajectory for the next few sessions after this one. Are you happy to do that now, Yoren?'

'Sure am.'

'Now, I can see that you're being more present in your relationship with Mel and attentive to her needs, and that's great,' said Grace. 'However, when we look into your profile, we can see that you don't relate well to several qualities that typically play major roles in our relationships. In addition to your relationship with Mel, family members, friends and the people you work with, your entrepreneurial journey will require you to build effective relationships with others, including clients, staff and so on. You might build commercial partnerships, work with suppliers and contractors, and you'll want to turn your one-off customers into delighted long-term clients. You might also decide to partner with others who could end up being part of your co-founding team. And, down the track, you might need investors and a board of directors if you grow the company to that level. Essentially, building a company requires stakeholders beyond yourself. Can you see that, Yoren?'

Yoren listened attentively and with an open mind, but he didn't answer Grace's question immediately. While everything she said seemed obvious at face value, he realised he wasn't necessarily seeing things from the same perspective. It was as if she and the profile were suggesting he was more focused on what was in it for him now and in the immediate future rather than thinking about the bigger picture. He grappled with the idea that this had been reflected in the health of his relationship with higher purpose.

Finally breaking the silence, he said, 'You're right, Grace. I wouldn't have viewed relationships this way before my recent experiences with Mel. But I can definitely resonate with this now. When I realised how much I'd been neglecting Mel, I found it hard to accept. Neglecting her wasn't a conscious choice. I was so caught up in my own world that I failed to consider how everything we were going through might have been occurring to her. I now see how self-absorbed I was – and still am to a degree – and how I often isolate myself. And to be honest, I find that a bit scary because I can see how inauthentic it is to even think I don't need relationships with others. What a fool I've been!'

Grace sat back, giving Yoren the freedom he needed to open up. As a coach, she knew his vulnerability and openness were vital to his transformation, so she let him express all that he needed to communicate.

When she was sure he was finished, Grace asked, 'Now that you're so present to what's missing and what's shifting in your relationships, what would you like to work on next, Yoren?'

'I'd like us to spend the next few sessions focusing on the qualities around relationship-building,' he replied.

'Okay, let's have a go at mapping out the sub-model around relationships together. As you might have noticed last time, my drawing skills leave a lot to be desired!' she laughed as she picked up her pen and started drawing on a blank sheet of paper. 'Let's put 'relationships' in the centre as that'll set the trajectory for our next few sessions together. Would you like to have a go at suggesting what to put next?'

Rather than be assertive and tell Grace he'd prefer her to create the sub-model for him as he was unclear on the qualities to add, he nodded and appeared deep in thought. Realising he was unsure, Grace tentatively added self-expression and contribution to the page.

'In the context of relationships, I propose coaching on self-expression, your unique being and your contribution to the world, which in your case and within the context of this coaching journey, is through the vehicle of entrepreneurship,' she replied.

'I'm a bit confused on this one, Grace. Could you please clarify what self-expression has to do with relationships?' Yoren looked puzzled.

'I'm suggesting self-expression because unless you can be with yourself, it's virtually impossible to be with others. We'll explore this Primary Way of Being in detail in an upcoming session. We'll also explore some of the Aspects of Being that contribute to your ability to build healthy and sustainable relationships with others, starting with Mel. After all, you mentioned before that you'll have little hope of building a successful business unless your future wife's on board!' laughed Grace. 'Then we could also explore the potential for you to need business partners and how to approach that from a being perspective.'

Grace added empowerment to the sub-model. Noticing he looked confused, she explained that although they'd explored empowerment in their last session, it would be useful to recontextualise it from the perspective of relationships. Satisfied with her suggestions and clarification, Yoren nodded his approval enthusiastically.

Suddenly enlightened about the connection with relationships, Yoren came up with a few of his own suggestions. Through discussion, they decided to add higher purpose, presence, partnership, accountability, care, commitment and awareness to the page. Although they'd also explored awareness before, Yoren agreed that it would be good to consider it in this context.

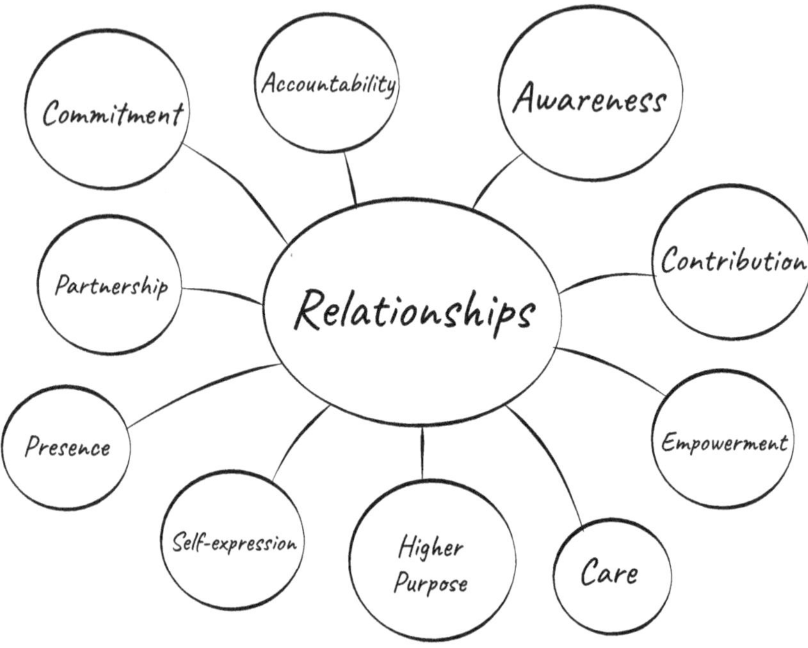

They created a plan for the next six sessions, including the rest of the current session. As always, Grace assured Yoren he could always change the flow as they went, as these were his coaching sessions and he was in charge of the direction, albeit with her professional guidance and support.

Grace refilled their glasses from the beautiful crystal decanter on the table and took a long sip. Lowering her glass onto an elegant coaster, she looked Yoren in the eye and asked, 'Are you empowered, Yoren?'

Clearly caught off guard by the question, he replied, 'What do you mean?'

Referring to the framework's distinction for empowerment, she invited Yoren to read the first paragraph aloud.

'Empowerment is living life from the viewpoint of being able to fulfil your intentions while enabling and inspiring others to fulfil theirs.

Empowerment is how you relate to your power, capabilities and real or perceived limitations,' he read.

'Considering this passage in the context of your relationships with others, would you say you're empowered, Yoren?'

'I'd say sometimes,' he responded.

'Great! Can you see how we're now looking into empowerment in a different context and perspective from the one we considered in our last session?'

'Yes, I'm starting to see that,' said Yoren, silently re-reading the paragraph.

'In the context of relationships, I'd like you to consider the importance of being receptive to other people contributing to your empowerment,' said Grace.

'I'm a bit confused. I understood empowerment to be a quality that comes from within or the quality that enables me to contribute to the empowerment of others,' said Yoren.

'You're correct to a certain degree, Yoren. However, empowerment isn't just an individual matter. You're not just empowered to fulfil your intentions and support others in fulfilling theirs; it also relates to how receptive you are to having other people contribute to your empowerment. Does that make it clearer for you?'

'Yes, I can see it from that perspective now,' said Yoren. 'One observation, though. Although we haven't explored contribution yet, looking at empowerment from this perspective and in the context of relationships makes it seem very similar to contribution as a way of being, at least how I imagine it to be.'

'That's a great observation, Yoren. You're right; the same is true with contribution as a way of being. Let's read the contribution distinction together,' Grace said as she pulled it up on her laptop.

Contribution

Contribution is when you are available to support and compelled to be of service to others to achieve what they are committed to and are also willingly available for others to support and serve you. It is an outward manifestation and expression of your care for others and humanity.

A healthy relationship with *contribution* indicates that you mostly experience being compelled to make a difference to other people and are open, receptive and comfortable in allowing others to make a difference to you. You experience satisfaction and fulfilment from being a contribution as well as being contributed to. Others may experience you as being intentionally supportive of them and what they are committed to.

An unhealthy relationship with *contribution* indicates that you mainly deal with challenges and breakdowns on your own. Others may experience you as unreceptive, disinterested or unavailable for support. You may lack the willingness to participate and add value to others, particularly if you know there is no immediate benefit for you. Your sphere of influence and impact on the world often occurs as narrow and limited. You may experience being unappreciated or consider that what you have to offer is of little value. You may also be resigned and cynical towards other people and question their motives. Alternatively, you may interfere instead of influence and give advice when it is neither asked for nor required. You may also pester others for help without due consideration of the impact on them.

Yoren listened attentively as Grace read the first paragraph aloud. He was intrigued to learn that some ways of being – like contribution – could have a two-way relationship.

'How does this land for you, Yoren?'

'It makes so much sense. I've always maintained that I'm here to contribute and to be empowered. But I never thought about being receptive to other people's contributions and support in empowering me! Before having this conversation with you, I considered it a weakness to rely on the contribution of others. As an independent, self-made man, I've always believed that a strong person doesn't need anyone's support. I didn't even feel good about my father contributing to me. I wanted to show him that I could be self-sufficient.'

'Great, Yoren. Can you tell me if anyone other than you has contributed to your growth?' asked Grace.

'Well, for the most part, I've created my own success and prosperity. Even back when I was at uni, and most of my friends and fellow students were partying and having fun, I chose to knuckle down and study without any prompting from anyone, even my parents. That decision got me to where I am today. And now, as you can see, I'm taking my success to the next level.'

Forgetting that Grace could see through his momentary lapse into invulnerability, Yoren continued to state his case, raising many more concrete examples and over-exaggerating some of his accomplishments and stories from the past in an effort to save face and demonstrate his independence. He was so accustomed to feeling the need to prove himself to others that he kept going until Grace politely but assertively interrupted him.

'I understand and appreciate the pride you must feel in all you've achieved, Yoren, but you didn't answer my question. I asked if you think anyone other than you has contributed to your growth.'

By Yoren's body language, Grace could see he was triggered and defensive. She waited silently for his next move. Rather than defend himself, he took a deep breath, emptied the contents of his glass in one gulp – spilling a few drops of water on his shirt – and settled back into a more relaxed posture. The entire execution led Grace to see the vulnerability-contribution and vulnerability-empowerment relationships of Yoren's being with razor-sharp clarity. She took some notes. She also realised that one more Aspect of Being needed to be added to the sub-model: gratitude. Rather than adding it now, though, she took note of it as a reminder to raise it with him later and gain his agreement.

They continued to focus on coaching around empowerment and contribution in the context of relationships, particularly Yoren's availability to being contributed to and empowered by others. Grace also referred to some case studies that demonstrated how the world's most visionary and top-performing leaders and entrepreneurs tap into other people's resources, including skills, labour and other outputs to grow their organisations. In this way they generate wealth for many of their employees by creating new jobs and opportunities that didn't exist before, as well as creating profits for their shareholders, business partners and themselves. She acknowledged that this could be misinterpreted as exploitation by some; however, in reality, all they're doing is leveraging their efforts to shift economic resources from areas of lower productivity to areas of higher productivity and yield, which is the very definition of entrepreneurship as coined by Jean-Baptiste Say. Grace also acknowledged that people who don't have a healthy relationship with contribution might not utilise other people's resources with integrity, which is when the shadow can manifest as exploitation.

'In addition to not shying away from asking others for support and contribution, top-performing entrepreneurs actively seek to create opportunities to leverage other people's resources, using the talents and skills of employees, contractors, consultants and so on,' said Grace. 'They hire or engage intelligent and talented people, not to tell them what to do, but to ask them what needs to be done to fulfil their organisation's objectives and vision. For example, they might get investors on board to inject capital into the business or seek the contribution of an advisory board to help them actualise their intentions. When leaders empower their people, they enable them to be creative, think for themselves, collaborate with their peers and, ultimately, fulfil the organisation's mission. Any visionary person who is up to big causes needs alliances with others. So can you see how empowerment is a two-way street, Yoren?' she asked.

'Yes, I can, Grace. I just haven't looked at it from that perspective before.'

Although, as a small business owner and leadership coach, Grace didn't have much experience in entrepreneurship and startups herself, she was able to paint a relatively clear picture for Yoren around empowerment and contribution. She'd completed a few courses while building her coaching business, had been supported by business coaches on various projects, and continued to work with mentors and advisors. Furthermore, her extensive experience in coaching executives, startup founders and SMEs, particularly on people and culture-related matters, had fuelled her belief that leaders are responsible for building and nurturing the culture within their organisations and for supporting and empowering their people. Ultimately, she knew that inspiring and effective leaders prioritise the development of their people. Consequently, their people are more inclined to willingly contribute to the organisation's growth.

'As you know, Yoren, this isn't business coaching or advice,' said Grace. 'I'm not qualified to do that, and I'm more than happy to refer you to an appropriate business coach if you're interested. But in the context of this conversation on contribution, consider that you'll need the contribution of many people, just as there are many ways in which you'll be contributing to others as you grow your business.'

'Sure, I'm aware this isn't business coaching or advice, Grace. But I value your contribution so I'm interested to hear more about this, just in terms of the Aspects of Being we're exploring today,' said Yoren.

'Okay, let's consider a high-level example to make it clear why contribution matters so much in business and the economy. Consider that all startup founders need to find a market: a group of people with a burning pain to solve. They also need to create job opportunities so they can shape a team to support them. These opportunities become their contribution to their employees, and then together, they can build products and services to serve their identified customers and resolve their burning pain. The products and services they produce are their contributions to those customers, and the customers' willingness to exchange money for those offerings are their contributions to the startup. Remembering that this is very high-level, how is this landing for you, Yoren?' she asked.

'Your explanation really clarifies how contribution is a two-way street in business. Would you mind if I have a go at giving you an example?' asked Yoren.

'Sure, go ahead.'

'Let's say I take on investors and shareholders down the track. Then, as managing director, it would be my responsibility to contribute to them by ensuring the company is profitable. That way, they'll not only recover the initial investment they made as a contribution to my company, but they'll also receive dividends as my company's contribution to them. Then the other directors and I can take our slice of the pie, which would be the company's financial contribution to us.'

'Excellent, Yoren! And consider that beyond all the materialistic parts, you can't ignore the meaning and satisfaction every person involved will gain from all these exchanges of service and contributions. In short, entrepreneurs create the vision, align people and build teams. They shift economic resources and their team's talents and labour from areas of lower productivity to areas of higher productivity and yield. They create synergy, and that synergy consists of many people's contributions. Then, when customers exchange their money for the product or service delivered by the organisation, it generates revenue. That revenue is used to contribute towards paying the employees and company debtors. And if all of this is done effectively and with authentic awareness, it might generate surplus value or profit, which may be issued to shareholders as dividends.

'Let's take this a step further. Suppose you consider money as the medium of exchange for the value created and delivered, and revenue generation as the outcome. In that case, if you were to focus merely on the accumulation of money instead of giving first, you would technically be expecting the results of something that hasn't been created and delivered yet. Generally speaking, this chain of contribution makes money flow through the economy and contributes to a healthy and thriving economy. Can you see now how contribution and empowerment go both ways, Yoren?'

'Yes, that all makes sense. Wow, this is great, Grace! It puts a whole new spin on business ownership. I've always imagined a business where I could contribute to others, not just with a product or service but in so many other ways. It's all about contribution, not just in business but far beyond that. Businesses contribute to the growth of the economy. Employers contribute by creating jobs and paying wages. Employees contribute their skills, knowledge, experience and labour to the organisations that employ them. Entrepreneurs contribute by creating opportunities for investors and shareholders and they, in turn, contribute to the company with their injection of capital. Then the company contributes to the shareholders through dividends. And let's not forget how businesses contribute to the consumers they serve by fulfilling their needs while the consumers contribute by voluntarily exchanging their money for the business's products or services. And in doing so, they're contributing to the business's survival and growth. It really is all about contribution!'

They continued their conversation, and Grace asked Yoren several questions and encouraged him to keep checking the validity and authenticity of his earlier statements about the lack of contribution he receives from others. They agreed that he should use the conception worksheet to work on contribution and empowerment during the week and continue journaling his Moods. Just before the end of the session, Grace looked down at her notes and was prompted to bring up gratitude and its connection to everything they'd discussed. They read through the gratitude distinction together, and Grace suggested they add it to the sub-model and explore it further in their next session. Although hesitant at first, since he saw gratitude as 'just a soft skill', Yoren could see the relevance to his intention and life in general after reading through the distinction and was on board with the decision.

On his way home, Yoren was deep in thought. He realised how inauthentic his perception of contribution had been. It opened his eyes to all the tremendous contributions made to him by so many, including his grandparents, parents, Jen, Mel, his close friends, and particularly Dylan, a friend from high school who'd suggested he apply for his current role. Thinking about Dylan brought back memories of how much his friend's emotional support and presence had helped him during some of the most challenging and confronting times in his life. Knowing Dylan was always there for him, whether to listen or contribute with an idea or a solution, had made facing difficulties much easier. He made a mental note to get in touch with him and arrange a get-together. It had been way too long between catch-ups.

As he drove, Yoren also thought about the tremendous opportunities afforded him by his family's sacrifices when they migrated from their homeland to a foreign country on the other side of the world. He considered the contributions made by his teachers, university lecturers and tutors, some of his ex-bosses and other senior members in his field and how they'd all supported him to become the person he was today. As he paid attention to his surroundings, he even thought about the contribution from a societal perspective and how all the infrastructure he took advantage of today was contributed by others. It made him see and appreciate the bridges, buildings, the car he was driving and even the tolls he paid in a new light.

He decided to pull over and write down all the contributions he'd previously taken for granted and was suddenly aware of on the conception worksheet. Now that he was seeing reality through a different lens, the worksheet exercises had become habitual and were no longer a chore. What he didn't realise was that his conscious awareness and appreciation of all those contributions also conveyed his developing relationship with gratitude, particularly considering someone with a healthy relationship with this way of being clearly sees and appreciates the blessings in life, even when circumstances may suggest otherwise, and doesn't take things for granted.

Arriving back home, he took a shower and put on his favourite cologne, a high-end brand he normally reserved for meetings and outings with others when he wanted to make a good impression. He couldn't wait to see Mel and continue their conversation about their future plans, hopes and dreams. But at the same time, he felt extremely nervous about opening up to her completely. He wasn't sure if he was ready to be totally vulnerable with her about all the thoughts and feelings spinning around inside his head, especially his doubts and fears.

What if I'm wrong? What if building this business is beyond my capabilities? What would Mel think of me then?

So many what-ifs. So much hesitation, doubt and wavering. He decided to keep that part of the conversation to himself that night, in so doing, suppressing his expression of self. He wanted to be crystal clear and very confident about the next steps before sharing them with Mel.

CHAPTER 11

A Drop in the Ocean

Sitting in Grace's office for the next session, Yoren expressed how quickly the week had flown by, as he'd been extremely busy at work. However, he no longer used being busy as an excuse not to complete his challenges for the week. They went through Yoren's conception worksheets and journal together and Grace addressed Yoren's questions. She was pleased when he suggested that his work on contribution would be a great way to transition into gratitude.

It quickly became apparent to both Grace and Yoren that they didn't need to spend much time on gratitude as a way of being. It was clear from the work Yoren had already done that he'd developed a reasonable conception of this quality and its link to contribution, especially when it came to his relationship and being contributed to. Grace acknowledged his work on gratitude and challenged him on some minor areas with a few deep, open-ended questions. She made a note to add a gratitude challenge to his other tasks for the week. Thinking that now would be the perfect time to focus on self-expression, particularly in the context of relationships, Yoren suggested they explore this Primary Way of Being in today's session.

'Self-expression is a great idea, Yoren. I'm delighted you suggested it because it's impossible for any of us to be with others, to be in partnerships and be a contribution and available for others' contributions unless we can first be with ourselves,' said Grace.

'What do you mean by "be with ourselves", Grace, and how does that relate to me? I'm pretty sure I know who I am, and I'm definitely confident in my own skin and comfortable in my own company,' he said, his voice dripping with sarcasm.

He leaned back in his seat, arms crossed, but suddenly realised he had overreacted, noticing his invulnerability and inauthenticity. He relaxed his posture but remained silent.

'Allow me to explain, Yoren. Being with oneself requires authentic and vulnerable awareness. Remember when we talked about the exposure triangle early on in your coaching, the model that centres on awareness, vulnerability and authenticity?'

'Yes, sure, the one using the camera analogy,' he replied.

'That's the one. Well, when it comes to self-expression, the subject being studied and around which we're intentionally gaining awareness is the self. And by self, I mean how each of us is being in relation to the qualities we share as human beings and also who each of us is as a unique being: a one-of-a-kind person who, deep down, is primed and ready to be self-expressed.'

'Aren't we self-expressed every time we voice an opinion, Grace?'

'That's a good question, Yoren. You see, there's a distinct difference between merely expressing oneself and being self-expressed. We're always expressing something, whether or not we're conscious of it. But self-expression is being intentional and authentic around what you're expressing and also how you're expressing it. When you're clear on what you are as a human being and how you, as an individual, relate to your human qualities, then having authentic awareness around the what and the how allows you to polish your relationships with those human qualities. This will support you to gradually discover who you are: your distinct self or unique being. And once you know who you are deep down, you can express yourself authentically to the world.

That's what we call being self-expressed.'

'Could you explain what you mean by "distinct self" in a bit more detail, Grace?' asked Yoren.

'Sure,' Grace responded. 'Simply put, your distinct self is who you are deep down, far beyond your surface-level qualities. It's the essence of you or your calling, the thing that lies dormant until you discover it, tap into it and project it to the world as your unique contribution. For many people, this unique contribution is what gives their life meaning and purpose. Consider that unless you're clear on your distinct self, you can't position yourself appropriately on the canvas of existence. Not knowing our place in the world or confusion around the self is perhaps the number one challenge people face in life. Some people go through their entire lives not knowing. Others spend their lives ignoring or neglecting reality. Those who, for whatever reason, don't want to become present to who they are deep down live life in frequent confusion, like particles floating in orbit. If you're unclear on your distinct self, you risk never discovering your unique being, the most precious asset you have.'

'So would you say this is the greatest loss of all, not only personally, but also for all those who end up missing out on our unique contribution?' asked Yoren.

'Absolutely! Imagine if your unique potential remained unexpressed and unfulfilled. Imagine a world without the contribution of the most accomplished scientists, doctors and researchers, the great poets, writers, thinkers, artists, chefs, musicians, entrepreneurs, architects, sportspeople and so on. A world void of our contributions because we fail to express our distinct self would be an emptier world. We can only expand the reality out there – just as the greats throughout history have done – when we're present to reality and then harmoniously express ourselves as part of that reality. In your case, you've chosen the vehicle of entrepreneurship and business as the primary channel to express yourself.'

Throughout the session, Grace skillfully guided the flow of questions, encouraging Yoren to look deeper, reflect and then share his thoughts. When Yoren queried how people could express themselves at all without fully understanding their unique being, she invited him to notice that while many people who are considered expressive communicate all kinds of things, self-expression requires a person to be in a state of surrender. She added that a state of surrender cannot be achieved unless they choose authentic awareness as their ontological perspective in life – ontology being whatever constitutes reality and truth to them – and epistemological approach, which is the way they choose to examine reality.

'Thanks, Grace. I can see how the framework we've been using helps here because of how it breaks down the reality of human beings into a series of relatable qualities. I think I can see a link with authenticity here, too,' said Yoren.

'You're right, Yoren. Self-expression is directly linked to authenticity. Imagine you've created a fake persona and are projecting it to others, which is inauthentic. If you attempt to polish that fabricated persona, it might still shine, but the shine won't come from within if it isn't aligned with who you are meant to be: if it's not consistent with your unique being. How is this landing for you so far, Yoren?'

He looked thoughtful as he reflected further on the link between self-expression and authenticity.

'Let me see if I'm understanding it correctly,' he said. 'So, what you're saying about a fake persona is that no matter how much you polish it, it won't come from within and it's still fake. The bling might look mesmerising to others; it might even attract them like a fake diamond, but that doesn't make it a real diamond. So by polishing something, you might give it the 'bling factor', but it's not a reflection of reality. For us humans, polishing a fake persona is all about the appearance on the surface, not who we really are. It's what many of the influencers on social media seem to do.'

'Spot on, Yoren. Even though polishing the facade and the pretence that goes with it might deceive some people, it won't have much impact on the reality of who you are as an individual human being. Unfortunately, many people don't want to face the reality of who they are deep down, and there could be various reasons for that. They might have a desire to fit in; they might want to avoid upsetting someone or keep the peace, and so on. No matter how effective your pretence might be, it will never change anything inside of you. Focusing on polishing the facade and neglecting the unique being within is like building a house without a solid foundation,' offered Grace.

'I can see how your explanation highlights the importance of authenticity in self-expression, Grace,' said Yoren. 'I can also see that it's not just about being self-expressed. It's also about knowing what we are being as humans, who we are being in relation to that awareness and how we express ourselves. Would you say that's just as important?'

'Yes, absolutely.' Grace smiled as she observed Yoren's deepening interest in and understanding of the topics they were exploring.

He mirrored her smile as he saw the similarities between today's coaching conversation and his discussion with Jen about the projection process. He recalled how she'd explained that every human being constantly projects themselves to the world, like a drop of water into the ocean of existence, and how this creates a ripple effect.

'Can we look at the distinction of self-expression together, just to confirm I'm understanding it correctly?' he asked.

'Sure. I was actually about to pull it up,' she replied, opening her laptop.

Self-expression

Self-expression is when you intentionally and authentically communicate who you are and how you are, including (but not limited to) your points of view, beliefs, values, feelings, emotions, moods and experiences. You may express yourself freely and creatively in many ways: through your work, speech, body language, facial expressions, music and other creative arts or ways. It is the state of being uninhibited and resonating with life and everything in it and may evolve to become your unique contribution to humanity.

A healthy relationship with *self-expression* indicates that you mostly experience being free to project yourself in various ways with others, regardless of circumstances, leading to satisfaction, joy and fulfilment. You are self-expressed when you unleash your qualities to be seen, heard and appreciated.

An unhealthy relationship with *self-expression* indicates that you may frequently experience being suppressed, restricted and constrained in how you interact with others, commonly leading to a lack of both fulfilment and satisfaction. Others may experience you as inhibited, quiet, reserved or shy in different circumstances or to have hidden or rarely seen talents and qualities. You may hide your passions or interests from others for fear of judgement or ridicule. Alternatively, you may have few filters and be considered blunt or overbearing. You may disproportionately value your contribution and feel the need to outshine others. You may also be uncomfortable with silence or not being the centre of attention.

Yoren read it aloud and paused thoughtfully.

'What are you present to, Yoren?'

'There are a few parts that particularly resonated with me. For example, I can relate to sometimes being suppressed, restricted and constrained in my interactions with others. I also resonate with the part about hiding my passions or interests from others for fear of judgement or ridicule. And if I'm being truly vulnerable, I would say there are also times when I might disproportionately value my contribution and feel the need to outshine others.' He grinned self-consciously.

'Great! And thank you for your vulnerability. So how would you link this to your intention of building your own business?'

Yoren looked down, deep in thought. His mind was such a whirl of thoughts and emotions that he didn't realise Grace had asked a question. Snapping himself back into the present moment, he said, 'Sorry, Grace. Could you repeat the question, please?'

'Sure. How would you link your self-expression with your intention of building your business?'

'I can now see that it's possible to integrate my passion and life outside of work with what I do for a job. But until now, I had seen them as being two separate things,' he responded.

'Yes, many people believe that passion is one thing and work is another. They believe that integrating the two is either unrealistic or unfeasible,' said Grace. 'What else is coming up for you? For instance, how do you think your expression of self channels itself apart from the fundamental ways like speech, body language and facial expression?'

'I can clearly link my self-expression and how I relate to it with my career,' said Yoren. 'I can see my career – or my future business-building journey, to be more precise – as a vehicle for making my unique contribution to the world.'

'Okay, and what do you think are some of the major by-products of that unique contribution for you?' asked Grace.

'A sense of meaning and satisfaction is the first thing that comes to mind. If I don't consider what I do for work just as a means of making money and managing the impression I have on others, but genuinely integrate it with what I have to offer and what I truly care about, it makes a huge difference.'

'Great, Yoren! Can you see how self-expression connects with contribution?'

'Yes, I think I'm starting to see the connection,' he replied.

They continued discussing the relationship between self-expression and contribution for several minutes, and Grace listened as Yoren linked it to his intention of starting his business.

When Yoren had finished expressing himself and they'd covered the topic thoroughly, Grace asked, 'Would you like me to show you another model that might support you to clarify this further? It's called the contribution quadrant.'

Yoren nodded his agreement as he found that diagrams and models often supported his understanding of concepts. Grace pulled it up on her screen.

Care about AND Effective at	Don't care about BUT Effective at
Care about BUT Not effective at (yet)	Don't care about AND Not effective at

'The contribution quadrant highlights the four ways we can all choose to contribute in life,' said Grace. 'On one side of the model, we can see that someone might engage in an endeavour they care about and are already effective at, or they might actively engage in something they care about but are not yet effective at. The other side of the model highlights how someone might engage in an endeavour they don't care about but are effective at, or they might engage in something they neither care about nor are effective at. Can you see where your intention to start a business from the point of view of contribution lies in this quadrant, Yoren?'

'Well, it's something I really care about, but I know I've got a lot to learn before I can become effective at it. So I'd say it sits in the second quadrant: care about but not effective at (yet),' he replied.

'Yes, I agree with you,' said Grace. 'Those who sit in the third and fourth quadrants are people who would generally refer to what they do as a 'job', while those who sit in the first two quadrants would have a career, meaning they're typically pursuing their endeavour long term and not just to put food on the table and pay the bills. Any questions?'

'No, that's clear,' said Yoren. 'So if someone intends to contribute in the most effective way they can, they would pursue a career and aim to engage in something they care about and are either already effective at or are willing to put in the effort to become effective at it, correct?'

'Yes,' said Grace. 'This is where someone can maximise their potential to contribute their skills and knowledge in the most effective way possible, Yoren. And if they also manage to tap into their unique being and focus on what they both care about and are effective at, their contribution might be a first of its kind, or at least rare. That scarcity makes them less replaceable and increases the value of their contribution in the market, to an organisation or a relationship, and life in general.'

Grace paused to allow her explanation to sink in.

After reflecting for a few minutes, Yoren said, 'Okay. So in planning my business, the most powerful way to contribute and express my unique being to the world is to shape my business and offering around the areas I care most about. Is that what you're saying, Grace?'

'That's right, Yoren. And then, ideally, you'd align yourself with others, from business partners to employees, who also care deeply about the business and its offering. That way, even if they're not yet effective at what they're doing, they'll be eager to learn and develop the skills to get there and become valuable contributors.'

After further animated discussion about the relationships between care, contribution and self-expression, Grace wrapped up the session. Before Yoren left, she gave him his challenges for the week, which were centred on self-expression and included an exercise on gratitude. He left feeling thoughtful but positive. The pieces of the puzzle were all coming together.

— ∎ —

Instead of driving home after the coaching session, Yoren headed towards the golf club where he was a member to have lunch with his close friend and former work colleague, Dylan. It was a cold, rainy day, but nothing could dampen Yoren's spirits. He was excited to see his friend and tell him what he'd been up to. It'd been several months since either of them had been there. Under normal circumstances, they would catch up regularly, usually for a round of golf followed by lunch or a few drinks. But both had been so busy in recent months, Yoren with his coaching commitments and Dylan with job hunting, that time had gotten away from them. After resigning from the firm a few months ago, Dylan had been actively looking for the right job opportunity.

The two friends embraced warmly before sitting at a table by the window overlooking the ninth hole. Over lunch, Yoren shared what he was going through in the coaching process and how impactful it had been. He also talked about how well his relationship with Mel was progressing and asked Dylan to be his best man at the wedding. Dylan was chuffed to be asked and didn't hesitate to say a firm yes to the honour of standing beside his best mate to witness him marry the woman of his dreams. He then updated Yoren on his job hunting and how frustrating he was finding it all, adding that he was over the corporate world and wished he could do something else.

They'd finished their lunch and ordered one last drink before Yoren mustered up the courage to tell Dylan he'd registered his company. It had been over a year since he'd raised his intention of building a startup with Dylan, so he was nervous about sharing his latest news with him now in case the business eventually failed or he decided not to proceed. But when he saw how receptive Dylan was to his update, he felt more comfortable opening up to him further. He told him he felt ready to jump into the unknown.

'Congrats, mate,' said Dylan sincerely. 'Something's changed about you, Yoren. But I can't quite put my finger on it. More confident perhaps? I always knew you had it in you, though. I only wish I had the guts to build something of my own. You know what I'm like with money, always thrifty and putting money away for a rainy day. I think I'm too risk-averse to part with my hard-earned savings to start a business on my own that could end up going nowhere. But I'm so sick and tired of the corporate scene, and going for interviews is doing my head in. I just can't seem to find the right job. I've had a couple of offers, but they just haven't felt right.'

Yoren looked thoughtful for a few moments before looking Dylan squarely in the eye and suggesting excitedly, 'Why don't you join me? We could build a partnership. I know I'm being a bit impulsive right now, but if you think about it, I'm building a software-as-a-service company. With my sales, marketing and financial expertise and your technical skills, this could be a match made in heaven!'

'Are you serious, Yoren? Hmm, perhaps this warrants serious thought and further discussion.'

The pair chatted excitedly about a potential business together and what that could look like as they finished their last drink. Before they went their separate ways, they agreed to meet again very soon to further explore the idea of a partnership. On his way home, Yoren decided not to tell Mel about it yet, only letting her know that Dylan had agreed to be the best man at their wedding when he got home, which she was thrilled about. She'd always liked Dylan and could see he was a good supportive friend to Yoren. She could even imagine the two of them partnering in business one day but kept that thought to herself.

— ■ —

Over the next three weeks, Yoren and Grace explored presence, accountability, higher purpose, care and commitment, as well as revisiting awareness. They focused on how these Aspects of Being impacted how Yoren was being with others, in line with the six-week sub-model they'd created. While Yoren was quite engaged in all the conversations, he particularly resonated with higher purpose: the ability to go beyond oneself and consider others' needs, wants, differences and preferences. He also learned that, as a way of being, higher purpose is going beyond the current time, forsaking instant gratification and immediate rewards to become a visionary leader. He particularly found the principles and practices around higher purpose quite useful and significantly relevant to his major intentions at this stage of his life to create a business and build a healthy relationship and thriving family with Mel. He discovered how his short-sightedness or unwillingness to take even the closest people in his life into consideration in his critical life decisions, coupled with his lack of generosity and, at times, selfishness, prevented him from fulfilling his intentions.

Through a series of enquiries and coaching conversations, Grace supported Yoren to see that it wasn't just about him. 'It's about living life as though none of us is isolated from others,' she explained.

As he challenged the idea of being the epicentre of the universe and succumbing to the shadow side of his ego, he realised he'd come to a critical milestone in his transformational journey. Looking back, he could see many times when he'd fallen victim to the shadow side of these recent Aspects of Being and how he'd irresponsibly let that run the show. Back then, all he had was a dream and a bunch of excuses for why he did nothing but wish, complain and blame everyone and everything but himself for not pursuing it. Had he not attended that info session and decided to complete the profile assessment and debrief and commit to the subsequent coaching, he was sure he'd never have moved forward with his business. He couldn't believe the difference between the man he was before embarking on this coaching journey and who and how he was being today. Going through these transformative conversations and experiences was so impactful; it was as though they were changing his DNA and altering the very fabric of his being. Consequently, the coaching was already making significant differences in how he was showing up, how he was being with Mel and, even more importantly, how he was being with himself.

Yoren had benefited greatly from journaling his Moods in combination with the conception worksheet exercises between coaching sessions, particularly over the last several sessions. Despite their simplicity and ease of use, he could clearly see how these tools contributed to him going through multiple rounds of transformation in line with the methodology. With each passing week, the conception worksheet, combined with the Transformation Methodology's iterative application process, made him more ontologically responsive. This meant that rather than reacting in an ad hoc manner, he was bringing a higher degree of appropriacy to his decisions and behaviours. He'd become quite adept at catching himself whenever an Aspect of Being's constituent parts were missing or malfunctioning and would make concerted efforts to restore its integrity as quickly as possible. For example, when he was on the verge of portraying a fake persona, demonstrating a shadow side of authenticity, he stopped and then chose to be himself and express an authentic point of view. He was also gradually becoming more adept at reading other people's being, especially when they were being inauthentic or invulnerable. This developing skill made him see many of his work colleagues and the friends in his and Mel's social circle in a new light.

— ∎ —

Yoren was alone with his thoughts in the living room, lounging comfortably on the sofa. Daydreaming as he gazed at the ocean view, he had a burning desire to set his and Mel's life back on track. It was like he had a new drive to move forward. He saw the road ahead as so bright and full of opportunities that he couldn't find the right words to articulate it. While some uncertainties remained, he was slowly becoming accustomed to these radical new feelings of optimism and confidence. The picture of that potentially more prosperous and meaningful future danced before his eyes. He suddenly had the urge to tell Mel everything.

He was so engrossed in his thoughts that he didn't hear Mel enter the room. Suddenly, she was behind him, her hands resting on his shoulders as she leaned forward to nuzzle into his neck, her dark hair trailing down to rest softly on his chest. He grabbed Mel's hand and guided her to sit beside him.

'I'd like to discuss our future with you,' he said. The smile on his face and the gleam in his eye belied the seriousness of the topic and the urgency in his voice.

Returning his smile, she responded, 'Sure. Tell me what's on your mind, darling.' She was still getting used to the new Yoren and loving his warmth and openness. He was always in a hurry to be somewhere or do something before.

They discussed their wedding, chose a tentative date for the ceremony in December and planned their honeymoon. Yoren also finally opened up to her about how serious he was about his new business and told her about the work he'd been doing with Grace to prepare him for the next steps. Mel was extremely receptive to what he had to say, and together they decided that he would tender his resignation in the next few months – once he had greater clarity about his business concept. She told him he had her full support. They openly discussed needing to rely on her income until the business became profitable. She said she was willing to ask her boss about increasing her work week from four to five days, and they agreed that her working full-time would be the best way forward, at least for now. They also agreed to sit down and work out a budget to reduce their living costs as much as possible. They decided they could reduce their debt by paying off the credit card while Yoren was still employed and agreed to sell one of their cars and make do with one for a while and put aside the savings as a buffer. Their lavish lifestyle to date meant they had very little in reserve.

Returning to their wedding plans, they excitedly chatted about the details and agreed that the ceremony should be far less extravagant than their original ideas. Mel suggested that an intimate wedding in Fiji would enable them to combine their wedding and honeymoon in one trip. That way, they would be back for the Christmas/New Year period, during which Yoren could put his head down and focus on getting the business off the ground.

They also discussed and managed to resolve a number of issues that had been allowed to fester and remain incomplete for far too long. Yoren surprised himself with the relative ease and flow he brought to the conversation. He was far more open than he used to be and attributed this to his recent coaching on presence, freedom, higher purpose, partnership, empowerment and contribution. Mel also noticed the remarkable difference in him. She particularly loved that he was not trying to be 'right' all the time. Yoren's vulnerability was having an impact on the way Mel was communicating with him too. She was being far more forgiving and generous than she used to be. While their communication was by no means perfect – now and then, they still disagreed on certain things, particularly on their radically different interpretations of some past events – there were no critical deal-breakers. The afternoon quickly turned into evening, and after more animated conversation over dinner, they retired to the bedroom, high on life and filled with desire.

Mel lay awake for some time, content but deep in thought while Yoren slept soundly beside her.

> *Interesting how it felt like we were just a few conversations away from being in sync with each other today and finally having a working relationship when it wasn't that long ago that our communication was so broken that I was entertaining the idea of going our separate ways. How could things have turned around so quickly? For it to feel like there's real hope for our future together? Perhaps I should look into this being conversation. It's pretty obvious that the changes in his behaviour have been happening since he started coaching with Grace. I doubt that's a coincidence.*

Her curiosity sparked, Mel began researching being and the framework Yoren had been introduced to. The more she read, the more intrigued she became. She decided to contact Jen to see if she could lend her some books or articles on the subject.

The next morning, Yoren arose at dawn and decided to go for a jog on the beach. As he ran, he reflected on his discussion with Mel. He found it challenging to have to ask her to shoulder the financial burden for an uncertain amount of time. Having grown up believing that the man of the house should be the chief provider, he felt a tinge of shame, blame and weakness around it, as if her offer somehow made him less of a man. He smiled as he remembered how present Mel was to his sensitivity around this issue, and he knew she'd been very careful not to hurt his pride. He felt a sudden rush of emotion as he realised how blessed he was to have such a wonderfully supportive life partner. It meant so much to him, knowing she was by his side. He noticed how feelings of shame, blame and weakness quickly turned to positive anxiety, the kind of anxiety that Grace told him is healthy because it keeps us on our toes. As the sun rose over the ocean, heralding the dawn of a new day, he made a commitment to stop wavering and procrastinating and finally set the wheels in motion.

— ∎ —

Seated in Grace's office for the fifth session of six on the relationships sub-model, Yoren could barely contain his excitement. When Grace asked him to share what he would like to express, he rattled off all the items he couldn't wait to tick off on his rapidly-growing business establishment to-do list.

'Now that I've got the ball rolling, I can barely think about anything else, Grace.' He spoke quickly and in a rambling fashion.

Grace sat back, listening patiently as he continued, 'It's all so exciting! I've come up with a draft design for the logo and have requested a few quotes for merchandising collateral, from pens and notepads to T-shirts and caps with the logo printed on them. I can already visualise my staff wearing the gear! I've also got lots of ideas for the website and social media pages, and I'm even considering future projects and potential new business ventures …'

Yoren continued in this fashion for about 10 minutes, barely stopping to take a breath. It was clear to Grace that he lacked focus and was way ahead of himself, as she knew he was still unclear on the market need and business offerings, let alone the brand. When he finally paused and sat back, the look on his face indicated that he was anxiously awaiting an equally enthusiastic response from Grace.

She smiled and said, 'I admire your passion and enthusiasm, Yoren. And it's wonderful to hear that you're moving forward with your plans. However, do you think you might be trying to focus on too many things at once?'

'Well, there's a lot to do. And I'm just eager to get the ball rolling.'

'I understand. But are you crystal clear on the needs of the market and the business offerings to meet those needs, Yoren? Do you think that certain tasks and decisions need to be prioritised first?'

'Yes, I suppose you're right, Grace.' He sat back in his seat and looked somewhat deflated.

'Don't worry, Yoren. Having too many priorities is a common phenomenon. It's human nature to get excited once we make a decision about an intention that's been sitting in the back of our mind for a long time. Do you recall when we talked about care several sessions ago and that a healthy relationship with this Mood means you can prioritise matters effectively? And remember how one shadow side of care is flitting from one thing to the next or caring about whatever comes your way to portray yourself as a caring person, both of which usually result in nothing being completed?'

'Yes, I remember. I just assumed that my passion and action indicated how much I value the business and genuinely care about it,' Yoren responded.

Grace reminded him that the framework that underpinned her coaching conversations was judgement-free and that there were no right or wrong answers. However, there could be more effective ways to go about matters if someone wanted to fulfil their intentions. She suggested they use the session to focus on the relationship between responsibility, care and commitment to help him hone in on the areas to focus on first and why this was important. Seeing the value in her proposal, Yoren agreed.

They spent the remainder of the session exploring how a healthy relationship with responsibility, care and commitment leads to focus. Grace explained that while there's nothing fundamentally wrong with spontaneity, focus is paramount to fulfilling one's objectives and intentions. They discussed how it's easy to be reactive rather than responsible when there are too many priorities and how the resulting lack of focus draws us away from what we care most about. He learned that while other Aspects of Being also come into play, responsibility, care and commitment are the key determinants when it comes to focus. By the end of the session, Yoren was clear on what he needed to do and committed to creating a realistic business action plan. The plan he brought back to show Grace the following week was significantly trimmed back and carefully prioritised.

During the final session of their coaching around relationships, Yoren brought up his recent meeting with Dylan and how they'd talked about the possibility of joining forces as business partners. He explained his relationship with Dylan, his experience and skill set and how they would benefit the business, and that Dylan had resigned from the firm and was actively looking for work. He also opened up about his recent conversations with Mel and how she'd committed to supporting him by switching to full-time work. Yoren suggested it was the perfect time to be coached on partnership. Considering that he'd raised the idea of a potential partnership with Dylan, Grace agreed that it was a great idea to explore this Primary Way of Being now. It was also the last remaining Aspect of Being in the relationships sub-model they'd created.

Grace began by asking Yoren a series of questions to gauge his current perception of partnership and why he was drawn to the idea of bringing in a co-founder for his startup. Yoren explained that he'd been researching the steps required to build a business from scratch and looking into the common mistakes made by others so he could avoid those pitfalls. After reading multiple articles, watching several YouTube videos and speaking to people he knew who'd experienced the entrepreneurial journey, he said it was worth considering having a co-founder to share the load and the risk. He had a feeling that Dylan was the best fit for him and had already scheduled a meeting to discuss it further. Sensing Yoren's perception of partnership was not fully aligned with its distinction as a way of being, Grace suggested he read it aloud.

Partnership

Partnership is living from the viewpoint of being in union with other human beings, an entity, team or organisation in the pursuit and fulfilment of a common purpose. It is when you are available to join with others who may share the same values, goals or commitments to create a disproportionate outcome in comparison to what each of you could possibly achieve alone. *Partnership* is the state of confluence where you embrace others and are available to influence each other. It is when you choose to powerfully collaborate and empower each other, irrespective of circumstances.

A healthy relationship with *partnership* indicates that you mostly experience being together, where common purpose, vision, intentions and goals are fulfilled. Others may experience you as being on the same journey with them. You appreciate the company of others and experience being connected, belonging and moving towards the same mutually fulfilling outcomes. You are steadfast in your relationships and will appropriately challenge and support others to bring out their best.

After reading the distinction, Yoren shared his surprise at discovering that partnership as a way of being was about more than just romantic relationships, but also about other people you partner with in life, making it relevant to business. He recalled how he'd misunderstood that connection in answering his assessment questions. Grace said this was a common misconception for many people. She supported Yoren to see that a partnership or relationship established between two or more people is a separate entity. She explained there are three entities in a two-person partnership. In the case of Yoren and Dylan – assuming he would make a suitable business partner – the third entity would be the business they created together. For Yoren and Mel, the third entity was the relationship and upcoming marriage they were building.

Yoren and Grace enjoyed an in-depth discussion throughout the session, and he asked several questions that demonstrated his growing conception of partnership as a way of being. Grace explained that when partners bring their best to a relationship or partnership, they allow parts of themselves to merge into the third entity. In this way, when two or more people with a healthy relationship with partnership and other relevant Aspects of Being come together, the outcome is often far greater than the sum of the individual parts. The result is that they can achieve far more than they could ever hope to accomplish alone. However, if one or both have an unhealthy relationship with partnership, the outcome can be disastrous. Grace was also careful to point out that when two or more people join forces, they bring with them both their healthy and unhealthy relationships with various Aspects of Being, meaning they share not only their strengths but also their shadows.

Given the importance of each person's relationship with partnership and other critical Aspects of Being, Grace said, 'Now that you've developed this lens into your being, Yoren, it's important for you to make yourself present to Dylan's being as well, especially since you're considering bringing him on board as a co-founder. And it would really benefit you both if you were able to speak the same language from a being perspective. So it would be great for Dylan to experience the assessment and debrief for himself. I can definitely support him if he's open to it.'

Seeing the value in Grace's suggestion, Yoren said he would raise the idea with Dylan. Knowing him as well as he did, he was confident he'd be open to it. He secretly thought he would likely be keen on coaching with Grace as well.

They finished the session with a recap of all they'd covered over the last six sessions on relationships and set the trajectory for their final two sessions together.

'Given we have just two sessions remaining in this round of coaching, based on our original agreement, tell me: what do you think will make the biggest difference for you in these last sessions together?' asked Grace.

After contemplating her question for several minutes, Yoren replied, 'I think I'd like to work on my relationship with assertiveness. I used to see myself as extremely assertive, but my profile report suggests otherwise. Reading through the distinction, I can also see how my lack of assertiveness sometimes acts as a roadblock and prevents me from moving forward.'

Assertiveness was a challenging subject for Yoren, and he'd avoided bringing it up before, despite wanting to understand it better. But he realised he could no longer avoid it; it was now or never, at least in this round of coaching. Grace wrote down assertiveness and suggested they add reliability to the plan. They agreed to cover those two qualities – both Secondary Ways of Being – as their final two.

As Yoren packed up his notes to leave, he casually asked, 'Grace, this might sound like a silly question this late into my coaching journey, but we keep talking about being, and even though your explanations have been great, I'm still a bit unclear on it.'

'No question is silly, Yoren. I'm glad you asked. Do you have to leave immediately? I don't start my next session for another half an hour. So, if you have a spare 15 minutes, I'd be more than happy to recreate it for you.'

'That'd be great. Thanks, Grace. So tell me, what exactly is being?'

'Dare I describe the indescribable!' she laughed. 'Only joking. Bear with me as I do my best to create it again as clearly and succinctly as possible. If we zoom out on the being of human beings in general, we are referring to our nature, our 'what-ness' or essence. Put simply, it's what constitutes being a human being: the series of attributes that each of us possesses and relates to, regardless of sex, race, faith or the era or culture we are born into. For example, we all relate to fear, anxiety, care, vulnerability and courage. Do you recall how you used to think it was possible to be literally fearless before we explored fear as a Mood, Yoren?'

'Yes. I used to see fear as a weakness,' he responded. 'I didn't think of it as something we all relate to. Now I know that the healthier our relationship with fear, the more likely it is that we'll be able to step forward despite being afraid.'

'That's right, Yoren. We're also vulnerable to many things, whether or not we acknowledge it and regardless of whether we consider that in the way we behave or how we make decisions and take action. And this can make us anxious and fearful. While care encourages us to prioritise certain matters over others.'

'I remember I struggled to understand the link between care and prioritising things before you coached me on it,' said Yoren.

'Yes, and when it comes to being vulnerable to the matters and circumstances life throws us, we are all relatively autonomous beings with the ability to respond, regardless of the source,' Grace continued.

'You're referring to responsibility as a way of being here, aren't you, Grace,' asked Yoren in a rhetorical manner.

'Spot on. Remember how you understood responsibility only from the perspective of duty or blame back then?'

'I do. It's amazing how we get caught in our own web of perceptions!' laughed Yoren.

'To zoom back out again for a moment, when we talk about being in the context of the framework we've been using in our coaching sessions, we're referring to the primal qualities we *all* have in common. Failing to acknowledge that we all possess these qualities is inauthentic; it conveys an incongruent conception of the nature of human beings. Any questions?'

'Just one. Aren't there other qualities than the ones in this framework that are common to human beings, Grace?'

'Absolutely. In fact, there are many more. However, this model has been designed within the scope of human performance and how we operate in life. So it focuses on the fundamental qualities or Aspects of Being required for effective leadership, whether leading others or being the leader of our own lives. In part, the framework's ontological model brings together an essentialist definition of certain human qualities by distinguishing what we are as opposed to what we are not, while acknowledging that we also have subjective sides. Does that make sense to you?'

'Yes, it does; but I do have another question,' said Yoren. 'So far, you've explained being from the perspective of what we are as human beings and the qualities we have in common. But how does it support us to look into our subjective sides?'

'Great question, Yoren. We consider our subjective sides by asking ourselves two key questions. The first is, *how* am I being? This is also referred to as 'how-ness'. This is where we consider how an individual, as an instance of the class: human being, relates to all these Aspects of Being. Here we're also considering how the way we relate to the Aspects of Being forms our mental model, including our web of perceptions, which we then tap into when making decisions and taking action. These decisions, actions and the way we behave go a long way to determining our results, including the consequences of our actions, and lead to our unique experience of life. Naturally, we can't ignore the part that external factors play in all of this. But here we're focusing on what we have immediate access to and control over – our own being. Remember how you used to think many of these qualities are fixed, that they can't be transformed, Yoren?'

'Yes, but you can't blame me for that,' laughed Yoren. 'It's what many schools of thought lead us to believe.'

'That's so true. You've experienced some significant transformations over the past few months. The assessment tool we used leveraged the 'what' by providing the ontological model with a list of these constituent qualities, and based on your answers, it assessed the health of your relationship with each quality at the time you completed it. And then the profile report helped me to coach you around how you were being. It gave you awareness, which is the first step towards transformation.'

'I'm truly amazed at how far I've come since completing that initial assessment,' said Yoren. 'You mentioned two key questions to consider when looking into our subjective sides, Grace. The first is the how or how-ness. What's the second one?'

'The second key question to ask is: *who* am I being? This is also referred to as 'who-ness'. Unless we're clear on the what and the how, we won't have access to who we are, which might lead to confusion in understanding ourselves and inauthenticity around our self-image and persona. In more extreme cases, it could even result in dysphoria around our sense of self or an identity crisis.'

Grace could see a look of confusion sweep across Yoren's face. 'Bear with me, Yoren. I know this part isn't the easiest to grasp. Who you are is very subjective. It's your unique being or distinct self that you carry with you for life. The framework we've been tapping into for this coaching has supported you to dig deep and dive into the dimensions of your unique being through your intentional consciousness and express those dimensions outwardly. You'll recall from our coaching on self-expression that your unique being can be described as the mysterious thing within that calls you, which is why it's often referred to as a calling. It comprises your innate talents and the potential that you may or may not end up fulfilling and expressing to the world in the form of your unique contribution. In contrast, how you are being is basically the way you relate to the Aspects of Being in the model and other qualities beyond the model. Any questions?'

'I'm not totally clear on this part. Could you give me a tangible example?' asked Yoren.

'Sure. For example, when we explored responsibility as a way of being, you learned that one person may choose to relate to it as duty, obligation, to be blamed, or to be at fault, while another may choose to relate to it as autonomy and being an active agent in their life, as per our distinction. We all have a cognitive model or web of perceptions for how we relate to various things in life. And how we relate to an Aspect of Being primarily determines how we act upon it. In other words, how we relate to it largely influences our decisions and behaviours, which are then reflected in our actions. When combined with external factors like where we were born, our society, religious and cultural beliefs, how we were raised and the prevailing economic conditions, how we are being leads each of us to have a radically different and unique experience of life.

'So, not only do we study the ontology of human beings in terms of our what-ness – the qualities we all have in common as members of the same species – but as coaches, we also support our clients to study themselves as unique individuals through the lens of how-ness. The idea is for you as an individual to discover more about yourself, first who you are deep down and then how you are in relation to the Aspects of Being in the framework. For the most part, your coaching has focused on the how-ness side of the equation while at the same time being guided by the objective what-ness through the ontological model.

'I then supported you to see how you were relating to each Aspect of Being, uncovering your mental model and determining how you could transform some of those relationships to shape the future you, a Yoren who is more aligned with what he wants to achieve. We did all of this to uncover and explore the subjective sides of you, Yoren, because you can transform how you relate to all of these qualities. That's why, with every conception worksheet exercise you completed, you always started with a degree of awareness and worked towards acting on your conception of those qualities before moving on to transform your behaviour through the application phase of the Transformation Methodology.'

Grace could see she had captured Yoren's interest with her deeper explanation of being.

'Do you feel you have a better understanding of the meaning of being now, Yoren? Although I bet you didn't expect such a lengthy, detailed response when you asked. Maybe now you wish you'd remained silent!' she laughed.

'No, I'm very glad I asked. And, yes, you answered it brilliantly. Thank you for the extra time. I really appreciate it, Grace.'

'My pleasure. Looking into yourself isn't meant to be easy. I know how complex it can all seem and how challenging it can be to get your head around it. That's why people like me spend years learning and practising all of this. We devote our time and energy to it so that we are equipped to not only apply it to ourselves because we believe in it, but also use it to support our clients. The point is anyone, no matter where they are in their journey, can benefit from studying their being. So, it's up to you how deeply you want to get into it and how you want to use it. Polishing and transforming your being is like modifying your car to make it a high-performance vehicle. But then determining how you want to use it – or your intention for that vehicle – is up to you. Similarly, in life, we all choose our own meaning, purpose and direction.'

Grace was thrilled to see Yoren showing such a keen interest in the philosophical background of the being discourse. Chatting as they walked towards the door, she mentioned an online resource library of lectures and articles that she used on the subject of being and offered him access to a recorded self-paced course on the subject. She also recommended some other books he could buy to explore the topic further. Just as Yoren opened the door to leave, Grace beckoned him to wait a moment and returned with a book in her outstretched hand. He recognised it as the one she always seemed to have close at hand in their sessions and noticed it was more than a little worn.

'It's yours, Yoren! It explores the philosophy of being in a lot more depth than the other book I gave you earlier. I know you'll enjoy it. You might even find you want to read it more than once,' she said, smiling. And before you express any concern about taking it from me, don't worry; I have a couple of copies.'

Yoren accepted her gift with gratitude and drove home deep in thought, occasionally glancing at the book on the seat beside him. He couldn't wait to turn the first page.

Philosophy! Who would've ever thought?

CHAPTER 12

Daring to be Assertive

Mel's curiosity about the being discourse was growing by the day. It was late, and she knew she had to be up early, but she couldn't sleep as questions consumed her mind. She decided she would call Jen first thing in the morning. While the two women weren't overly close, they always got along well whenever they came together during family gatherings. While others engaged in small talk around the table, Mel and Jen would often find a quiet corner or wander through the garden to discuss topical societal and political issues. Although their views weren't always fully aligned, they found ease, flow and joy in these intellectual conversations. However, Mel wasn't the kind of person who could easily open up to others about her personal life and emotions. She avoided asking others about themselves, fearing they might reciprocate that line of enquiry. So, while she knew about Jen's seemingly impressive career and her wonderful relationship with Nader and her family, she'd never tried to understand or get to know who Jen was deep down.

Calling Jen on her way to work the next day, Mel was nervous as she waited for her to pick up. After several rings and expecting the call to go to voicemail, Mel was surprised to hear Jen's cheery voice on the other end. Realising she was genuinely happy to hear from her, Mel relaxed. She explained that she had a few questions about the being discourse work that Yoren had been doing with Grace and wondered when she might have time to talk about it. Jen wasn't surprised to hear from Mel, given the conversations they enjoyed at family gatherings and the curiosity she believed Mel would be experiencing after observing the changes in Yoren over the last few months. Without a moment's hesitation, she invited Mel for brunch the following morning.

Mel thought about Jen and the life she'd built with Nader on their beautiful property on her way home from work. It had been a while since she and Yoren had visited. She smiled as she pictured the two of them, laughing and carefree, looking and acting far younger than their years and always standing out from the more conservative members of the family. But this time, she wasn't going to Jen and Nader's for a family gathering. She was heading there with a purpose: to learn the secret behind Yoren's remarkable transformation. All she knew was that the changes in him were positively impacting their relationship in ways she hadn't expected and had dramatically enhanced the quality of their life as a couple and soon-to-be growing family, which she was so excited about.

Mel had always been obsessed with human beings and how people interacted with one another. Even as a youngster, she'd been curious about her parents' relationship and the way they engaged with each other. In adolescence, she was regarded by her peers at school as quiet, shy and reserved. Instead of gossiping and chatting about boys, makeup and fashion with the other girls, she would sit back and closely observe people's behaviour. Almost everything she did, from listening to the news and reading a novel to performing in school plays – which she enjoyed despite her outwardly reserved nature – was done through the lens of attentiveness to human behaviour. Over time, she developed a passion for volunteering and worked with several charitable organisations. But she was most drawn to charities that supported people in need, such as the Red Cross, the local homeless shelter and the Salvation Army, and often imagined what it would be like to be in other people's shoes.

After graduating from high school, Mel opted to study human resource management, knowing it was an area that was both aligned with her interest in human beings and would lead to a secure, relatively well-paid job. However, once she started actually working in the field, she became increasingly disillusioned. She was shocked and dismayed to discover how some corporations treated people in the hiring process, reducing them to little more than their functionality. It was a similar experience when it came to their handling of performance reviews, payroll cuts, redundancies and terminations. Even working for different employers made no difference. At one point, she tried working for a recruitment agency, only to resign on the spot after discovering those issues were even worse in that environment.

Eventually, even the term 'human resources' would trigger Mel. She found it a derogatory way to refer to people at work because, in her opinion, it conveyed a lack of care for people as complete human beings and reduced employees to nothing more than what they do rather than who they are. She eventually concluded that, no matter which corporation she worked for, HR in action was far from her vision of a profession that made a real difference to people. So while she maintained her care for human beings and compassion for humanity and continued to work in HR, doing her best to make a difference for the people she worked with, she always felt something was missing from the profession. She just couldn't put her finger on what that was, let alone articulate it clearly.

Over the last couple of years, Mel had built a sound professional persona. However, she lacked ambition and chose to only work part-time because her hopes and dreams about the impact she could have in HR had been crushed by reality. Her priorities had also shifted since becoming engaged to Yoren, and their relationship and plans to start a family were now her main areas of focus. She hoped her catch-up with Jen would not only shed light on the reasons behind Yoren's transformation, but also help fill the gap between her passion for human beings and the disappointing reality of working in the field. In the past, she'd been mildly curious about some of the being-related topics Jen talked about, but never took them seriously. This time was different. Something beyond curiosity sparked the urge to dig deeper and learn more.

With a sense of excitement, Mel drove to Jen and Nader's. On arrival, the two women hugged, and Jen explained that Nader was out, so they had the place to themselves. She led Mel out into the garden, where she'd set up a small table and two chairs under the shade of a magnificent oak tree. On the table was a large timber tray carrying a delicate bone china teapot, matching cups and saucers and a simple but delicious-looking continental-style brunch with rustic bread, pate, goose salami and various cheeses and fruit. Jen was dressed casually, her feet bare beneath a flowing floral dress, her hair falling in waves over her shoulders. It was a beautiful, sunny day and, being spring, the temperature was pleasant and the garden was alive with fragrance and colour. Daisy and Bella were sunning themselves on the lawn nearby. To Mel, it was the picture of domestic bliss. She momentarily fantasised about her and Yoren's future, living on a beautiful property, their children running around the yard with the dog.

Jen poured them each a cup of tea and invited Mel to help herself to the food. Over a leisurely brunch, they chatted about the coaching approach that had guided Yoren's transformation, and Mel subtly looked for ways to learn how to be trained in it. They discussed some of the principles behind the framework Grace and Jen had adopted and how it both differed from other disciplines, but also leveraged some of the existing paradigms. Although Mel found everything Jen said interesting, she conveyed her intellectual scepticism through her carefully worded questions. She wanted to learn the 'why' behind everything and kept comparing the principles and practices they discussed with her existing knowledge of the realm. Accustomed to this line of questioning, Jen responded to every one of Mel's questions with finesse. Although Mel didn't fully grasp everything Jen told her, she found the conversation enlightening and thought-provoking.

The women were so deeply engrossed in the conversation that time seemed to stand still, and before they knew it, more than three hours had passed. Jen stood to stretch, her fondness for yoga evident in the way she moved. Casually reaching into a canvas tote bag hanging over the back of her chair, she pulled out a book on the being discourse, which she handed to Mel, and then used her phone to share links to some white papers, articles and videos that she recommended Mel look into on the subject. The book was familiar to Mel as she'd seen the same one in Yoren's briefcase. These days, it went everywhere with him.

Walking back to the house, Jen suggested Mel might like to experience the assessment tool and debrief that Yoren had been through for herself. She offered to connect her with a colleague who could deliver her debrief session and who was responsible for running the introductory accreditation program if Mel was keen to pursue it further. When Mel expressed interest in tapping into the framework to support people at work, Jen offered to send her some information and case studies highlighting what's possible when the framework is introduced within an organisation. And as Mel was leaving, Jen encouraged her to call any time if she had more questions or wanted to know more.

On her drive home, Mel couldn't stop thinking about the morning's conversation. Although Jen had clarified much of her confusion, she felt she was leaving with more questions than she'd come with, questions like: What's the background to all of this? How can an HR specialist leverage it? Is it just for individuals, or can teams also benefit from it? How scientific is it? The discussion had ignited her curiosity even further. Simultaneously excited and nervous, she couldn't wait to get home and start reading. She suddenly remembered she'd planned to call into the shopping centre on the way home to buy Yoren a gift for the rapidly approaching anniversary of their first date. The book would have to wait.

— ∎ —

As Yoren drove to Grace's for his second-last coaching session, he reflected on the past six months. He was so accustomed to meeting with Grace weekly that it was hard to imagine the journey coming to an end. Not only was Grace expertly guiding and supporting him to actualise his growth potential by addressing the shadow sides to his Aspects of Being, but she was also someone he could vulnerably share with, an enormous benefit in itself. Imagining how hard it would be to fill that void in his life, he pushed that thought aside and cranked up the volume of the classical music he enjoyed listening to while driving, focusing on the road.

Arriving in the nick of time, Yoren hastily rang the doorbell. He'd already decided that he'd begin today's sessions by giving Grace an update on where things were at with Dylan. When she opened the door, he noticed she seemed a little flustered. Suddenly, he became aware of a boy who looked to be around eight, seated in a wheelchair beside her.

'Hi Yoren, please come in. I'd like you to meet my son, Prosper.'

The boy smiled and extended his hand.

'Great to meet you, Prosper,' said Yoren, bending down to shake the boy's hand. Not accustomed to children, he felt a little awkward.

'You'll have to excuse me as I'm running a bit behind schedule this morning,' said Grace. 'Please take a seat in my office and make yourself comfortable. I'll be with you in just a few minutes.'

Yoren had just sat down in his usual spot on the sofa when Grace called out from the adjacent room, 'There's fresh water in the decanter on the table, and help yourself to a blueberry muffin. I baked them this morning so they're lovely and fresh.'

Pouring himself a glass of water and filling Grace's glass, Yoren thought about Grace's son and couldn't help but wonder why he was in a wheelchair. Was he injured? Did he have a disability? Consumed by those thoughts, he didn't hear Grace enter the room.

'My apologies for the delay, Yoren. Normally, my husband, Justice, is home on weekends to be with our three kids while I work. But he was called away urgently for business, so I've had to make some last-minute adjustments. Prosper was born with cerebral palsy and, as you can imagine, requires more care and attention than the average nine-year-old. He's the sweetest, most loving boy you'll ever meet. Our eldest, Heavenly, is twelve, and our youngest, Celeste, is seven. The girls are spending some time with their cousins, and I just needed to set Prosper up in the other room. My sister's on her way over to sit with him. He'll be fine till she gets here.'

Yoren nodded as he listened attentively. He was so present to how Grace seemed to have successfully managed to gracefully integrate her career with her life that he completely forgot his urge to tell her about his latest meeting with Dylan. He wondered if he could be as forgiving of disruptions and challenges as Grace seemed to be if he became a father one day. Would he harbour resentment when schedules became disrupted? Or would he take it all in his stride like Grace seemed to do? The thought of having to make sacrifices and be generous with his time to take care of others while building a business instilled fear.

Sensing his lack of presence, Grace asked, 'Yoren, Is there anything you want to share so that you can be present for the session?'

'Hearing you speak of your children and the unexpected disruption to your schedule made me suddenly aware of what it might take to have kids,' he said. 'Mel and I are talking about it, but to be perfectly honest, I think I'm scared.'

Grace could see his vulnerability and knew it was a big deal for him to admit his fear.

'Before we had our first child, I was scared too,' she responded with a smile. 'Yet, despite my fear, I took the step forward, and I'm so glad I did. Would you like us to change the contract for today's session and explore your concerns over being with uncertainty instead?'

'No. I appreciate the suggestion, but there's a more immediate matter I'd like to discuss with you. Let me update you on where things are at with Dylan, and then perhaps we can continue with assertiveness as we planned.'

'Sure, I'm all ears, Yoren.'

'I've had a few face-to-face and phone conversations with Dylan since our last session. And from everything he's told me, it seems that, deep down, he doesn't really want to take another job. I guess my telling him about my business idea has intrigued him enough for him to consider it. He also knows how compatible we are since we've worked together before. At this stage, we've agreed to keep the lines of communication open.'

'It all sounds positive to me, Yoren. So what's the issue? I sense that something's worrying you.'

'I wouldn't say there's a specific issue. But Dylan's my best friend, and I love what we already have and don't want to risk the friendship. I know there'll probably come a time when we'll disagree over business decisions. And I'm afraid financial and commercial commitments could negatively impact our relationship or even ruin it. I'm really nervous about that. Other than that, though, I really feel like we'll complement each other, both from a being perspective and in terms of skills.'

Grace could see Yoren had more to get off his chest, so she remained silent.

'The other thing I'm feeling anxious and a little overwhelmed about is the idea of starting a family,' he continued. 'Not only are Mel and I getting married very soon, which is a huge commitment in itself, but I've already said yes to trying for a baby soon afterwards. It's all happening so fast and at a time when I'm choosing to walk away from my high-paid, stable corporate career. I'm sure many see what I'm doing as foolish, especially knowing I'm jumping into something as risky as entrepreneurship, which I've never done before. Not only that, but I'm also entertaining the idea of drastically changing the nature of my relationship with Dylan. I'm feeling the pressure to make confident and assertive decisions to avoid everything piling up and biting me in the back.'

'There are many aspects of your life that are shifting right now, Yoren. How are you being with all this uncertainty?' asked Grace.

'Something inside me tells me I can now be with this tremendous level of discomfort and uncertainty, which is very new for me,' said Yoren. 'A few months ago, I'm pretty sure I would've avoided a lot of this, even in my mind, let alone in terms of action. But I can't help but feel scared and a bit overwhelmed.'

'In what way are these feelings still blocking you?' she asked.

'It's like I'm sucking in my fears and suppressing myself to an extent. There are many conversations I should be having with Mel, but for some reason, I keep holding back. So things remain unsaid and unresolved. What do you think I should do?'

Tempted to succumb to Yoren's request and tell him what she thought he should do, Grace quickly pulled herself together. She was present to Yoren's concerns and could clearly read his vulnerability and reception. Her attentiveness to how he was being and what he was going through made her even more confident that assertiveness was the most appropriate Aspect of Being to explore in today's session.

'I see. Let's start with a few questions, Yoren. In discussing your relationship, the upcoming wedding and starting a family with Mel, do you think you're ever overly agreeable about something you're perhaps not ready for?' asked Grace.

'Well, when it comes to our relationship, Mel is definitely the right woman for me. Our decisions are aligned in so many ways. But with regard to the wedding, there are several things I would've done differently, such as not inviting certain people. But I just tell myself to go with it as she's the bride and I know how much it means to her for the day to be perfect. So, yes, I recognise I'm being overly agreeable and not challenging her on certain things when it comes to the wedding plans. But aren't I supposed to be like that as the groom? Mel sees the wedding as one of the most important days of her life. It's also very important to me, but I thought I'd let her lead it and compromise my wants and needs to make her happy. I guess I'm just trying to be nice.'

'What does 'nice' look like to you, Yoren?' asked Grace.

'Well, I suppose what I'm trying to say is that there are certain things I'm not fully on board with, but I say yes just to please Mel. I guess that's not very authentic either,' said Yoren.

'Okay, and … ?' Grace asked, pausing to encourage Yoren to continue.

'At other times, I avoid bringing up a conversation for fear that it could lead to conflict. I just don't want to ruin the experience for either of us. Happy wife, happy life, right?' Yoren regretted the cliché as soon as it slipped out of his mouth.

'What happens when you don't speak up about these things,' asked Grace.

After pausing to ponder Grace's question, Yoren replied, 'I end up disengaging, and sometimes that makes me resentful.'

To confirm they were on the same page, Grace asked, 'So are you saying there are certain hidden conversations you've been keeping to yourself, and you're holding resentment around some of them?'

Grace's words touched a nerve. Sitting forward, Yoren exclaimed, 'Absolutely! And I can give you a good example. Mel wants to invite a man to our wedding who she had feelings for and even dated for a while when they were both teenagers, and I know he was just as keen on her. Just because they were neighbours and their parents are still friends doesn't make it okay for an old flame to be at our wedding! Why the hell does she think that's okay?'

His breathing had quickened, and he was visibly angry and upset. From his sudden outburst, it seemed he'd been carrying resentment over this issue for some time but had bottled it up.

'I see,' said Grace calmly, pausing to give him space to continue.

'I don't understand why she insists on this idiot coming to our wedding!' he said.

He paused for some water, and Grace remained silent.

Relaxing his posture, Yoren looked up and apologised. 'Sorry, Grace. I didn't mean to be rude, but Mel inviting that guy really bothered me. Even though the two families are close and they've both moved on, I can't help how I feel about it. It might be irrational, but it's just the way I feel.'

'Why haven't you brought this conversation up with Mel?' asked Grace.

'I didn't want her to think I was jealous or insecure. What would she think of me then?'

'What do you think, Yoren?'

'Oh, I don't know … I guess I am. But I don't think that was my intention. I guess I just don't think Mel would appreciate how I feel about her inviting an ex. How could she? She's not a man. What do you think I should do?'

'I'm not here to tell you what to do, Yoren. However, I encourage you to consider what just happened. Do you recognise any hidden conversations? Can you see how your concern over your perceived need to be nice, considerate and polite – to use some of your words – caused you to become angry and upset, and led to your outburst?'

'Well, yes, but I was angry. What was I supposed to do?' asked Yoren.

'Consider that your urges aren't entirely controllable. You can't fully block them, but you can redirect them,' said Grace. 'If you don't adequately channel what's there for you to express, it will burst out at some point, and not in the most effective and healthy way. I imagine there are probably many conversations buried deep, not just ones you haven't had with Mel but also with others. Can you see how you aren't doing anyone any favours, including yourself, by being overly agreeable or accommodating?'

'I thought it was easier to just go along with it rather than rock the boat,' said Yoren.

'If you keep saying unassertive yeses, which means they're not genuine, they'll eventually rise to the surface in the form of anger, as they did just now when you opened up about the wedding,' said Grace.

'So how should I have addressed my anger over Mel inviting an ex?' asked Yoren.

'Let me ask you, Yoren: how do you think you could have handled it differently?'

'I guess I could have been more vulnerable and told her how I felt about her inviting him instead of thinking on her behalf and creating my own narrative about the situation,' he replied.

'And what might have been the outcome if you'd been more vulnerable and assertive,' asked Grace.

'Well, I suppose Mel could have been more sensitive to my feelings and either not invited him or openly shared her point of view about why it's so important to her to have him there,' replied Yoren, his eyes fixed on the floor. 'Perhaps this would've led to a healthier conversation between us and maybe a resolution we would both have been comfortable with,' he added somewhat sheepishly, now aware of the dysfunction in keeping the conversation hidden.

'Is there anything else you'd like to share on the subject of hidden conversations before we move on, Yoren?' asked Grace.

'As a matter of fact, there is. When I arrived this morning, and you said you had to make some last-minute changes to ensure your kids were looked after while you worked, I questioned whether I was ready to have children and make those kinds of sacrifices myself. To be honest, I was already questioning it. I only said yes to Mel because I didn't want to disappoint her. She desperately wants to have children and start our family now. But do I want that too? What if I told her

I wasn't ready? Would that make her question our relationship? The truth is, I've always wanted to win, no matter what game I enter. If I thought I might not win, I wouldn't enter the game from the get-go. What if telling her I'm unsure I'm ready to have kids causes her to leave me? I can't afford to lose her.'

'What do you think might happen if you try to force an outcome, Yoren, even if there are other people involved?' asked Grace.

Suddenly feeling embarrassed and humbled, Yoren responded, 'I suppose you're right. I failed to acknowledge that Mel isn't something to win. She's a human being. The thing is, I know I want children one day, but …'

Seeing he was struggling to get to the point, Grace said, 'How about you consider it from another angle, Yoren? Whether you're being overly submissive, excessively disagreeable and unwilling to negotiate, or you're rigid or passive-aggressive, none of it works,' said Grace.

Aware that the conversation was no longer directly aligned with Yoren's primary objective for the coaching, Grace asked, 'Yoren, would you be happy if we also bring in examples around assertiveness that are more directly related to starting your business?'

'Yes, sure.'

'Great. I'd like you to consider that not saying your real yeses and noes is detrimental in all relationships, not just personal ones. For instance, you touched on your relationship with Dylan and raised your concern that partnering with him in business could affect your friendship. The point is you need to be assertive if you want any relationship to work. You might frequently go along with what others decide to avoid conflict. You might also use inappropriate humour, sarcasm or underhanded comments to manipulate, control or put others down. But none of these will lead to you being effective and fulfilling your intentions, particularly in building your business. The same is true in building your relationship with both Dylan and Mel. Consider that all hidden conversations can potentially cost a relationship, personal or professional. This is where working on your relationship with assertiveness can help.'

'Would you mind if we read the distinction of assertiveness together again to put it into context?' asked Yoren.

'Sure. You took the words right out of my mouth,' laughed Grace.

Assertiveness

Assertiveness is when you express yourself effectively and stand up for your point of view while also being respectful of others. It is the willingness to express your thoughts and feelings and communicate your needs and expectations firmly and directly while being considerate of others and aware of any subsequent consequences of being assertive. *Assertiveness* is being resolute, straight, firm and effective.

A healthy relationship with *assertiveness* indicates that you are predominately straight and unambiguous in your communication with others. You rarely resort to threats or attempt to manipulate outcomes and are transparent with your motives. You are bold in communicating your and others' needs and expectations in terms of the outcomes required or expected. You are comfortable letting others know how you feel and express yourself without emotional outbursts.

An unhealthy relationship with *assertiveness* indicates that you may be unreasonably submissive, agreeable or aggressive, or that you predominantly rely on manipulation and domination to get your way, express yourself and communicate with others. You may frequently go along with what others decide to avoid conflict. You may also use inappropriate humour, sarcasm, teasing or underhanded comments to manipulate, bully, control or put others down. Alternatively, you may frequently threaten or use the tone of your voice to dominate or exert your will on others. As a result, they may consider you manipulative or dominating, even though that is not always your intention. Your conversations may quickly spiral or escalate emotionally while issues remain unresolved.

After re-reading the distinction, certain parts grabbed Yoren's attention and he lingered on them. Grace didn't interrupt, allowing him to relate the distinction to the hidden conversations he'd shared with her.

'An unhealthy relationship with assertiveness indicates that you may be unreasonably submissive, agreeable or aggressive [...] Alternatively, you may frequently threaten or use the tone of your voice to dominate or exert your will on others. As a result, they may consider you manipulative or dominating, even though that is not always your intention. Your conversations may quickly spiral or escalate emotionally while issues remain unresolved,' he read to himself.

Hmm, this basically describes what I've been doing.

Yoren could now clearly see and resonate with the distinction of assertiveness, especially the part that described how an unhealthy relationship with this Secondary Way of Being might play out.

'This describes many of my interactions with Mel, my boss and my father,' said Yoren. 'I can now see that when I'm being overly accommodating with certain people in my life, trying to be 'nice', how that can easily backfire and swing into nastiness or aggression.'

'That's very observant of you, Yoren. Interestingly, what you're describing is exactly how it's conveyed in the framework. Just like a pendulum, one's relationship with assertiveness can quickly swing from being submissive or overly agreeable to being aggressive or overly disagreeable.'

Grace showed Yoren a diagram illustrating her point.

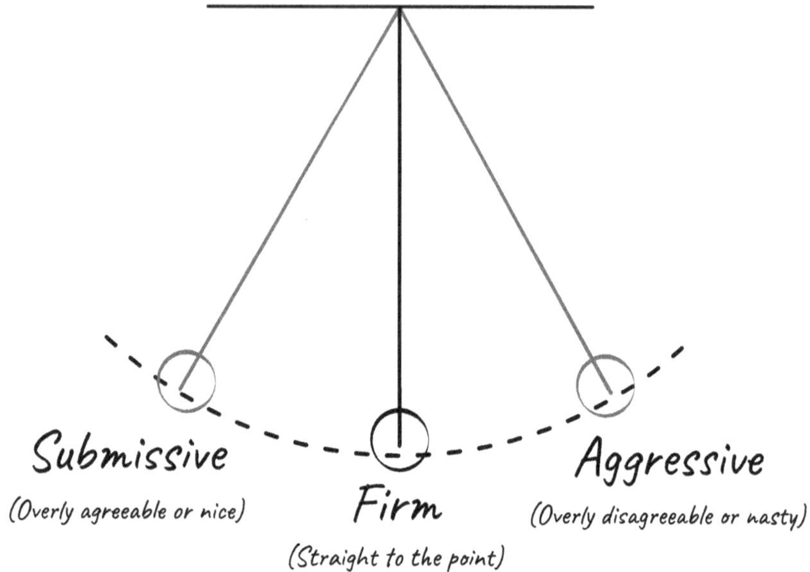

Yoren could think of many instances where those kinds of swings had occurred. It was as though he was unconsciously creating a conception worksheet in his mind. Just as he'd practised for the last several months, he also considered the alternatives, trying to see how many of those instances could have been different if he'd been assertive instead of submissive, overly agreeable, disagreeable or aggressive.

His self-reflection and contemplation lasted several minutes and Grace gave him time to be with his thoughts. Looking down, his fingers interlocked so tightly that his knuckles began to whiten and his breathing suddenly became heavier as he became present to a major root cause of the dysfunction in various areas of his life. A combination of emotions and feelings circulated throughout his entire body; he could feel them everywhere, from his head to his toes. Shame, sorrow, anger and rage mingled with excitement, liberation and peace of mind.

'How are you feeling, Yoren? Are you alright?' asked Grace softly, nudging a box of tissues towards him.

Yoren was so overcome by emotion that he couldn't find the words to respond. Tears welled, blocking his vision. However, his eyes had never been more open, and it felt like he could see more vividly than ever before. On the one hand, he was overwhelmingly present to the burden he'd placed upon himself by not being assertive in the past. On the other, he felt an overwhelming sense of relief because he now knew how to prevent that in the future. Looking down at his feet, his tears began to flow. He felt strangely at ease being emotional in Grace's presence. She gave him space to be with his newfound awareness, and they sat silently for several minutes while he regained his composure.

Grace brought to Yoren's attention that, as a Secondary Way of Being, assertiveness had other more subtle Aspects of Being contributing to it. She then encouraged and guided him to map out a sub-model by coming up with the Aspects of Being he thought most contributed to his assertiveness. Aware that they were approaching the end of the session, Yoren took the initiative to come up with his own challenge for the week.

'How about I work out the instances of my unhealthy relationship with assertiveness and their tangible costs to me and my life this week, and explore how the outcome would be different if I related to assertiveness in a healthier way? I'd also like to keep journaling my Moods in the context of assertiveness,' he said.

'Excellent suggestion, Yoren.' Grace was visibly impressed. 'Now, as we're approaching our final session, I invite you to complete the profile assessment again. That way, we can see how our work to transform your relationships with the various Aspects of Being we've been working on is reflected in your results.'

'Great. That should be interesting!' said Yoren.

'Oh, and one more thing,' said Grace. 'This time, when you complete your conception worksheet, I'd like you to bring forward the timeline even further: to the last month on one worksheet and to the present moment on another.'

'Could you please remind me why we need to keep reducing the timeframe, Grace?' Yoren asked.

'Sure. We started with a longer timeframe because it's much easier to reflect retrospectively and find instances of your shadows of different Aspects of Being in the past than to consider them in the present moment. We're gradually narrowing the timeframes as you become more proficient at the exercise, because shorter timeframes make it more challenging to identify instances and manifestations of your shadow sides. It requires a higher degree of awareness, authenticity, vulnerability and presence to pick them up in the moment.'

'Okay, that makes sense. So, start by bringing the timeframe forward to the last month?' he asked.

'Yes. Then, as you develop your sensitivity even further, you'll become more adept at identifying and catching the manifestations of your shadows in real time. Given that you want to become more competent at polishing and addressing those shadows, I encourage you to focus on an even shorter timeframe on the second worksheet, right up to the present moment, so you can start to catch yourself out in action,' she explained.

'Sure. But would you mind giving me an example of what to look for to make it more tangible?' asked Yoren.

'Of course. Let's say you're in a meeting or talking to someone. Reflecting on assertiveness, you'll look for instances when you're about to not be assertive. The idea is that you'll become so adept at identifying these that you can pause and then choose to be assertive right there and then. So you'll stop reacting in the moment and acting upon your impulses. And instead, you'll respond to the situation. In other words, rather than reacting from the shadow, you'll let your relatively healthy relationship with each and every Aspect of Being positively and effectively influence the decisions you're about to make and the actions you're about to take. Does that make sense?'

'I think so. But just to confirm that I understand it properly, why is the time factor so important in relation to transformation?' asked Yoren.

'Sure. Consider that you're working towards becoming responsive in the moment. When you're being responsive, you tap into your wisdom by passing the urge to react through your Moods, Primary and Secondary Ways of Being. This enables you to bring self-control, relevance and grace to your decisions and actions. Being responsive is distinctly different from reacting to impulses or urges initiated by your temperament or triggered by external factors. It's when you no longer act under the influence of your shadows and only catch yourself out afterwards. Instead, you become adept at catching yourself when you're about to be influenced by the shadow, in this case, when you realise you're on the verge of being unassertive. This is the state of being ontologically responsive or ontological volition. We want to leverage the power of the Transformation Methodology to achieve that state of being responsive.'

'Thanks, Grace. Now could you please recap the stages of the Transformation Methodology and how the conception worksheet helps to facilitate that process?'

'Absolutely. The Transformation Methodology is an iterative process that begins with the three stages of awareness: **Reception** > **Perception** > **Conception** and progressively leads to integrity or wholeness and greater degrees of effectiveness, from competency to proficiency and, ultimately, mastery. Integrity and effectiveness increase the probability of fulfilling the intentions you care so deeply about. It's what allows you to sit in the driver's seat when responding to matters in life, regardless of their source. It's about getting to the point where you can maximise your ability to influence what you can and surrender to the rest, because, as human beings, there are limits to what we can influence.

'Now, to move from awareness to effectiveness, we go through rounds of the Application Phase of **Execute** > **Track** > **Learn** > **Refine** and back to Execute again. This phase is repeated over and over until transformation is achieved, for example, when you've transformed your relationship with assertiveness and no longer relate to the person you were before, the one who often lacked assertiveness in various situations. The conception worksheet facilitates the iterative Awareness and Application phases by helping you clarify your thinking and develop a deeper conception of the area you wish to transform. My approach has been to support you to adopt this paradigm and develop the habit of identifying the shadow sides of the Aspects of Being we've worked on via the three stages of awareness. Then you gradually conceived a more authentic and congruent understanding of that fragment of reality in each round of the iterative process before executing or acting upon that more refined conception. Does that clarify it for you, Yoren?'

'Yes, got it. Just out of curiosity, is there a state beyond what you just described, an even more refined state of responsiveness that enables us to influence a matter on-the-spot and in real time?' Yoren asked.

Smiling, Grace replied, 'Absolutely. It's a state where you can predict what might happen before it does. To clarify, as human beings, we can develop our vision and discernment to predict the consequences and outcomes of circumstances and events that haven't happened yet. I'm not talking about being prophetic. I'm simply pointing out that a highly aware and responsive person has the ability and foresight to develop high-quality guesses, or predict the consequences of certain matters and respond accordingly in advance. This ability comes with maturity and is one of the keys to developing wisdom. Consider this one of the most essential qualities any visionary leader can possess.'

Once Grace was satisfied that she'd fully addressed Yoren's questions, she continued coaching in line with the contract for the rest of the session. She asked Yoren relevant questions about how he related to being responsive in the context of starting his business. Each question required him to think deeply and provide an in-depth response.

As he gathered his things to leave, Yoren paused, looked at Grace and said, 'I have to confess that this session impacted me more profoundly than any other. The conversation around assertiveness was so real to me that I can feel it with every fibre of my being.'

Grace smiled. 'I'm so pleased, Yoren. I could tell that this session was especially impactful for you.'

'If it's okay with you, I'd like to sit with the conversation for a while. Would you mind if we postpone our next session until the week after next?' asked Yoren.

'I think that's a great idea. You can always contact me if you need my support in the meantime,' said Grace.

Once Yoren had left, Grace sat in her office to reflect on the session. She, too, had been deeply impacted by the conversation and Yoren's reaction to it all. At that moment, she felt intense satisfaction in her chosen career. While she'd loved coaching from the very beginning, there were times in the past when she felt as though she swapped her energy for her client's pain, leaving her depleted. These days, however, she usually left a coaching session feeling energised and empowered. Looking out at the garden, she took a moment to reflect on her day with gratitude, a practice she frequently enjoyed. She thought about the peaceful stillness of the dawn and the beautiful sunrise she'd witnessed in quiet solitude, a luxury she'd created for herself by getting up well before her children to get organised for the day. She recalled the delicious aroma of the muffins she'd baked from scratch this morning as a special request from her eldest child, Heavenly. She thought about her sister and how she'd willingly changed her plans for the day to be with Prosper so she could work. She thought of her own coach and smiled as she realised their next session was coming up soon. So many things and people to be grateful for.

It was midday, and realising she had no specific plans for the rest of the day – a rarity for her – she decided to take some time out to relax with a book and some lunch in the garden, knowing her sister was there to support her. Then tonight, she and her sister had planned a movie night at home with all the cousins, complete with popcorn and drinks. The kids were so excited and, she realised, so was she.

Metamorphosis

As Yoren approached the end of his coaching journey with Grace, he found himself increasingly reflecting on past events. It struck him how many times he could have easily averted his gaze from reality and turned his back on the opportunity to shift the course of his life. He recalled how one night, in particular, had almost ended the journey before it even began …

Yoren always berated himself for agreeing to attend a get-together at his parents' place. Sunday night's dinner was no exception. It was just the four of them: he and Mel, Stewart and Sahar. As usual, Stewart disagreed with some of Yoren's decisions and actions, leading to a heated argument. Meanwhile, Mel and Sahar tried their best to calm things down and save the evening. Predictably, their efforts proved to be in vain. Before Sahar had even had a chance to serve dessert, Yoren grabbed Mel's hand and announced they were leaving. On the drive home, he silently questioned his decision to trust Jen's recommendation to embark on a coaching journey with Grace, that seed of doubt planted by his father's snide remarks over dinner. Before that evening, he'd been filled with hope about the future. Now, the more he questioned himself, the more he wondered if coaching was the solution to his problems. The evening left him with a bitter aftertaste that lingered for days.

— ∎ —

Sahar was a gentle soul who worked hard to maintain peace within the family, especially between Yoren and his father. Born in Australia as the eldest of three children to Hanan and Aisha, both of Palestinian descent, Sahar grew up having enormous respect for people forced out of their homelands. For this reason, she decided early in her life to pursue a career that would enable her to support migrants and other refugees.

Hanan's parents fled Palestine during the first of three waves of migration in 1948, years before he was born. His father was an influential politician, so he sacrificed a great deal to leave all that behind and come to Australia. However, he and his wife felt they had little choice at the time. Hanan was born in Australia and enjoyed a life of relative privilege and freedom far from his parents' troubled homeland. After finishing school, he studied information technology at university, followed by a Master of Information Systems with a major in business analysis. His qualification opened many doors. However, lacking ambition at the time, he settled for a corporate career in the banking sector and was happy to do his job and go home at the end of each day rather than pursue more ambitious goals. As a self-proclaimed ethical and 'nice' person, Hanan was a pacifist who did his best to avoid conflict and not hurt anyone; however, his people-pleasing ways didn't always work in his favour. At times, his overly agreeable nature led him to put pressure on himself or play victim through self-sabotage. Despite this, he was generally content to accept whatever life brought him.

Aisha's parents also fled Palestine during the first wave to make a life for themselves in Australia, settling in a community dominated by other Palestinian refugees. Through this community, Aisha later met Hanan and shared an almost instant attraction. They married a year later and had three children, Sahar, Sana and Omar.

Temperament-wise, Aisha was far less agreeable than Hanan. While they enjoyed a good life as a family, she wished her husband was ambitious like she was. After studying natural medicine, Aisha became a herbalist, successfully integrating her career with motherhood. As a natural health practitioner who drew on a wide range of proven traditions, Aisha was well-respected within the Palestinian community, and there was usually a lengthy waiting list to see her.

Keen to see her eldest daughter follow in her footsteps, Aisha encouraged Sahar to study medicine. However, Sahar had other plans and dropped out in her first year to pursue social science. She met Stewart at university, and they married in their early twenties, producing their first child, Yoren, soon afterwards. Choosing to be the primary carer at home, Sahar worked part-time as a social worker and counsellor and, inspired by her heritage, was passionate about supporting migrants and refugees. For many years, Stewart and Sahar tried unsuccessfully to have another child. Eventually, they succeeded and welcomed Sophia into their family.

While Yoren had a strained relationship with his father, he was close to his mother. She had played a significant role in his upbringing, particularly in fostering the positive qualities later revealed through his coaching journey. As a nurturing and open female influence in his life, Sahar taught Yoren to be compassionate, loving, kind, forgiving and caring, although he spent much of his life ignoring and neglecting these qualities. Nevertheless, having a relatively healthy relationship with qualities like love and care made the coaching journey far easier for Grace than coaching someone who hadn't experienced these qualities much in their formative years. In raising Yoren, Sahar influenced him in ways beyond what was visible on the surface.

— ▪ —

Yoren's resentment after the interaction with his father over dinner hung over him like a dark cloud. Sitting alone in the living room the next evening, he absentmindedly stared at a soccer match on television while contemplating the day's events. It had not been a good day, and he blamed everyone but himself for how things had panned out.

He'd gone to work all fired up and ready to negotiate a pay rise and a higher commission rate with his boss, only to be denied. Then, to top it off, a colleague who Yoren believed had achieved far less for the company than him suddenly announced he'd been promoted. Yoren was furious, telling himself he'd only been overlooked for the position because he didn't suck up to the boss like his colleague did. As much as he tried to calm himself, he couldn't help but feel resentful and envious.

Yoren was so consumed by his inner chatter, a cacophony of confusion and self-doubt mixed with bitterness and envy, that he didn't hear Mel enter the room. She could see his eyes were glued to the screen and was perplexed as she knew he didn't follow soccer. He suddenly caught a glimpse of her in his peripheral vision.

'How are you, darling?' he asked.

His tone was warm and friendly, but Mel could tell he was acting on auto-pilot, fully self-absorbed and oblivious to her mood. He had no idea how much she'd longed for him to ask her that one simple question, a question that could potentially open Pandora's box if she answered it authentically and if he gave her the time to truly listen and be present.

Realising Yoren wasn't in the right frame of mind to be open to any meaningful conversation, Mel shrugged and replied nonchalantly, 'I'm fine. How about you? How was your day?'

'It was okay. Same old, same old for a Monday,' he responded without looking up, continuing to stare at the screen.

She turned and hastily made her way towards the bedroom, throwing herself onto the bed and allowing the tears to flow once behind closed doors. She blamed Yoren for failing to notice how she really was and making no attempt to decipher the unspoken words between them. Not once did she consider that her inauthenticity, lack of assertiveness and invulnerability might be the culprits behind her self-sabotage and growing habit of playing the victim.

— ▪ —

Sitting on a bench in the park during her lunch break, Mel toyed with her half-eaten salad as she fantasised about starting a family, a dream she'd had since she was a little girl, and thought back to her childhood. She'd grown up thinking her conservative parents were far too traditional and outdated for the era she was born into and often rebelled behind their backs. However, she ignored the fact that they'd gone against their own parents' wishes by entering into an interracial marriage, making them far more progressive than she'd ever given them credit for.

Mel's father, Robert, was steered into a trade by his devout Catholic, ultra-conservative parents, and he left school early for a plumbing apprenticeship. After qualifying as a tradesman, he married his high-school sweetheart. However, that marriage ended in heartbreak and divorce two years later when his wife announced her preference for women and moved in with her girlfriend, a close family friend. Completely blindsided, Robert couldn't bring himself to trust another woman for more than 10 years. He only reluctantly agreed to ask Linh, an attractive, younger Vietnamese woman, on a date after meeting her through a mutual friend. Despite their differences, lack of family support and Robert's continued wariness, they hit it off immediately and married six months later. The following year, the couple welcomed a daughter who they named Melara or Mel, as she became known. As much as they desperately wanted more children, Linh was unable to fall pregnant again.

Robert and Linh ran the local corner store, and her father continued to do plumbing jobs on the side to bolster their income. So Mel was accustomed to spending time on her own and never objected to helping out with the day-to-day running of the household. However, remembering how lonely it was growing up without siblings, she vowed she would have at least three children of her own one day.

As a teenager, Mel was increasingly influenced by popular culture and began to question the traditions her parents lived by, particularly around the institution of marriage and family. After leaving high school, she attended university and adopted a progressive and liberated approach to sexuality and relationships. However, she eventually became disillusioned with this way of life, especially after realising it didn't align with her dream of starting a family. Her ideal partner was someone who shared that vision. And this made her look at marriage in a different light and recall one of her mother's favourite and most frequently spoken sayings, which she'd adapted from a biblical verse: 'The house built on sand will never stand the test of time.' Knowing her mother's words were directed at her, Mel ignored them, especially when she went through her rebellious phase. But they often sprang to mind over the ensuing years.

By the time she'd graduated from university and embarked on her career, Mel had developed the maturity to recognise that many of the traditions she used to look down upon, including those instilled by her parents, were meaningful and relevant. She came to understand that her so-called 'progressive lifestyle' had lured her away from the values that had become her priority. She found it both amusing and intriguing how things she'd always considered a 'vice' could become a 'virtue' and vice versa after exploring them from a different perspective. While these thoughts made her feel deeply humbled, they also prompted her to wonder why human intellect and rationality don't always work in our favour.

Finding relevance in matters that her rationale and logic previously made her question, Mel began to see the traditions handed down by her parents in a different light, particularly once she reached her early thirties and felt her body clock ticking. Furthermore, knowing her mother couldn't conceive after having her made Mel anxious that she might experience similar challenges. But she kept these thoughts close to her chest. She learned the hard way to tread lightly around the topic of parenthood with the men she dated after discovering they would often take off as quickly as they could after it was broached. She carried this fear into her relationship with Yoren, even after they'd declared their love and commitment to one another through their engagement. Deep down, she resented feeling unable to speak her mind about a subject she believed should be an obvious next stage of life.

Fatherhood was the last thing on Yoren's mind until recently. He longed for the 'perfect life' complete with the dream home, the best car, travel to exotic places and the most impressive career and social status. He'd also been intent on meeting and dating as many women as possible before committing to 'the one'. Even after proposing to Mel, he intended to continue enjoying the high life with her for as long as possible before bringing a baby into the picture. From what he could tell from friends and colleagues, kids were demanding and time-consuming liabilities, and he was nowhere near ready for that 'burden'. He was pretty sure Mel was on the same page; she seemed more interested in building her career and being financially independent than becoming a mother. She also enjoyed the lifestyle they'd built together as much as he did or so he thought.

Unbeknown to Yoren, Mel's priorities had shifted dramatically, particularly in the last year and a half. Disillusioned with her work in HR, she found the idea of having a baby and becoming a mother was once again at the forefront of her mind. She assumed Yoren wanted the same thing. However, their hidden conversations about parenthood threatened to rip their relationship apart. It seemed their individual interpretation of what their future together would look like was becoming increasingly disparate over time. Based on her past experience with men, Mel was afraid that if she raised the baby conversation too early, Yoren might panic and take himself out of the equation, just like the others. She loved him too deeply to risk making the same mistake.

— ■ —

Yoren continued to mindlessly stare at the screen, unaware Mel was upset when she left the room. His mind was a whirl of emotions as he tried to ignore the dark shadows clouding his judgement. But his efforts were in vain. He was consumed by his own inauthenticity, which he interpreted as not being who he'd always wanted to be. And no amount of external success was filling that gaping hole. He recalled something Erik had said in the information session: 'Often the greatest shadow of all is an unactualised potential, which is when we become present to not yet being who or where we hoped we'd be at a certain stage in our lives.' His sense of inauthenticity was so strong that he suddenly realised he was failing to consider matters and people beyond him, most notably, his beautiful, intelligent and loving partner in life, Mel.

Deep down, Yoren knew how much Mel wanted to start a family, but he noticed she hadn't raised the subject with him in a while, which suited him because he was more than happy to be inauthentic and avoid it with willful blindness. He wanted everything in his life to be sorted and perfectly engineered before taking that step. At the same time, Mel knew in her heart that Yoren wasn't ready to have that conversation. But withholding her thoughts and feelings from him was slowly killing her inside. There were even times when she could have left him, frustrated over his wavering and lack of confidence, commitment and communication. But then she reminded herself that up until the last year and a half, she'd also deprioritised starting a family to focus on her career. So she could resonate with him to a degree.

On the upside, she was encouraged that he'd chosen to embark on the coaching journey. She could already see glimpses of increased awareness and care in him and that he wasn't as self-absorbed as he used to be. This gave her hope and a higher degree of optimism about their future. While they each had different perspectives about the current state of their relationship, they both knew they were out of sync and that there were unspoken conversations between them. They were also aware of how they were deliberately avoiding those conversations.

— ∎ —

Suddenly snapping back to the present moment, Mel realised her mouth was dry, her heart was racing and her breathing was shallow. It felt like she'd been holding her breath while events from the past played like a newsreel on the screen of her mind. Shaking herself to remove the cobwebs, she cleared her vision to take in the beauty of the scenes playing out beyond her bedroom window. It was like she was seeing the view for the first time. The ocean's transitioning hues from aqua to turquoise to deep blue on the horizon. The way the sun's rays flirted and danced with each newly formed wave. How the offshore sea spray resembled the manes of a hundred white horses galloping in the wind. She could see surfers fighting for the best position to catch and ride the next wave, people sunbathing on the golden sand, couples walking hand-in-hand along the foreshore, families enjoying a picnic, and children building sand castles and flying kites. It was mesmerising.

Observing the scenes beyond the window, Mel became present to the blessings in her life. She couldn't believe how much Yoren had transformed over the past six months and the impact his transformation was having on their life together. He was calmer and more attentive. He was also more present, which encouraged her to be more forgiving of herself and the mistakes they'd both made in the past. Watching the families on the beach brought a smile to her face. She imagined a future when that would be her, Yoren and their children and wondered why she'd pushed that dream aside for so long for the sake of a corporate job she found unfulfilling. Suddenly missing her fiancé and wishing he was by her side to witness all this beauty, she grabbed her phone to call him, but then remembered he was meeting with Dylan at the golf club. So instead, she decided to iron her outfit for tonight's anniversary dinner date at home, wrap his gift and start preparing the ingredients for the three-course menu she'd planned. She couldn't wait to see him.

— ∎ —

Yoren and Dylan had caught up several times, both in person and online, to further discuss the possibility of joining forces. They both enthusiastically spent hours and hours together exploring various ideas, analysing their potential market and researching the landscape to determine if there were any existing solutions to the SaaS product they planned to build. However, this time was different. Today they intended to confirm their commitment to one another. As Yoren walked into their usual meeting place at the club, he beamed when he spotted his friend and soon-to-be business partner.

Over lunch, they openly expressed their feelings about going into partnership, including the pros and cons. In the end, they decided the pros outweighed the cons. Shaking hands, Yoren and Dylan committed to the partnership, no matter what happened, despite not yet fully knowing what their SaaS product would look like, let alone the problems it would solve. Their ideas had changed considerably, particularly over the last two weeks. Despite the unknowns, they chose to value their partnership more than the actual business idea or concept, convinced they would work it out as they go.

Before they wrapped up the meeting, Dylan raised the subject of coaching, as he'd been curious about the process since learning of Yoren's experience with Grace. Pleased that Dylan had brought it up, Yoren suggested he contact Grace and consider coaching for himself. He told him enthusiastically that he believed it would make a massive difference to their business partnership, particularly in facilitating effective communication around building and growing the business through a mutual language and thought process concerning how things work in the real world, also known as a 'shared mental model'. Dylan was open to the idea, especially after witnessing significant changes in Yoren since he committed to coaching with Grace. He wondered how it might support him too.

On his drive home, Dylan reflected on the major commitment he'd just made. He felt an overwhelming sense of excitement and antic-ipation. Knowing he lacked the courage to start a business on his own and would never have initiated the idea of building a business in partnership with someone had Yoren not raised the idea, he was deeply grateful to his friend. He also couldn't help feeling relieved that he no longer had to apply for jobs, knowing he had ample funds saved to live on until the business got off the ground.

Stopping to buy a bunch of flowers for Mel on his way home, Yoren felt profoundly grateful for both his personal life and his career. Not only had he established a wonderful partnership with Mel, but he'd also just committed to a business partnership with his best friend. His bond with both of them had never been stronger. He knew he also had an incredible support network in Jen and Grace. What more could he want? Interestingly, he'd always had access to all of this; he just wasn't present to it.

— ∎ —

Seated opposite Mel at the dining table, a candle flickering in the centre, Yoren thought he'd never seen her look more beautiful. Like him, she'd dressed up for the occasion of their third anniversary and had prepared a delicious French-inspired meal. They took their time to savour each course, chatting excitedly about the wedding, the status of their professional lives and their future together. Mel was delighted to see this new, authentic and vulnerable side of Yoren. She recalled that it wasn't long ago when he would have found her efforts to create the perfect romantic atmosphere for an anniversary dinner excessive and clichéd.

Yoren told Mel about his partnership agreement with Dylan – news that delighted her because she knew what a genuine friend he was to Yoren – and they discussed the best time for Yoren to tender his resignation. Mel shared that she'd already spoken to her boss about returning to full-time work and confirmed her commitment to be the main financial provider for a while. She also revealed that she'd agreed to work with Jen and her colleagues to develop herself as a coach and how excited she was to add all of this to her arsenal as an HR practitioner. She was curious to see what this new knowledge and skills could bring to the table, hinting at the possibility of doing some coaching on the side and potentially making it her future career. She shared that she could envisage running a coaching business while raising their children. Unlike in the past, Yoren was happy to chat about their plans to start a family. However, they both agreed it would be best to wait until the business was reasonably well-established before she fell pregnant.

It was clear their relationship had reached a new level. There was clarity and willingness to deal with a much higher degree of uncertainty. There was also hope and a vision for the future. They were far more in sync and ready to move forward with their plans. Careerwise, Mel now had renewed direction and meaning. She also felt a profound sense of satisfaction that she was tangibly contributing to Yoren's dream to start a business and their overall financial wellbeing and prosperity. Growing up, her parents had taught her the importance of a husband and wife being there for one another through all the ups and downs. Despite all the uncertainties and unknowns, Yoren felt blessed and grateful for his life with Mel. They were both acutely aware of renewed commitment in their partnership.

— ∎ —

Yoren was working on his coaching challenges during his lunch break when he suddenly had the urge to call Grace, wanting to confirm that he was on the right track with his assertiveness challenge. Although he'd asked for a fortnight between sessions rather than the usual week, he realised he was missing that regular interaction. He messaged Grace to see if she was available and she called him a moment later as she was between clients. After chatting for several minutes, Yoren felt confident he was on the right track. Before they ended the call, Grace told him she'd heard from Dylan and how, after a brief conversation, he'd agreed to complete the assessment and meet with her to explore the possibility of entering into a coaching agreement. Yoren was delighted to hear it.

After work, Yoren was eager to get home for his weekly video catch up with his sister, Sophia, who was on a six-month working holiday in Europe. At 23, Sophia was much younger than Yoren, but they'd always shared a close bond. With her rebellious, curious nature, bubbly disposition, natural good looks and bohemian style, she reminded him of their aunt Jen, both in character and appearance. Sophia enthusiastically told him about her new experiences and the diverse people she'd met. She explained that she'd just been in Vienna, was currently in Amsterdam, and was heading to Andalusia in a few days to find fruit-picking work.

Seeing his sister light up the screen as she chatted excitedly about her adventures brought back fond memories of his own travels at a similar age. That time seemed so long ago now. Looking back, he realised how much he'd changed. It was almost like he was a different person back then and he wondered what Sophia's life would look like 10 years from now. His recollections made him reflect on how different stages of life bring varied perspectives that ultimately lead us to shape a more comprehensive and potentially congruent conception of reality. He realised that the more perspectives we tap into, the more effectively we can relate to life, leading to better decisions and the ability to adapt our priorities in line with our changing values and goals.

— ■ —

Dylan was grateful to Yoren for referring him to Grace, especially now that he'd completed an assessment and debrief with her, which he found fascinating and eye-opening. During their conversation, Grace told him how coaches often use the being discourse to support their clients to build or transform the culture within an organisation and to enhance team dynamics. This gave Dylan a deeper insight into why Yoren had suggested he consider coaching: to support them in building the company culture they wanted.

Reflecting on the session afterwards, Dylan found he'd connected most with the conversations around courage, fear, anxiety and assertiveness. He realised these were all areas he desperately wanted to work on as he could see that his lack of courage and assertiveness, combined with his fear and anxiety, had been getting in the way of him finding fulfilment for much of his life. He decided to give Grace the go-ahead to coach him and couldn't wait to tell Yoren.

— ■ —

Yoren and Dylan were now meeting weekly to plan their business. They started by contacting the people they knew in an attempt to entice them on board as investors and created a preliminary budget for the first 12 months, deciding that if they stuck to the plan, they'd make it work. Their aim was to develop a predictive plan for both the technological aspects of their business and the commercial side, particularly sales and marketing. While they knew they were working with estimates at this stage, as a lot was still unclear, they figured the numbers would at least give them an estimate of the capital they'd require upfront.

They agreed they would need to bring some software developers and engineers on board immediately, but thought they could handle the product testing themselves. They estimated a marketing budget based on a comprehensive go-to-market strategy and considered a minimum wage for themselves as the founders. The more their plan unfolded, the more they could see the numbers adding up exponentially. By the time their budget was complete, they realised they would require enormous capital upfront to get the business off the ground. So they got to work creating their first pitch deck presentation, together with a comprehensive business plan and implementation roadmap, using a template and informative video they found online. Yoren toyed with the idea of approaching Samuel, his grandfather – whose entrepreneurial journey he'd always admired – about seed funding if all other avenues proved unsuccessful. But for now, he held that card close to his chest.

— ■ —

Samuel Healy was eight years old when he, his two younger sisters, Leah and Rachel, and their parents, Gerald and Stella, emigrated from Dublin to Tel Aviv in 1950, just two years after the establishment of the State of Israel. Like many Irish Jews, they left their homeland willingly, out of ideological and religious convictions, and looked forward to building a new life for their family. What they didn't know at the time, however, was that the newly established state was facing a deep economic crisis. As well as recovering from the devastating effects of the 1948 Arab–Israeli war, the nation was forced to absorb hundreds of thousands of Jewish refugees from Europe and almost a million from the Arab world. Consequently, Israel was financially overwhelmed. The resulting economic crisis led to a policy of austerity to reduce public debt and shrink the budget deficit. This policy was in place from 1949 to 1959. Unemployment was high, and foreign currency reserves were scarce. So within months of their arrival, Gerald and Stella felt quite isolated in their new homeland and missed their tight-knit community in Dublin. But there was no turning back. They had no choice but to raise their three children in this environment of hardship in a country that lacked political, social and economic stability. They realised they would need to draw on every ounce of available strength to keep their family going.

In 1952, Israel and West Germany signed an agreement stipulating that West Germany would compensate Israel for the persecution of Jews during the Holocaust and for Jewish property stolen by the Nazis. Reparations over the next 14 years significantly contributed to the Israeli economy. Around the same time, the Israeli Declaration of Independence coincided with the Palestinian Catastrophe, also known as the Nakba. This saw the destruction of the Palestinian homeland and society, as well as the permanent displacement of Palestinian Arabs. What began in 1948 with the persecution, displacement and occupation of Palestinians in the West Bank, the Gaza Strip and Palestinian refugee camps throughout the region led to the exodus of over 700,000 people, the denial of the Palestinian right of return and, ultimately, the obliteration of Palestinian society.

As Samuel grew from child to teenager, he began to question why those in power in Israel were doing to others the same sorts of things that had caused their people so much suffering. He was not yet mature enough to fully comprehend the cultural and societal conflict, let alone the irony of it all. At 19, he met 18-year-old Uriel through match-making, and they married a year later. In the same year, the barely 20-year-old Samuel lost his father to an aggressive cancer, and he assumed responsibility for supporting his mother and younger siblings. He decided to try to create his fortune by starting his own business. However, after several attempts and multiple rounds of failure over the next 10 years, he realised he was fighting a losing battle, given Israel's socialist-leaning economy. As the economic system wasn't market-oriented, it didn't favour an ambitious, determined young entrepreneur like Samuel. By then, he and Uriel had produced three children – Stewart, Jenna and Igor – and, with a deep-seated desire to take the family's financial prosperity beyond what he thought was possible in Israel at the time, he decided to move the family to a new and distant land.

It was 1978, and Samuel had just turned 36 when the Healy family made the long journey to Australia. Ironically, Israel implemented an economic stabilisation plan seven years later to combat crippling inflation. The subsequent introduction of market-oriented structural reforms reinvigorated the economy and paved the way for its rapid growth in the 1990s. The plan became a model for other countries facing similar economic crises. However, it was too late for Samuel to take advantage of the reforms as he was now well-established on the other side of the world.

Arriving in a foreign land so far from Europe and Israel, Samuel and Uriel quickly grew to love Australia's breathtaking landscape and laid-back culture. At the same time, Samuel was deeply present to the changes occurring within the Australian economy, which he found aligned more with what he believed would work in his favour as a businessman. They had arrived when the Australian Government was led by Malcolm Fraser. Influenced by the economic ideas espoused by American Nobel prize-winning economist and statistician Milton Friedman, Fraser tapped into supply-side economics, or 'economic rationalism' as it was known in Australia. It was an approach that tended to favour economically liberal policies such as deregulation, a free market economy, the privatisation of state-owned industries, lower direct taxation and higher indirect taxation. In other words, it was an economic policy based on the supposed efficiency of market forces, characterised by minimal government intervention, tax cuts, privatisation and the deregulation of labour markets. However, the term was also used to describe advocates of market-oriented reform within the Australian Labor Party, whose position was closer to what became known as the 'Third Way', an attempt to bring people together by reconciling right-wing and left-wing politics to promote moderation, balance and integrity. Studying all of this made Samuel convinced that the economic environment would lead to a relatively thriving economy that would favour his intentions. So he felt ready and willing to venture on as an entrepreneur.

By the age of 42, Samuel had built a substantial financial portfolio; however, he remained laser-focused on continuing to grow his financial empire. His primary business involved supplying jewellers with diamonds and other precious gemstones and he'd also built a successful wedding catering company, while his growing investment portfolio included shares in various financial institutions. Despite his focus on business, Samuel remained deeply family-oriented. He chose to sacrifice many things to continue supporting his mother and siblings in Israel, in addition to Uriel and their children, as he hoped to give his family a level of stability he never had.

It was also important to Samuel to create generational wealth and he hoped his children would continue the tradition. However, all three chose very different paths. Stewart opted for academia, while Igor went into politics. Jenna was the only one of the three who wanted to be 'self-made' like her father. However, this proved to be a double-edged sword for Samuel as it meant she refused to join him in what he'd hoped would be a family business. It was only after Jenna resigned from the corporate sector and started working part-time as a coach that she decided to support the management of her father's investment portfolio by taking a seat on the board.

Samuel later learned more about Australia's harsh history and the abhorrent treatment of its First Nations peoples. It made him realise that human-led atrocities have occurred globally since the beginning of time. Being present to all of this, from the persecution of the Jews and Palestinians to the mistreatment of First Nations Australians and others, he wondered how we human beings could cause such pain and suffering to each other and how the role of victim and offender can change over time. His observations, studies and experiences led him to be ambitious yet humble in business – always endeavouring to make ethical decisions – and sparked a passion for altruism. This gradually shaped who he became and the businesses he created. At 81, Samuel was still Chairman of his holding company, but no longer as hands-on. While he continued to oversee the investment portfolio from a high-level perspective, he spent most of his time in philanthropic pursuits with Uriel, supporting people in need through charity work and, particularly, through micro-financing.

— ▪ —

The night before his final session with Grace, Yoren lay awake while Mel slept peacefully beside him. She'd fallen asleep reading the book Jen had given her, exhausted after a long day at work. He'd gently removed it from her grasp, marked the page she was on and placed it on the bedside table. He smiled as he thought about how she was becoming increasingly curious about the being discourse and that the more she read, the more questions she had.

He was deep in thought. What a journey it had been so far, a journey that had opened his eyes to possibilities he hadn't considered before. Never in his wildest dreams had he imagined he would choose to enter into a business partnership with his best friend and be so open to becoming a father at this stage of his life. He thought about the secure, well-paid corporate career he was about to leave. Despite disagreements at times, deep down, he had enormous respect for his boss. He also valued the brand he worked for and, for the most part, enjoyed working with and managing his team. He was present to the value his team and organisation were bringing to the world. There were so many factors that could have kept him there. But his heart was no longer in it and he would be betraying himself and others if he stayed. It just wasn't authentic for him to work there anymore.

He remembered his discomfort and insincerity at the beginning of the coaching journey and how sceptical he'd been about coaching in general. Now he was deeply present to how inauthentic it had been for him to generalise an entire profession when the framework a coach chooses to leverage, how they facilitate the coaching process and the coach themselves make all the difference. He realised consistency, integrity and goodwill were evident in every interaction with Grace and he now had a sense of what it took for a person to become as polished and well-rounded as she was. Most importantly, he learned that the effectiveness of coaching also depends on how the coachee chooses to relate to it. He could now clearly see why it was so important to be sincere and not just curious, and how critical it was to have a clear intention to want to fulfil and to bring intentionality to the coaching process. Furthermore, after six months of regular sessions, Yoren was so accustomed to having a coach that it felt odd to think the process was about to end. Even beyond the coaching, he liked Grace so much as a person that he knew he'd miss her. She'd impacted him in more ways than he could articulate.

He was still consumed by his thoughts when a notification on his phone jolted him back to the present moment.

That's got to be Jen. Who else would text me at 10 minutes past midnight?

How's it going, legend?

I'm fine, Jen. How about you? Do you realise what time it is? Shouldn't you be asleep?

Haha, yes, but you know me; when a thought pops into my head … Are you and Mel free to join Nader and me for dinner at our place on Sunday night?

I'm up for it. But I'll confirm tomorrow after checking with Mel.

Great. Text or call me in the morning.

Will do. Did you know I've got my last coaching session with Grace in the morning?

Wow, that's gone quickly! Enjoy. And don't leave anything left unsaid or incomplete.

We'll talk later. Time to get some sleep. Good luck with your final session. Hope to see you both Sunday. Come at 6 and just bring yourselves. Good night, Yoren.

He closed his eyes and willed himself to go to sleep, unable to tell if he was nervous or excited.

— ▪ —

As usual, Grace opened the session by asking Yoren what he felt like expressing. He used the opportunity to update her on where he and Dylan were at with their business planning, including the budget they'd drawn up and their attempts at finding an investor. While she found numerous incongruencies in what he told her, based on what she knew about establishing a startup, Grace simply reminded him about the importance of authentic awareness as an approach to anything in life.

'Yoren, it's great to hear the enthusiasm in your voice and that you're moving forward with your plans. However, before we begin today's session, would you mind if I draw your attention to something beyond our coaching agreement?'

Yoren nodded his agreement.

'Before you take any action and make any decisions, particularly costly ones, I would strongly encourage you to consider the authenticity of your perceptions, including your perception of investment, capital injection and strategic business planning. I'm happy to refer you to a business coach I know who can support you if you like. His name's Connor O'Reilly. Just let me know if you're interested and I'll introduce you via email.'

Yoren was too excited to pay attention to Grace's suggestion and ignored it for now. His obsession with becoming a 'self-made successful entrepreneur' made him want to do everything himself.

Grace steered the conversation back to their contract for the coaching session, and they completed their conversations on assertiveness. They then moved on to reliability, the last Aspect of Being they had agreed to explore for this coaching contract.

'Grace, can you remind me why you suggested we leave reliability till last?' asked Yoren.

'Sure. I suggested we explore this Secondary Way of Being as our final one because reliability is one of the main outcomes of transformation. It's when you consistently perform as intended while completing what's expected of you or agreed to fully and on time. Being reliable means you produce consistent results in line with your promises and expectations. It means you can be depended on or trusted to be available, ready and fully present. As you have learned throughout this process, transformation is all about polishing yourself through the three stages of awareness – reception, perception and conception – which then leads you to be more integrous and effective. The more polished you are overall, the more reliable you become.'

'Got it. But isn't it just as important for me to ensure others are reliable too?' he asked.

'Yes, absolutely,' said Grace. 'Just as reliability generates trust in you from others, you may be unlikely to trust others unless you consider them reliable too. As social beings, we all need to rely on each other. Consider that a world without reliability would be unworkable.'

'Okay, so in my case, my partners, Mel and Dylan, expect me to be reliable, and I expect the same from them, correct?'

'That's right. And when you and Dylan eventually take on employees, you'll pay them based on the assumption that they'll be reliable in delivering what's expected of them.'

'That all seems pretty straightforward, Grace. I'm not sure I understand why we need to spend time on this when it's logical that we all need to be reliable for the business to work,' said Yoren, a little perplexed.

'You're on the verge of building your family and business, Yoren. Since reliability is critical for those partnerships to work, that's what I'd like to leave you with as we come to the end of this coaching journey. How about we re-read the distinction together,' suggested Grace.

Reliability

Reliability is consistently performing as intended while completing what is expected of you or agreed to fully and on time. When you are being reliable, you produce consistent results in line with promises and expectations. You can be depended on to be available, ready, fully present and show up when needed.

A healthy relationship with *reliability* indicates that you are acknowledged as someone who can be counted on to fulfil your promises. Others know that when you agree to something, it will happen as and when you said it would. You expect – and others expect you – to complete all tasks and projects you undertake as promised and on time.

An unhealthy relationship with *reliability* indicates that you often have difficulty completing tasks or seeing projects through to completion. You may be someone others choose not to count on. You may underestimate timeframes and push back deadlines. You may be frequently late for meetings and complain that you have too much to do or are running behind. You may be considered someone who lets others down, over-promises and rarely delivers as agreed. You may be unpredictable, overly spontaneous or frequently change course without considering the consequences. Alternatively, you may excessively go beyond what is required of you or necessary for the project.

They explored reliability further, including its shadow sides and Grace explained that awareness, all the Moods and all the Primary Ways of Being play a significant role in our ability to be reliable.

'Thanks, Grace. Now I can see why we covered it. I'd never really considered that an unhealthy relationship with reliability could manifest as being unpredictable or overly spontaneous. I can now see how that could be just as detrimental to the business as being unreliable,' said Yoren thoughtfully.

'Great. I propose we now briefly review your most recent profile assessment results. Are you happy to do that now, Yoren?' asked Grace.

'Absolutely! I'm keen to see the difference from the first time I completed it at the beginning of this journey.' Yoren edged forward in his seat, eager to get started.

They checked his latest results, comparing them to his first, and Yoren was thrilled at how far he had come. The report showed remarkable growth, particularly in certain areas, and highlighted the shadows, which he now saw as possibilities for future development.

'Before we finish, Grace, I just want you to clarify one last thing for me.'

'Sure, go ahead.'

'When I'm going through the iterative application phase of the Transformation Methodology, I understand that I need to execute, track, learn, refine and execute again. The part I'm struggling with is how to hold myself to account when I no longer have you as my coach to be accountable to. Any suggestions to help me keep making new commitments and holding myself to account to achieve them?' he asked sincerely.

'Sure,' said Grace. 'Remember how we explored ontological responsiveness in our last session?'

'Yes, but what does that have to do with holding myself to account?'

'Well, consider that the more ontologically responsive you are, the more self-discipline and self-control you have. It heightens your awareness and makes you more capable of catching yourself and changing course whenever you're about to cross a line you've drawn for yourself,' Grace replied.

'Ah, so I guess being proactive in that way would help me become quite adept at holding myself to account. Is that right?' asked Yoren.

'Correct. To recap, being ontologically responsive is the opposite of being reactive. It's when you catch yourself when you're about to be influenced by the shadow side of one or more Aspects of Being and then respond accordingly. In other words, you'll be able to preempt when you're on the verge of being unreliable or inconsistent, or when a shadow side of any Aspect of Being begins to take hold. Then, instead of a knee-jerk reaction, you'll respond more effectively.'

'So, in terms of holding myself to account, that's about making a commitment to myself and keeping it,' said Yoren. 'By being ontologically responsive, I'll notice when I'm on the verge of not meeting that commitment and respond accordingly.'

'That's right, Yoren. However, it's always beneficial to establish an agreement with someone else to support you in being accountable. It could be a business partner, life partner, mentor, coach; it doesn't matter, as long as an agreement is established so that both parties are on the same page.'

'Ah, yes, I get it! It's all so clear to me now,' he said, beaming. 'To be a powerful leader, I need to be reliable, both for myself and others. And I can only be reliable if I'm intentionally aware, integrous and effective. And that won't happen unless I value ontological responsiveness and take charge of my actions, decisions and behaviours.'

Yoren felt their conversations around reliability and responsiveness made everything they'd explored over the last six months so much more tangible and relatable. Grace could see, from the look in his eye, that it had all come together for him and confirmed that they'd left nothing incomplete.

Wrapping up the session, she commended Yoren on how far he'd come and on his willingness to be vulnerable and allow the process to unfold with ease and flow. She handed him a list of suggested further reading and told him that if he ever felt the need for further coaching support down the track, she was only a phone call away.

Realising the session was wrapping up, Yoren reached into his bag for the thank-you gift he'd purchased.

'Grace, I can't find the right words to express how much I appreciate your support. I know I haven't always been the easiest person to work with and I've no doubt challenged your patience at times. But what you've given me is the gift of literally transforming the trajectory of my life, personally and professionally. And I can't thank you enough for that. Please accept this gift as a small token of my appreciation.'

He handed her the gift, and she accepted it with gratitude. It was beautifully wrapped and included a handwritten card. Grace was visibly touched.

Inside was a velvet box containing a delicate crystal butterfly paper-weight. Carefully removing it from the box, Grace held the crystal up to the window and it reflected the sun's rays, creating tiny rainbows on the wall.

'Yoren, it's absolutely beautiful, thank you!'

'I'm so pleased you like it,' Yoren responded with a smile. 'I chose a butterfly as I found it a fitting way to depict the metamorphosis I feel like I've experienced during this coaching journey.'

CHAPTER 14

Crescendo

L ounging in his favourite chair on the balcony of their apartment, Yoren marvelled at the changing colours in the sky as the sunset heralded the end of a glorious October day. He was filled with a deep sense of humility and calmness as the evening sun cast long shadows on the dancing ocean and expanse of golden sand. A few eager surfers remained in the line-up, peering out to the horizon for a sign that their final wave of the day was building momentum. The last beachgoers were busy packing their belongings and gathering their children for the journey home.

Yoren cast his mind back to how sceptical he'd been when first introduced to the being conversation during the online information session he'd attended so many months ago. He vividly remembered how Erik's words had initially triggered feelings of anger and resistance before attracting his attention with certain points that hit home. He reflected on his many conversations with Grace, Jen's valuable contributions, and all the conception worksheets he'd completed. He thought about the invulnerability, inauthenticities and resistance he'd shown. He was suddenly deeply present to how this entire journey had supported him to where he was now and couldn't believe how the trajectory of his life had changed so radically through a series of intentional conversations and practices. He realised he could no longer relate to himself the way he was just months ago. The Yoren of the past had become a total stranger.

He thought about how distrustful he used to be and how doubt, hesitation and an overall lack of integrity had prevented him from taking ownership of his life with Mel: the beautiful, intelligent and caring woman he now knew would be by his side for the rest of his life. He marvelled at how happy and excited he was to be building a business with his best friend and wondered how he could have been so ignorant of Dylan's value in his life before. Ironically, many of the things he longed for were right in front of him all along. But he was too distracted and blind to see them back then. It took the coaching journey with Grace to not only make him present to the blessings in his life but to help him relate to them differently and commit to acting upon this new way of being.

Deep in thought, Yoren was oblivious to how much time had passed until he realised, with surprise, that day had turned to night. A crescent moon shone like a silvery claw in the night sky. He looked up at the blanket of stars that stretched to infinity as though he was seeing them for the first time and was suddenly aware of how small and insignificant we beings are in the grand scheme of things, like a drop in the ocean of existence. And yet, he knew there would be no ocean unless all these drops were united. Realising the paradoxical significance of this reminded him of some of the statements Jen would share during their conversations, many of which he'd ignored at the time, finding them too esoteric for his liking.

> *Incredible how quickly time passes! It feels like only yesterday when I embarked on this coaching journey. Time really is fleeting. How easy it is to get lost in the past or hung up about the future when right now is the moment to seize.*

In reflecting on time, Yoren failed to recognise that his life would have little to no meaning if all he focused on was its passing, like a lit candle gradually burning down until extinguished. Far better to be present to the beautiful light it casts along the way.

Spellbound by the beauty of his surroundings and the profoundness of his thoughts, Yoren felt so relaxed and at peace that he dozed off, something the 'old Yoren' would never have done.

Mel arrived home quite late after another day of overtime, an increasing occurrence since she'd switched to full-time work. Yawning as she walked towards the glass sliding doors to the balcony to close the blinds, she was surprised to see Yoren curled up on the outdoor recliner. He looked so peaceful that she didn't want to disturb him. Although it was an unusually warm evening for spring, the sea breeze was quite fresh. So she grabbed a throw from the sofa and gently placed it over him. By the time she was ready for bed, Yoren had woken up and come inside. They chatted about their respective days, and Mel reminded Yoren about their dinner plans with her parents the next evening before they retired to the bedroom together.

The crisp early morning breeze through the open window touched Yoren's skin and woke him from a deep, restful slumber. Looking at his watch, he was shocked to see that it was 7 am. He couldn't remember the last time he'd slept this soundly and for so many uninterrupted hours. The sun poured through the window, lighting up the room and casting a golden glow on Mel's exposed shoulders, face and hair. He rubbed his eyes and surveyed the scene beyond the bedroom window. The sun's rays lit up the beach like an artist's brush strokes on canvas.

It was a Saturday. His routine for the past six months involved rising early for a run on the beach, followed by a shower, a leisurely breakfast while going over his challenges for the week and the drive to Grace's for his weekly session. It felt odd not to have anywhere he needed to be. Now that he was left to his own devices, he felt mixed emotions. While he was somewhat anxious, he was fiercely determined to be with his anxiety and make everything he'd been working on come together as planned. He realised what an exciting time it was and that he couldn't wait to move forward with it all. Looking at Mel as she began to stir from her peaceful slumber, he felt such an overwhelming sense of pride and love for her that it seemed his heart would burst with joy. Soon, he would be able to call her his wife. He couldn't wait.

It suddenly occurred to him how much more present he was now to the beauty and wonder in the world around him, even though nothing had physically changed. The sun was still the same sun, the moon was still the same moon, and the ocean was still the same ocean. All was as it always had been. He was grateful for having discovered his ability, as a human being, to transform.

— ■ —

Yoren and Dylan were now working feverishly on their startup plans. Their partnership official, they met three times a week and spoke daily by phone. It was clear to all who knew them that they'd been well and truly bitten by the entrepreneurship bug. After changing their core business concept a few times, the pair agreed on the product they believed would deliver the most significant impact on the market and therefore generate the greatest return.

Leaning into their corporate experience, they finally prepared a comprehensive business plan and used it as ammunition to raise funds to build the various business components they believed they needed from the start, including the software application, a development team, a market research budget, an R&D fund and sufficient funds to pay themselves a modest salary. Assuming they'd be invited to meet with potential investors, they dipped into their personal savings to develop a company logo, and ordered branded pens, business cards and other paraphernalia.

Filled with hope and optimism, they reached out to 15 potential investors and scheduled three initial meetings to test the waters. However, after the first two meetings, they were swiftly brought back to earth. Unperturbed, they reached out to a few early-stage angel investors. Although they received insightful feedback here and there, on the whole, their endeavours were unsuccessful. Those who took the time to respond indicated they were far from investment-ready.

And the angel investors didn't regard them as serious players, especially once they saw their expectation to receive a salary from the initial investment. Yoren still considered getting his grandfather on board at some point. But he continued to remain tight-lipped about that option, preferring it to be a last resort.

After looking into the statistics, Yoren and Dylan realised how few startups were lucky enough to land an initial investment. So they swiftly changed tack and decided 'bootstrapping' was their best option. Surfing the net taught them that bootstrapping is when you rely solely on existing resources, including personal savings, to start and grow a company. Although hesitant to use their own capital, they decided it was worth the risk. After reprioritising their requirements, starting with the software development components, they received a few quotes from various outsourcing companies. They settled on a software development company in the Philippines that claimed, after going through their idea on a quick video call, to be able to build the software they needed in just a few months and at a fraction of the cost. Ironically, their software design included several features they assumed their potential market needed and wanted even though they hadn't conducted any needs analysis.

Yoren and Dylan's hastily-selected outsourcing company's development team agreed in writing to build the software, including all the 'bells and whistles' they asked for. In the proposal, they were given a detailed list of the features that would be built and told that it would take four months and cost $90,000 to complete. While they'd heard that creating a prototype, testing and validation before committing to the build would be a far more effective plan, they felt extremely confident that their idea was different from anything else they'd seen. So, without hesitation, they dipped into their personal savings to contribute 50% each towards the development costs. They were naively convinced that outsourcing the development would free up their time to focus on marketing, sales and relationship-building in readiness for the launch of a product they were sure the market wanted, even though they hadn't undertaken the appropriate due diligence. Confident that their actions would also make the business more investment-ready, they both felt greater hope of eventually achieving the seed capital they needed.

— ∎ —

Yoren felt both happy and a little anxious as he drove to Darling Harbour to meet Grace for lunch. The last two months had flown by, and while he was looking forward to catching up with her, he was nervous about answering her inevitable questions about where he and Dylan were at with the business.

Waiting in a seafood restaurant on the waterfront, he stood and smiled broadly when he saw her approach.

'Hey, Yoren! It's great to see you!' said Grace.

'Yeah, it feels like ages since we've spoken. You look great, by the way,' Yoren responded warmly.

'Thank you. And thanks for inviting me to lunch. I rarely venture into the city these days. I'd almost forgotten how beautiful it is, especially on a warm summer's day like this.'

After ordering, Grace asked, 'Tell me, Yoren, how are things going for you?'

'Great! The wedding's only two weeks away now. All the preparations are complete, thanks to Mel, and we're both super excited.'

'Wonderful! I'm very happy for you.' Grace took a sip from her sparkling water before asking, 'And how are your business plans going?'

He paused to gather his thoughts. Clearing his throat, he said, 'It's going great, but it's far from where I thought we'd be by now. The reality of getting a startup off the ground keeps slapping us in the face! I can't figure out where we went wrong, though. We did everything right. We devised a detailed and accurate business plan conveying the concept for our product and how we intend to build and market it. We prepared a strategic plan, budget estimates and project plans, just as we've always done in our corporate roles. We even reached out to several investors. Considering our corporate backgrounds, we figured they'd automatically trust us.

'Turns out we were wrong. I guess getting a startup off the ground is a whole different ball game. In our previous roles, we always dealt with existing, mature products, fully developed sales systems, processes and procedures, and well-established, trusted brands. Whenever something wasn't in place, we could take the time to map it out because we knew we had plenty of support systems to back us. In the corporate world, you've also got access to management all the way up the hierarchy to rectify any issues. Most importantly, you don't have to worry about the cash flow situation because you know you'll receive your regular pay no matter what happens. I could keep going, but I'm afraid I might bore you with the details.'

'Not at all, Yoren. I'm really interested,' said Grace. 'Much of what you're communicating is actually very similar to what many other first-time entrepreneurs I've coached have told me. And I've built a business myself, too. So I understand the risks to a degree, although the nature of my business is significantly different from what you and Dylan are trying to build. Did you end up contacting Connor, the business coach I referred you to? He's very experienced at supporting and growing businesses based on the being discourse. I imagine that could be very helpful for you. It can't hurt to have an initial conversation with him.'

'Sure, I definitely should call him at some point,' said Yoren, while internally pushing the suggestion aside yet again. Deep down, he was convinced he and Dylan should do it on their own and become self-made millionaires.

'The thing is, Grace, now that we know predictive planning is not the way to go, we plan to adopt the Lean Methodology approach and go low budget, building it gradually, bit by bit, and then progressively scale things up. Also, have you heard of bootstrapping?'

She nodded, aware that Yoren's perception of her knowledge about business was inauthentic. In reality, she was relatively well-versed on the topic and knew a lot more than he did.

'Well, that's what we intend to do,' he said. 'We'll start by tapping into our own resources and capital as much as we can to build part of the technology and get a start on the marketing and sales strategies. We've already built a good relationship with an outsourcing company in the Philippines to help us build the software …'

He continued telling Grace about their plans enthusiastically and confidently, barely stopping to take a breath, let alone taste his perfectly cooked grilled salmon topped with dill, lime and asparagus.

Grace listened while enjoying her seafood bisque. She knew he was rambling and trying to big-note himself, a sign that the shadow side of vulnerability had once again begun to manifest. But this wasn't a coaching session, and she knew better than to interrupt with probing questions.

'Doesn't it all sound brilliant, Grace? Surely our new plan will work.'

'It certainly sounds like you and Dylan have put a lot of thought and work into all of this,' said Grace. 'The only thing I would suggest you consider before getting in too deep is the importance of authentic awareness, as we talked about in our coaching sessions. Without authentic awareness, it's easy to fall into the trap of assuming everything's fine and then making some huge and potentially costly mistakes. Have you considered that many of the problems you're encountering might not be unprecedented, especially for startups?'

'Of course. I'm sure that's why the failure rate among startups is so high,' said Yoren.

'Indeed it is,' responded Grace. 'But consider that you might not need to reinvent the wheel. By looking into the more common problems encountered by startups, you and Dylan might be able to avoid or at least minimise the same pitfalls. I'd also encourage you to check the validity and congruence of your views and beliefs, as we discussed when we explored the authenticity quadrant. They'll play a critical role in the effectiveness of your decisions and actions moving forward.'

As usual, Grace had a way of making Yoren see things from a different perspective. He was silent as he pondered her words while eating his meal, which by now had gone cold.

Once their empty plates had been taken away, Yoren looked Grace in the eye and finally broke the silence. 'You're right! I guess I've just been caught up in the excitement of it all and impatient to get things moving. I definitely should check the authenticity of how I'm relating to this business-building journey. Thanks for the reminder, Grace.'

'You're most welcome, Yoren,' she smiled.

Over dessert and coffee, Grace shared parts of her business-building journey with him, including some of the stories and mistakes she could now look back on with good humour, leaving them both in fits of laughter.

Just as they were finishing up and Yoren was settling the account, he said, 'Now more than ever, I see the value in having a coach. I realise only two months have passed since our last session, but it's amazing how quickly we forget. Your simple reminder just now was quite impactful.'

'I'm glad, Yoren,' responded Grace.

He looked thoughtful. After a few moments, he said, 'I've got an idea. How about we create another coaching agreement, only this time at a much slower pace? That way, I can have your support as my coach while building the business. What do you think?' He looked at Grace in hopeful anticipation.

'Of course, we can do that, Yoren,' she replied with a smile. 'How about I contact you later this week to discuss the details as I just need to head off to another appointment now.'

'That would be great. Thanks, Grace.'

'My pleasure. And thank you for a lovely lunch!'

Yoren walked back to his car with a spring in his step.

— ∎ —

Despite being busy with last-minute preparations for the wedding and full-time work, Mel didn't let anything stand in her way of learning as much as she could about the being discourse. She devoured the books and other background material Jen had suggested she read, completed two full-day workshops, attended a practical introductory program on the assessment tool and had enrolled in the community's coach training program.

The program was scheduled to commence in mid-January. So the timing fitted in perfectly with her and Yoren's wedding and honeymoon plans, as it would give her a week to organise herself after returning home from Fiji. Its completion also coincided with her return to work and, being the beginning of a new year, she knew it would be the ideal time to introduce some fresh new ways of thinking into the organisation. However, she had no intention of rushing things, as she wanted to ensure she was fully across the material and well-practised in its application first. After Mel discussed her plans to introduce the assessment tool to the company with her boss and other key decision-makers, they welcomed her initiative to make some much-needed changes. Their teams were experiencing considerable dysfunction, and workplace morale was relatively low. They were also intrigued to know more as the concepts, principles and practices she explained were unlike anything they'd seen or heard of before.

For Mel, being introduced to what she saw as a relevant approach to understanding and working with human beings in the context of performance, wellbeing and effectiveness changed how she perceived her role at work. Craving meaning and purpose, she now saw possibilities where she'd previously felt limited in her capacity to support the organisation and the people she cared about. She also found it rewarding to be the primary breadwinner, supporting Yoren so that he and Dylan could focus on getting their startup off the ground and work towards their future financial prosperity. Knowing that she'd taken on more significant responsibilities and commitments, she felt both nervous and excited. However, the excitement won out when she thought about all the incredible things that were happening in her life. She was about to marry the man she loved, build the family she'd always longed for and embark on the next stage of her career with a renewed sense of meaning and joy. It was like all the pieces of the puzzle were finally coming together. She became present to a deep sense of fulfilment.

— ■ —

Meanwhile, Dylan was embarking on a new journey of his own. Having completed an assessment and debrief with Grace and committed to fortnightly coaching sessions, he had high hopes after witnessing remarkable changes in Yoren through his coaching journey. However, since he had very different assessment results from Yoren, Grace knew she would face some unique challenges in coaching him.

Intelligent, highly educated and a team player, Dylan was every employer's dream. However, beneath his positive, confident and agreeable exterior, and despite earning a high salary in his previous role, he yearned for more. That's precisely why he jumped at the chance to partner with Yoren in building a new business rather than trying to secure a new corporate role. But now he found himself in unfamiliar territory. Accustomed to thinking things through carefully and logically before making decisions, let alone embarking on a brand new journey, Dylan found that taking such a leap of faith had left him with tremendous uncertainty and fear. He was intelligent enough to know that the skills and knowledge that got him to this point in his life would not be enough to get him to the next stage. However, he was prepared to be challenged to become the person his new intention and goal required of him.

— ■ —

With so many things happening simultaneously, time flew by, and before Yoren and Mel knew it, they were boarding a flight bound for Fiji. Mel's planning and preparations for their tropical island wedding had come together without a hitch, so they could sit back on the plane and relax, knowing everything was taken care of. While excited about the wedding, both were eager for some downtime, and they congratulated themselves on their decision to marry and honeymoon in the one destination.

The wedding proved to be everything they'd hoped for and more. With only close friends and family in attendance, it was an intimate affair, giving them plenty of time to mingle and savour every moment. Dylan stood proudly beside his best friend and business partner and felt honoured to witness Yoren marry the woman who had finally captured his heart. Despite being the wet season, the rain held off, so they were able to marry on the beach. Mel looked stunning in a simple white gown with a floral wreath in her hair, and everyone – including the bride and groom – was bare-footed, much to Jen's delight. After the ceremony, they held an open-air reception at the resort, where they enjoyed a traditional Fijian feast before dancing late into the night.

After farewelling their guests, Yoren and Mel took full advantage of their beautiful, tropical surroundings and private, lavish accommodation to relax, unwind and enjoy being newlyweds. They were content to simply be with one another, often spending the entire morning in bed or lazing on the outdoor daybed to talk, laugh, be intimate or catch up on sleep after long nights of passion. They also relished the downtime knowing the work ahead of them. But for now, the work and the rest of the world could wait.

Epilogue

Yoren sat on the terrace of their sprawling mansion with a coffee and his laptop. It was a beautiful Saturday morning, and he was casually responding to emails, scrolling through some property listings and checking his share portfolio. He smiled as he spotted Mel on the lawn being chased by their children, Eden and Bruce, in a game that had them all in fits of laughter. Archie, their Standard Poodle pup, did his best to keep up. It was a picture of domestic bliss.

At 43, Mel was now the Director of People and Culture for the organisation Yoren and Dylan had built. She was thriving in that role, and Yoren was in awe of her ability to integrate her career with her parental responsibilities and fulfil both roles with so much love and care.

After five years of challenges, with some extreme highs and lows along the way, Yoren and Dylan's business venture turned a corner three years ago, thanks in great part to Mel's contribution in creating an incredible company culture, and it was now a highly successful global concern. Valued at over a billion US dollars, it had recently attracted acquisition offers from two independent investors, both multinational giants. However, after consulting Samuel, they decided to become a publicly listed company instead. As CEO and COO, respectively, Yoren and Dylan now proudly led a company that served users in more than 37 countries and was growing exponentially.

They had recently met their goal of surpassing 200 million dollars in annual revenue.

Reflecting on how far he'd come, the now 45-year-old Yoren knew none of this would have been possible without the support of so many people. Jen, who set him on a trajectory of change with one phone call all those years ago and who continued to support him and Mel in so many ways. Grace, who'd coached him through his initial transformational journey and was still coaching him today and who, along with Jen, sat on the advisory board for their business. Dylan, who was not only his best friend but had turned out to be the best business partner he could have hoped for. Samuel, who'd offered much-needed seed funding as an angel investor at the start of their journey and who also sat on the advisory board. The business coaches and mentors who advised them as they grew. And last but not least, Mel, for her unwavering support through all the ups and downs and for giving him two beautiful children.

Deep in thought, Yoren didn't hear Mel approach him from behind. Suddenly, she threw her arms around his neck and kissed him on the cheek, her hair falling in ribbons down his chest. Yoren loved how she still surprised him like that. It was like the flame of youth still burned brightly within her.

Taking a seat beside her husband, she said, 'Don't forget the family's coming for dinner tonight to celebrate your grandfather's birthday. The forecast says it'll be clear and quite warm, so how about we set up the table on the terrace?'

'Sounds perfect, my love. I can't believe Samuel's turning 90 tomorrow! That man has more energy than many people half his age,' said Yoren.

'Absolutely! Although, since we lost Uriel last year, he's not been quite as jovial as he was, which is completely understandable. It must be devastating losing the love of your life, especially after being together for so many years.'

'Yes, I've noticed that too. But he's still as sharp as ever, and his ongoing passion for philanthropic work is truly inspiring.'

'Yes, I've always admired that about Samuel,' said Mel. 'I'm so glad Dylan and Kylie are joining us too. Not long now till the arrival of their little one. They're going to be such wonderful parents!' beamed Mel as she went inside to prepare morning tea for the children.

Yoren took a sip from his mug, shut his laptop and sat back in his chair, musing over how far he'd come in just eight years and realising how deeply content and happy he was. Recalling that the state of fulfilment comes and goes, he made a conscious decision every morning to be present and enjoy every moment. But the intense hardship and pain of those first five years was never far from his mind. He often recalled the sleepless nights and the countless times his and Dylan's plans were shattered by unexpected circumstances, many beyond their control. He'd almost lost track of the number of iterations they'd been through, those times when they'd failed to generate interest from the market for their product because they hadn't done their due diligence. And he winced as he reflected on how close they'd come to walking away. Where would they be now if it had come to that?

In hindsight, it was clear to see how naive they'd been in assuming their corporate experience was all they needed to build a startup. How ignorant they were in thinking any half-astute investor would back them when they were nowhere near investment-ready and far too cocky for their own good. He also reflected on the many times when his relationships with Mel and Dylan had been tested, sometimes to breaking point. What a rocky road it had been, full of twists and turns, heartache and despair, failures, tough lessons and, eventually, triumph.

Yoren finally understood and appreciated why Mel doggedly journaled and carefully documented every step of their journey. Although it had irritated him back then, as she would take copious notes and remind him of commitments he'd made, he'd become grateful for her efforts. Mel had always enjoyed journaling and secretly dreamed of writing a book one day. This urge was further ignited after witnessing firsthand the realities and hardships of entrepreneurship and its sometimes brutal impact on relationships and families. It opened her eyes to how sustained effectiveness and financial success were inseparable from how polished the people involved were. It also made her realise how many startup hopefuls only saw the glistening tip of the iceberg but failed to see what lay beneath the surface. She longed to save others from making the same mistakes.

Yoren suddenly recalled the turning point, the moment that had changed it all. He could almost hear Jen's voice inviting him to that first information night. He could almost feel that same tightness in his chest when he resisted, and yes, he'd definitely resisted.

How different would my world be now? One simple invitation. One conversation. Who would have thought?

About the Author

Ashkan Tashvir is a best-selling author, thinker and philosopher with a profound interest in and knowledge of metaphysics, ontology, epistemology, phenomenology and ethics. He is also an engineer and the founder and CEO of Engenesis, a business movement of global venture-builders, investors, business management consultants, advisors, practitioners and coaches.

Ashkan's interests extend beyond theory and abstracts of philosophy to their application in the real world. One of the greatest challenges he has faced in this regard has been to make his intellectual bodies of work relatable and accessible to as many people as possible to broaden their reach globally and maximise the benefits received. With accessibility and relevance in mind, he applied a structured and holistic approach to the study of human consciousness, leadership, transformation and being through a series of practical frameworks, tools and methodologies. One of those frameworks is the Being Framework™, which incorporates an ontological model consisting of 31 Aspects of Being, the Being Profile® and the Transformation Methodology™. Today, this readily accessible and relatable framework supports people worldwide to derive fulfilment from their contributions and be more effective and integrous human beings. The framework is also applied within organisations for team effectiveness and company-wide transformation.

Committed to supporting human beings to raise their awareness by shaping a more congruent, authentic and accurate conception of reality, Ashkan's overarching mission is to facilitate transformation in the world, one human being at a time. The Being Framework supports him in achieving his mission by offering practitioners a methodology and tools that encourage individuals to focus on who and how they are being and leverage their potential to tap into and project the power and unique being that lie within.

When not writing, studying, coaching or building his businesses, Ashkan spends his time close to nature with his family and their beloved dogs. He also enjoys cooking, singing and playing the oud and harmonica.

Acknowledgements

Many people have directly or indirectly contributed to this book, my first work of fiction. My deepest gratitude to Ariya Chittasy, John Smallwood, Lucy Faulconer, Aydin Yassemi, Phaedra Pym, Caroline New, Odette Abrenica, Eric Hoek and Thymen Hoek.

I would also like to acknowledge our community of practitioners and coaches, whose stories significantly contributed to the narrative.

Last but not least, thank you to my wife, Atefeh, for her love and support. Without her, none of this would be possible.

Connect with the Author and Explore More Resources

Thank you for reading *BECOMING – The Emergence of Being*. To support your continued journey of discovery, you can connect with the author and access additional resources through the pathways below.

Website
Visit https://www.ashkantashvir.com to explore Ashkan's latest projects and related work.

Connect with Ashkan
Connect with Ashkan through the links below.

Linkedin
https://www.linkedin.com/in/tashvir/

Engenesis Platform
https://ashkan.engenesis.com

Further Reading
Check out Ashkan's other books and recommended articles for insightful reading on the topics of philosophy, human beings, transformation, performance and effectiveness.

- *BEING – The Source of Power*: https://beingbook.net/
- *HUMAN BEING – Illuminating the Reality Beneath the Facade*: https://humanbeingbook.net/

Recommended articles
How your way of being determines the results in your life:

https://engenesis.com/a/how-your-way-of-being-determines-the-results-in-your-life

How the integrity of our being is critical to an organisation's performance – The application of the Being Framework in the workplace:

https://engenesis.com/a/how-the-integrity-of-our-being-is-critical-to-an-organisations-performance-the-application-of-the-being-framework-in-the-workplace

Engenesis Publications
For enquiries about booking the author for interviews or media features, email publications@engenesis.com